A Secret Trial

Also by William Kaplan

A Secret Trial

Brian Mulroney, Stevie Cameron,
and the Public Trust

William Kaplan

McGill-Queen's University Press

Montreal & Kingston · London · Ithaca

For Robert S. Bothwell

© McGill-Queen's University Press 2004

ISBN 0-7735-2846-6

Legal deposit third quarter 2004
Bibliothèque nationale du Québec

Printed in Canada on acid-free paper.

McGill-Queen's University Press acknowledges the support of the Canada Council for the Arts for
our publishing program. We also acknowledge the financial support of the Government of Canada through the
Book Publishing Industry Development Program (BPIDP) for our publishing activities.

Library and Archives Canada Cataloguing in Publication

Kaplan, William, 1957–
A secret trial : Brian Mulroney, Stevie Cameron and the
public trust / William Kaplan.

Includes bibliographical references and index.
ISBN 0-7735-2846-6

1. Mulroney, Brian, 1939–. 2. Political corruption–Canada.
3. Corruption investigation–Canada. 4. Airbus (Jet transport)
5. Cameron, Stevie. 6. Kaplan, William, 1957–. I. Title.

FC630.K35 2004   971.064'7   C2004-903653-X

Design and typesetting by oneonone@arobas.net

Contents

Foreword

J.L. GRANATSTEIN

Bill Kaplan is a rarity. A lawyer and a well-known labour arbitrator, he is also a trained historian with a master's degree in history and a law doctorate in legal history. He deals with the law on a daily basis, and he continues to research and write history, publishing first-class work at a pace that puts law school professors and academic historians to shame.

He is, above all, a superb researcher, a scholar with the ability to find the documents that cast light on a story and the knack for getting the key participants in events to talk to him. Good scholars have this talent, but only a first-rate legal historian has the training to make sense of the complicated manoeuvres that play out in our courts and, quite often, in corporate boardrooms, police strategy sessions, the Justice Department, and the Prime Minister's Office.

Kaplan's book on the Airbus affair, *Presumed Guilty: Brian Mulroney, the Airbus Affair, and the Government of Canada*, published in 1998, was precisely the kind of book that showcased Kaplan's strengths. He won the cooperation of former prime minister Brian Mulroney and had unprecedented and unlimited access to Mulroney's files. He secured the cooperation of Mulroney's legal counsel as the former Progressive Conservative leader battled – ultimately with success – the Government of Canada and the RCMP to clear his name of the charge that he had been bribed. He talked to Mulroney's friends and allies. But Kaplan didn't stop there. As good historians must, he sought access to government documents and to those individuals pressing the government case. He was surprisingly successful.

Presumed Guilty sets out what Kaplan found. Despite the stories of sleaze and cronyism retailed in 1994 by journalist Stevie Cameron in her book *On the Take: Crime, Corruption and Greed in the Mulroney Years,* Kaplan found that Mulroney was innocent, exactly as he claimed, in the Airbus affair. Moreover, Kaplan demonstrated that Jean Chrétien's government had pursued what amounted to a political witchhunt against Mulroney – a cold and deliberate attempt to destroy Mulroney's reputation.

Kaplan was flying in the face of public opinion with his book. Canadians detested Mulroney, hated his closetful of Gucci shoes, revolted against his constitutional brinksmanship, and revelled in the way his successors had reduced the Progressive Conservative Party to a tiny rump in Parliament. They implicitly believed Stevie Cameron when she charged that Mulroney and his friends had been on the take. But historian Kaplan was undaunted. Fact was fact, truth was truth, and while Mulroney was certainly not right in everything he had done, he was clean on Airbus. The evidence was clear, and Kaplan laid it out fully and fairly. That is what historians are supposed to do.

Although *Presumed Guilty* sold well, it is probably fair to say that its publication did Bill Kaplan no good. Liberal supporters and Cameron's friends painted the Toronto lawyer as a Mulroney apologist, a sycophantic hanger-on, and a closet Tory sympathizer. Mulroney was guilty, the general response seemed to be, regardless of the evidence that cleared him. Kaplan would have been less than human if he didn't feel hurt by the response, and he might have been expected to hunker down in his legal practice to allow time for the wounds inflicted on him to heal.

But people kept talking to him quietly about the Airbus case, and documents about it and other matters continued to wend their way to him. He heard whispers about secret trials under way in Toronto and Edmonton, about RCMP raids, about continued investigations, and his acute historian's nose began to sniff at the hints of a good story. To his enormous credit, he let the evidence lead him forward, regardless of the direction in which it was pointing. What if Stevie Cameron had been right in some way about Mulroney's sleaziness? What if the Toronto journalist had been a confidential informant for the RCMP, so eager to get Mulroney that she passed on files she uncovered? What did that say about her professional ethics? More important still, what if Mulroney had taken money from Karlheinz Schreiber, one of the key players in the Airbus affair, albeit after he left office in 1993? What could that money have been for? What if Mulroney had been less than forthcoming under oath in describing his relations with Schreiber? What would that do to the former leader's carefully burnished reputation – a task to which he had devoted himself with extraordinary assiduity since leaving office in 1993?

But there were problems for Kaplan in all these stories too. What if he, Bill Kaplan, had got some of the inferences in the story wrong in *Presumed Guilty*? What might that do to his reputation as a professional historian? Few of us are ready to admit error; fewer still are the historians able to say that new evidence can change their minds. The books and articles stand as written, or so seems the unwritten rule of the historical profession. But Kaplan is different, a scholar who unfailingly goes where the evidence takes him and who is not afraid to admit that he might have got it partly wrong. That takes courage and a high degree of professional integrity, and Kaplan is a rare man.

A Secret Trial is an important book. It lays bare the seamy undersides of politics and journalism, and it exposes self-serving individuals for what they are. This is not the end of this story, for evidence continues to become available. What is striking, however, is how this book, written so close to the events it chronicles, has detailed what went on. Unlike most historical researchers, Kaplan did not have the luxury of playing Monday-morning quarterback. Still, there seems little doubt that he has got this tale right. In the process, he has raised troubling questions about those who govern us and about some of those who deliver us the news. Cameron's reputation, shattered by the weight of the affidavits the RCMP provided, may not recover. But what of the truly important person in this case – Brian Mulroney? How will historians assess him in the light of the material presented here? It is too soon to be certain, but Kaplan's evidence at a minimum will call into question the place in history Mulroney thought he had been restored to with his victory over the Chrétien government in the Airbus affair. The future will decide.

What we do know now is that, with courage and fine scholarship, Bill Kaplan has shed a pitiless light on the recent past, and we should all thank him for what he has done. Certainly the historians of the future will do so, for the story he tells here would never have emerged without his diligent search for the truth. It will be up to them to complete this unsavoury tale.

A Secret Trial

1 The Prince of Penne

"Thank you," Brian Mulroney said in his usual polite way when Karlheinz Schreiber passed over the large envelope containing $100,000 in cash. "Thank you very much."[1]

The story begins in late June 1993, not long after Mulroney stepped down as prime minister. He had bought a new home for his family on Forden Crescent in Montreal, high up on the hill in Westmount. It would be months, however, before the extensive renovations on the new house were complete. In the meantime, courtesy of his successor, Kim Campbell, the Mulroneys were staying at Harrington Lake, the rustic summer home for Canadian prime ministers in Gatineau Park, outside Ottawa. It was here that Schreiber says Mulroney arranged for a government limousine to pick him up at his Rockcliffe condominium and bring him over for a visit.[2] They talked and, before long, they met again at a hotel in Montreal to exchange that first envelope. Other meetings followed, including one at the Pierre Hotel, Mulroney's favourite, in New York City.

The two men had known each other for years. Schreiber, born Friedrich Karlheinz Hermann Schreiber in 1934 to a poor family in a small town in the Harz Mountains in Germany, was a natural-born salesman with winning ways and a knack for finding the big deal. His first job was selling Oriental carpets. Settling in Kaufering, Bavaria, he began working for a road-marking company with a unique product to sell. Instead of painting lines on roads, the company, Bayerische Bitumen-Chemie Ferdinand Heinrich GmbH, cut grooves into the road and filled them, permanently, with asphalt studded with reflective beads. Drivers could not only see the markings at night but feel them too. They lasted almost forever. Soon the ambitious, hardworking Schreiber owned the company. Thanks to his carefully cultivated friendship with Bavarian premier Franz Josef

Strauss, the business eventually had a lock on all the road-marking contracts in Bavaria. Schreiber began looking for other markets for this innovative product.

Schreiber made his way to Alberta, Canada, in the early 1970s. Realizing that government contracts required government contacts, he quickly went about making them among the reigning provincial Tories. Despite these contacts, the road-marking company did not do well in Canada and was eventually sold. Schreiber invested heavily in real estate, on his own behalf and for others. He made money and he lost money. But there was always a new project on the go, in Alberta, Newfoundland, Saudi Arabia, Costa Rica, Mexico, France, Switzerland, and, of course, Germany. Along the way he befriended a number of Canadian politicians, including Brian Mulroney. It was no surprise to Schreiber, then, when Mulroney summoned him to Harrington Lake for a chat that summer day in 1993. When it was time to go, Schreiber remembers Mulroney escorting him to the door and the waiting car.

The limousine kicked up dust along the dirt-and-gravel road out of the Harrington Lake compound and was waved through the white entrance gate by an RCMP officer. Three cameras mounted on poles recorded the exit as the vehicle bounced down the narrow road hugging the south shore of Meech Lake, one of three large finger-shaped bodies of water bisecting Gatineau Park. To the right, cliffs descended sharply to the road, dotted here and there with cottages. Soon they were in the quaint village of Old Chelsea, where, looking out the tinted window, Schreiber could see the summer tourists milling about, stopping at the popular brick bakery and the local pizzeria. The car turned onto No. 5, a four-lane divided highway, and the Ottawa skyline soon appeared on the right, the Parliament Buildings rising magnificently above the Ottawa River. Barely half an hour after leaving Mulroney, Schreiber later recalled, the car sped along Sussex Drive, beyond the prime minister's residence and the sprawling grounds of Rideau Hall, and delivered him home in Rockcliffe Park.

Less than one year after the last payment was made in December 1994, Mulroney and Schreiber were back in the newspapers, but it was unwelcome publicity for both of them. Early in 1995 the RCMP resurrected an old file, one filled with allegations of major wrongdoing by the former prime minister, Schreiber, and a third party, Frank Moores, the former premier of Newfoundland.

Born in 1933 in Harbour Grace, Moores was the son of a prosperous family of fish merchants. He had little formal education but tremendous street smarts. Hard working, hard living, and hard

drinking, Moores entered politics in 1968 as a federal Tory MP.
He quickly tired of Ottawa, however, and in 1970 returned to New-
foundland to challenge longtime Liberal premier Joey Smallwood.
Three years later, Moores was premier, a post he held for seven years.

In 1976 Moores nominated Mulroney in his first bid for the federal Progressive Conservative Party leadership. They had been
friends before and they have been friends ever since. When Mulroney was finally elected leader of the party in 1983 and then prime
minister in 1984, Moores moved to Ottawa and established the
number one lobbying firm in the capital, Government Consultants
International (GCI). In 1995, two years after Mulroney had left
office and Moores had left town, the RCMP believed that the duo,
together with Schreiber, had engaged in a criminal conspiracy to
defraud the people of Canada of millions of dollars. The Mounties
were convinced that unlawful commissions had been paid in Air
Canada's $1.8 billion purchase of Airbus aircraft, the Coast Guard's
acquisition of a dozen helicopters, and a stillborn plan to assemble
light armoured vehicles in Bearhead, Cape Breton. Among the recipients, the RCMP believed, were Brian Mulroney, Frank Moores, and
the German-Canadian middleman in all three transactions, Karlheinz
Schreiber. But the police investigation, first launched in 1988, had
run out of steam in Canada. The Mounties had their suspicions, and
little else. But, thanks to a secret police informer, the inquiry was
given a big boost and the RCMP were in a position to follow up on
some leads overseas. They wanted to ask the Swiss government for
assistance in divulging details about a number of secret Swiss bank
accounts supposedly belonging to Mulroney, Moores, and Schreiber
and containing some of their share of the spoils. To do so, the investigators needed to present a document called a Letter of Request.

The Swiss banking system is governed by two overriding principles: security and secrecy. As a result of international pressure, however, the Swiss had reluctantly agreed to assist foreign governments
in obtaining details about numbered accounts – provided the requesting government could assure them there was real evidence of
the commission of a serious crime.

The RCMP's 1995 Letter of Request fit this requirement. The letter from Canada did not beat around the bush. It said that Mulroney
had defrauded the Canadian people of millions of dollars. He was,
to summarize in three words, "on the take." Karlheinz Schreiber and
Frank Moores were also involved, with the trio receiving big kickbacks from Air Canada's purchase of Airbus planes, the Canadian
Coast Guard's purchase of helicopters from a German company

called Messerschmitt Bolkow Blohm (MBB), and also from an aborted attempt by Schreiber, on behalf of the German military/industrial conglomerate Thyssen, to establish a light armoured vehicle factory at Bearhead, Cape Breton. Some of Mulroney's share of the money, the letter asserted, ended up in a secret numbered Swiss bank account code-named "Devon." Later, another account, suspiciously named "Britan," came to light and was said by some to hold more of Mulroney's ill-gotten gains.

When Mulroney learned of the Letter of Request, he sprang into action and hired some of the finest legal talent around. They worked overtime to try to get the Canadian government to withdraw the letter and replace it with another request that did not outright call the former prime minister a criminal, before he had even been charged with a crime. But they failed.

The letter was leaked to veteran journalist Philip Mathias – who did the leaking is still a source of considerable speculation – and Mulroney filed a $50 million defamation action against Ottawa. The lawsuit was eventually settled in January 1997, when both the federal government and the RCMP said they were sorry and acknowledged that there was no evidence of any wrongdoing on Mulroney's part. It was an abject apology: "Based on the evidence received to date, the RCMP acknowledges that any conclusions of wrongdoing by the former prime minister were – and are – unjustified." And, it continued: "The government of Canada and the RCMP regret any damage suffered by Mr. Mulroney and his family and fully apologize to them."

Moores and Schreiber also got apologies, although they were different in content and in tone, given only as a matter of "logical consistency." The government and the RCMP apologized to them for some of the language used in the Letter of Request that indicated, wrongly, that the RCMP had reached conclusions that they had engaged in criminal conduct. Nothing was said in the letters to Schreiber and Moores about the evidence gathered about them. To an astute reader, the conclusion was compelling that whatever evidence the RCMP had collected about Mulroney at the time the letter was sent, along with any new evidence accumulated since, there was nothing to support any allegation of wrongdoing on his part. However, the same could not be said about Schreiber and Moores. In fact, anyone who carefully followed the story could not help but notice that, at the same time the RCMP and the Government of Canada were apologizing to Schreiber, German authorities had raided his Bavarian home and had him under active criminal investigation for a variety of serious offences. But Mulroney, it seemed, was completely cleared, a view reinforced when Judge Allan Gold was called upon to adjudicate the amount the government owed the former prime minister for payment of his legal fees and other expenses.

Gold, a well-respected Montreal jurist with a knack for settling large, intractable disputes, had assisted in negotiating the Minutes of Settlement resolving the case. When the two sides could not agree on how much money Mulroney was owed, Gold was called back into service and gave Mulroney just about everything he asked for. "I begin with the firm conviction that the intent and purpose of the Settlement was to right the grievous wrong that Mulroney had suffered through no fault of his own," Gold wrote in his award. "Simple justice and fair dealing required no less." In the end, the Canadian government reimbursed Mulroney a little more than $2 million for his legal and public relations expenses. The CBC's *Fifth Estate*, Canada's leading current affairs and investigatory television program, which first broke the story about mysterious Airbus commissions, had always made it clear that there was no evidence of any wrongdoing on Mulroney's part.

That was my view too, set out in my earlier book on the Airbus case, *Presumed Guilty: Brian Mulroney, the Airbus Affair and the Government of Canada*, published in 1998. One thing surprised me, though, when I went on the promotional tour for the book and appeared on radio talk shows across the country – the depth of dislike Canadians felt for the former prime minister and the way suspicions about him were extended, without hesitation, to anyone seen to be speaking on his behalf. I was, however, with only two exceptions, treated fairly and well by the press. In the end, my publisher sold more than ten thousand hardcover copies of the book.

In the years since the case was settled in early 1997, fortune has treated the three principals in the Airbus case very differently. Life never turned around for Frank Moores, the former King of the Rock, as he was known in Newfoundland. The Airbus investigation had cost him dearly, personally and financially, and his million-dollar account in Switzerland was still frozen, even though he had reportedly made amends with the Canada Customs and Revenue Agency and paid all his outstanding back taxes.

Schreiber was – well, Schreiber. He was fighting an extradition request from the Government of Germany. After raiding his Bavarian home and seizing, among other things, his diaries, which were then correlated to banking records obtained from the Swiss, the German authorities wanted to question him about a number of things.

Tax evasion, bribery, and political corruption were at the top of their list. Indeed, Schreiber was one of the key figures in a huge German fundraising scandal, one that continues to dominate German politics. In 1991 Schreiber gave one million marks, in cash, in a parking lot, to Liesler Kiep, a prominent businessman and the powerful treasurer of Chancellor Helmut Kohl's Christian Democratic Union Party.3 Less than ten years later, when the story broke, a political firestorm erupted. While Schreiber maintained the money was simply a donation, a parliamentary inquiry was called. Kohl was soon in trouble, as was his successor, Wolfgäng Schauble. The money had gone into an unreported bank account and had been used as a slush fund. Even though many of the records relating to the affair went missing, there was no shortage of inculpatory evidence. One senior German official committed suicide. A former deputy minister of defence went into hiding and is still a fugitive from justice. Several ranking Thyssen officials were convicted of corruption.

German authorities had many questions for Schreiber, but if his lawyer Eddie Greenspan has his way, their extradition request is unlikely to be finally concluded anytime soon. In the meantime, Schreiber is suing the Government of Canada for $35 million in a claim filed in Edmonton alleging abuse-of-process, defamation, and sundry other legal wrongs. Schreiber was also going after the CBC's *Fifth Estate* and Luc Lavoie – Mulroney's spokesperson – for millions more because of Lavoie's on-air observations about Schreiber and his reputation for telling the truth. According to Lavoie, Schreiber was "the biggest fucking liar the world has ever seen." This was not, apparently, just Lavoie's view: "That's what we believe," he added, suggesting that Mulroney was on board too. Before long, Lavoie wrote Schreiber an unconditional letter of apology – "My words were wrong and they were neither authorized nor condoned by Mr. Mulroney. Therefore I apologize to you without reservation and regret any damage caused by my words" – and his cheque for $50,000 followed quickly thereafter. The furniture just got moved around as Schreiber dropped his lawsuit against the CBC and ended up paying the broadcaster more than $50,000 for its legal costs.

While the lawyers wrangled over these various lawsuits and legal actions, Schreiber was, in effect, stuck in Canada, but he did not waste his time. He opened and then closed a chain of pasta restaurants (and he claimed to have discovered a form of spaghetti that cured cancer and reduced weight), attracted a number of blue-chip investors, and continued to enjoy the support and friendship of

Canadian politicians, most notably Marc Lalonde and Elmer Mac-
Kay, two former federal ministers, one Liberal, one Conservative,
who personally guaranteed Schreiber's bail when he was arrested by
the RCMP as part of a German government extradition request.

For Mulroney, life was good. He established probably the top
international law and advisory practice in Canada and was appointed to numerous important boards of directors. He was named a
Companion of the Order of Canada, the highest level and the greatest honour the country can bestow. He saw his only daughter married at a lavish wedding in Montreal, with former president George
H.W. Bush and his wife as his special guests of honour. His children
were all successfully launched, the house in Palm Beach was reno-
vated and enlarged, and Mulroney was prospering in Canada and
abroad. For a man concerned about his place in history, Mulroney's
contributions to Canada's economic well-being were increasingly
recognized and appreciated. Few dispassionate observers could dis-
agree with his claim made in the fall of 2003: "My policies are now
accepted by the majority of Canadians. Just look, my policies on
GST, free trade, on the United States and the Middle East, they are
back in favour ... My government wasn't perfect, but it is better
than the one we have there now ... the Liberals are ... systemati-
cally corrupt."[4]

Indeed, after the Airbus debacle, the Liberal government did look
very bad. Justice Minister Allan Rock and Solicitor General Herb
Gray seemed mean-spirited and ungenerous, while their boss, Prime
Minister Jean Chrétien, appeared nasty and vindictive. Many Canadians speculated about Chrétien's possible role in the affair, and there
was some reason to believe that the prime minister was not unaware
of the RCMP investigation into Mulroney before it became public
knowledge. However, even Mulroney's biggest critics were left with
little choice but to concede that the whole sad episode had been a
travesty of justice. "I always said that dog won't hunt," claimed
Stevie Cameron, Mulroney's longtime nemesis and most public enemy, through her bestselling book On the Take.[5] The RCMP announced it would continue to investigate.

That was just fine with Mulroney. Savouring his victory, he gave
an impromptu press conference outside his Westmount home in January 1997 the day after his lawsuit was settled. "I wanted any stain
whatsoever removed from my father's name," he told reporters hap-
pily, "and that's been achieved." What about the continuing RCMP
investigation? Mulroney just laughed. The Mounties could continue
their inquiries until "the cows come home." He had nothing to worry

about: "They won't find a single thing because we've never been involved in anything untoward." But even in his time of triumph, Mulroney conceded the story was not yet over. The case was, Mulroney continued mysteriously, very "unusual," and he would not be surprised if there were more "revealing developments."[6]

Philip Mathias again got the new story first, nailing it down in late 2000 and early 2001. Mathias began his journalism career in London, England, in 1960 when he was assistant editor of *Tin and Its Uses*. He joined Toronto's *Financial Post* in 1965. Between 1975 and 1980, he worked at the CBC's *Fifth Estate*, and stints at *Money Magazine* and *Venture* followed. By 1985 he was back at the *Financial Post*, which, in 1998, became the *National Post*. Mathias was obsessive about figuring things out. Humming, whistling, or singing away, and driving his newsroom colleagues nuts, he would stare at documents for hours to understand them and to satisfy himself that he had not missed something important. This time, the scoop was pretty straightforward: "Brian Mulroney was paid $300,000 in cash by German businessman Karlheinz Schreiber, the man at the centre of the Airbus affair, over an 18-month period beginning soon after Mr. Mulroney stepped down as prime minister in 1993."

The story suggested that the payments had nothing to do with Airbus or any wrongdoing asserted in the 1995 Letter of Request. Mathias noted that at the time the payments were made, Mulroney was re-establishing himself in the private sector, and there was no reason to avoid Schreiber, who was not yet embroiled in the various legal proceedings and political scandals that were soon to engulf him. The *Post* interviewed Schreiber for the story and quoted him as saying that the business relationship between the two was "normal," and that it was not up to him "to report on Brian Mulroney to the Canadian public." The story also pointed out that a fee of $300,000 was not unusual for providing legal and lobbying assistance in major transactions.

Mulroney declined to comment for the story, as did his lawyers. However, Mathias spoke to a "Mulroney confidant," who told him that "the former prime minister earned the fee in full by performing services for Mr. Schreiber after the fee was paid." Mathias was not told the nature of the work or when it was done. When the newspaper reporter asked why Mulroney did not make this matter public at an earlier time, the confidant replied that Mr Mulroney was "fearful of creating a false impression in the middle of what he described as a witch hunt over the so-called Airbus affair." The fear was hardly misplaced. It would certainly have made an impression if news about the multiple cash payments from Schreiber had come out at the same time that Mulroney was suing the federal government and the RCMP for claiming he had accepted a bribe from Schreiber.

While there is no predicting legal outcomes, one thing is near certain. Had Jean Chrétien, Allan Rock, and Herb Gray known in late 1996 and early 1997 that Mulroney had gone on Schreiber's payroll soon after leaving office and been paid $300,000 in cash, they would never have allowed the Department of Justice and the RCMP to settle the case. Mulroney had taken a huge gamble. Now Mathias had found out about the money and, although he greeted this information with his customary scepticism, he was determined to get the story in print. He immediately realized that the amount involved paled in comparison to the many millions Mulroney was alleged by the Canadian government and others to have received as a payoff for Airbus and the other transactions. Still, $300,000 was hardly insignificant. The payment in cash was also unusual. Mathias heard, but could not apparently confirm, that the purpose of the retainer was to assist in kick-starting the Bearhead project in Cape Breton, if possible, or, if politics demanded, in the east end of Montreal."

Mathias had been working on the story for months, to the exclusion of just about everything else, when he submitted a final draft in early January 2001, just weeks before his scheduled retirement. It went to the *Post*'s lawyers – no one would dare publish a contentious story about Mulroney without a libel check – and was approved. It emerged from editorial, fairly edited. Mathias waited and waited and waited. Nothing happened. Mathias began to ask questions. He pestered. Finally, he wrote to the dual proprietors of the *Post* – Conrad Black and the Asper family. In a letter dated towards the end of March 2001, he complained. He told the owners that Mulroney received the first instalment soon after he left office in 1993 and accepted the last payment in December 1994. Why, he inquired, was the story not published?

A few days later Mathias was summoned to a meeting with senior editorial staff in the main meeting room, which overlooks the newsroom on the inside and an ugly industrial parking lot on the outside. It was not exactly the Star Chamber, but Mathias became increasingly uncomfortable as the meeting did not go well. There was, he was told, no story. Why, he was repeatedly asked, was he pursuing it? Why, he was also asked, had he gone over his editors'

Philip Mathias – the journalist who first
got the story

heads? There was unproductive conversation. Finally, Mathias announced he had had enough.

Discussion then turned to the merits of the story. There was further exchange and a line-by-line dissection of the story. More observations were shared that it was not a story. Since there was no evidence that the payments had anything to do with Airbus, MBB, or
Bearhead, why refer to them in the story? There was something to
that. If the commercial relationship had nothing to do with the matters under police investigation, was it journalistically proper to con-
textualize it in this way? Yet the government had asserted that Mulroney and Schreiber were in cahoots, and that millions in bribe
money had passed hands. Did the story not require that background
information in order to place the payment, whatever it was for, in
appropriate context? The money, moreover, had been turned over in
cash. Surely that fact cast a shadow over the entire transaction.

That night the *Post*'s editor-in-chief, Ken Whyte, called Mathias
at home and said that the criticisms of the story reflected his view.
Whyte suggested that Mathias contact me, the author of *Presumed
Guilty*, which had been written independently of Mulroney but with
his complete cooperation, to get a comment. Mathias called me and
told me what he had learned. If Whyte expected me to try to explain
it all away, as Mathias suspected, he was sorely disappointed.

I could not believe what I was hearing when Mathias read me his story. After spending the better part of a year working on a book that defended the former prime minister and severely criticized the then current one, Jean Chrétien, among others, I learned that Mulroney and Schreiber enjoyed something considerably more than a casual, nodding acquaintance. Obviously, I had asked Mulroney about Schreiber and their relationship. In fact, at our first formal interview, it was the very first question I asked because it was the most important one to be answered. It was central. This is what Brian Mulroney said to me on December 2, 1997: "I knew Schreiber in a peripheral way. He was associated in my mind with the Alberta Progressive Conservatives. That was the limited extent to which I knew anything about him. I knew who he was and that he'd been involved in Bear Head."[7] Mulroney told me that he simply considered Schreiber's proposal to bring jobs to Cape Breton Island and that he was initially in favour, but, on the advice of his officials, he decided against proceeding with the project. I believed him – his answer was completely consistent with the written record – and moved on to interview him about other things. One of Mulroney's university friends is reported to have told the CBC's Larry Zolf, "Mulroney never met this Schreiber guy, Mulroney doesn't even know Schreiber, Moores may have brought Schreiber to a party, but that's all." However, I now learned that their post–prime ministerial get-togethers had to have been something more than "peripheral," and that the relationship between the two men actually went way back. I had been duped. Schreiber had been part of the Mulroney circle even before he entered public life. In fact, he had played an important behind-the-scenes role in Mulroney's road to power.[8]

In January 1983, 2,400 Tory delegates descended on Winnipeg. The only item on the agenda that mattered was a leadership review. Joe Clark had won the Tory Party leadership over Mulroney in 1976 and, three years later, at the age of thirty-nine, was elected the youngest ever prime minister of Canada. After just nine months in power, Clark squandered his government by losing a crucial and avoidable parliamentary vote on a budget of tax increases and program cuts. He then lost the election that followed. Clark won the first leadership review after his electoral defeat, and he claimed to welcome the opportunity for a renewed mandate. He was so certain of success that he raised the bar from the traditional two-thirds support needed for a leader to carry on to 70 per cent, though he had received barely more than 66 per cent in that first review in 1981.

While Mulroney publicly endorsed Clark, his people worked furiously behind the scenes to deprive him of victory. Frank Moores was the leader of the review forces, coordinating the entire operation by walkie-talkie from his hotel room, while Elmer MacKay, the Nova Scotia MP, was directing the many mutinous members of the Conservative Party parliamentary caucus. Schreiber, among others, lent a hand. His entrée to the group came through Austrian-Canadian businessman Walter Wolf and Montreal lawyer Michel Cogger, a former classmate of Mulroney's from Laval law school who handled Franz Josef Strauss's family business interests in Quebec. Wolf introduced Schreiber to Cogger, who in turn introduced him to Moores and other Tories working to depose Clark. Schreiber was happy to help out by ensuring that enough pro-business, pro-Mulroney delegates attended to deprive Clark of victory.

There was an especially large turnout from Quebec, funded by Wolf, Schreiber, and others anxious to dump Joe. Wolf was more than happy to donate money for the cause, but, he asked, "Why should I be the only one to pay?" As Schreiber later told the *Fifth Estate*, "It's expensive to travel, right?" Those travel expenses needed to be defrayed. Some of the delegates' wives needed money too, "to go shopping or whatever." Mulroney dismissed the claims at the time as "rumours and innuendo," and it is, of course, possible that he was kept in the dark about some of the efforts exerted on his behalf. Party elder Dalton Camp figured it out, however, and publicly denounced the "off-shore money." Joe Clark had no idea until later how well organized and financed his opponents were.[9] He did not even know who they were.

Schreiber and Wolf were working on the front lines, but they received some of their direction and, it appears, some of the money from overseas, from the premier of Bavaria, Franz Josef Strauss. Strauss was one of the founders and the undisputed leader of the right-wing Christian Social Union (CSU) party (the sister party to the federal CDU). Known as the "Bull of Bavaria," he served as West Germany's minister of defence, 1958–62, federal minister of finance, 1966–69, and premier of Bavaria, 1978–88. The son of a butcher, Strauss lurched from scandal to success and back and was, without a doubt, the most consistently controversial figure in post-war German politics. As defence minister he created a *Bundeswehr* of more than 400,000 men. The need for *matériel* was enormous, and the opportunities for payoffs were fully exploited. Whether for the purchase of tanks or planes, Strauss exercised influence on behalf of party, family, and friends in return for benefits. When the leading German weekly *Der Spiegel* published an article attacking him as an unprincipled and incompetent minister, he obtained arrest warrants for the magazine's editor and editor-in-chief, along with search warrants for its Hamburg headquarters and its Bonn office. Seven journalists ended up spending a total of almost three hundred days in jail.

In Bavaria, Strauss set the tone. The state was made a safe haven for tax evaders who had the good sense to direct sufficient funds to the CSU. Strauss was the chair of Airbus Industrie's supervisory board, and he played a key role in the creation of MBB, the Munich-based aircraft manufacturer, and served on its board too. He was a super-salesman for German industry and also became chairman of Airbus Industrie. He was determined to do what he could to export his particular brand of conservatism abroad, mostly by providing financial assistance to like-minded politicians. In Canada, Joe Clark, a Red Tory, had to go – he did not fit the bill. Brian Mulroney did, however. At the 1983 leadership review convention in Winnipeg, the Quebec delegates flown in by two big Boeings leased from Wardair voted against Clark and helped to deprive him of his quixotic 70 per cent. According to Schreiber, Strauss "was fully involved, he knew everything."[10]

It took a quarter of a million dollars in cash, according to L. Ian MacDonald, Mulroney's official biographer, to get the "pro-review delegates to Winnipeg." When Clark called the leadership convention – characteristically, he threw away his leadership just as he had earlier thrown away his government – Mulroney could not believe his luck, and, with due dispatch, he won the party leadership. Patrick MacAdam, a Mulroney classmate from St Francis Xavier University, became, in his words, "the gatekeeper" to the new leader of the opposition. Schreiber, he said, often accompanied by Max Strauss, the son of the Bavarian premier, was a frequent visitor to the future prime minister as the younger Strauss visited his "trap line" in Canada. In 1984 Mulroney easily won the general election, as the Canadian people were anxious to send the decayed Liberals and their hapless new leader, John Turner, into opposition. Strauss and Schreiber, who had long been business associates, had backed a winner – a national leader with a compatible political philosophy.

"Canada," Mulroney famously declared after being elected prime minister, "is open for business." The Foreign Investment Review Agency was disbanded and replaced by Investment Canada, which was given the mandate of facilitating investment in the country. The National Energy Program, which allowed the federal government retroactively to seize a share of Canadian oil discoveries, was dismantled. Canada, Mulroney told anyone who asked, was not built by expropriating the property of others. Thoroughly pro-business and attractively pro-American, Mulroney was a welcome break from more than twenty years of almost uninterrupted Liberal rule.

Schreiber, who had overseen many Strauss family investments in Alberta for years, assumed some new responsibilities. Around 1985, at the request of Strauss, he became the Canadian agent for MBB, which was trying to sell helicopters to the Canadian Coast Guard. He also became, again thanks to Strauss, the agent for Airbus Industrie, which was trying to sell aircraft to Wardair, Canadian Airlines, and Air Canada. This mandate was particularly lucrative, and one of its terms was especially interesting.[11] The contract between Airbus Industrie and International Aircraft Leasing, IAL, a company owned and controlled by Schreiber, indicated that the agreement requiring large payments to IAL for each Airbus sold would come to an end if there was a major political change in Canada. Wardair bought first, but instead of earning commissions on that deal, the agreement was amended to provide for larger payments in the event that Air Canada signed on. And sign on it did. In 1988, in the biggest acquisition in its history, the Crown corporation bought thirty-four Airbus A320 planes at the cost of $1.8 billion. Millions in commission payments immediately began to flow from a bank in France to Liechtenstein, where IAL was headquartered, and from there to bank accounts owned and/or controlled by Schreiber in Zurich. Quite a bit of that money, the RCMP claimed in the 1995 Letter of Request, had made its way to Mulroney, who had stashed his share of the loot in a secret numbered Swiss bank account. That allegation turned out to be incorrect, and Mulroney had no Swiss bank account. But he had later accepted money from middleman Karlheinz Schreiber in questionable circumstances.

Maybe Mulroney had an explanation, I thought, as Mathias outlined his story. In the meantime, I agreed to give him an objective comment. Personally, Mulroney is engaging, funny, and likeable. When I began working on *Presumed Guilty*, I told one of my colleagues at the University of Ottawa law school, where I was then teaching, that Mulroney had agreed to unlimited interviews. "That's too bad," she replied, adding that it was unfortunate I would have to meet and talk to him. But my experience was quite different. We had countless conversations and meetings, and I enjoyed them all. He was always considerate, and his wife, Mila, charming. But how could this story be true? The unpublished *Post* story did not make any sense: for Mulroney, a business relationship with Schreiber made no sense; cash

The inscription under this picture speaks
for itself:
"for my friend, Karlheinz
with gratitude and best personal regards
Brian Mulroney"

payments made no sense. Nothing about this account made any
sense. The story raised serious questions – and Mulroney was the
only person with the answers.

Meanwhile, Mathias continued to press for the publication of his
story – but he got nowhere and eventually gave up. The environment
for its publication, he reflected a few years later, was just not right.
In fact, it was downright hostile. An experienced reporter with very
good sources, Mathias had been working on different angles of the
story ever since the 1995 Letter of Request. Now he had uncovered
what he thought was one of the biggest scoops ever, and, instead
of getting the front-page coverage the story objectively deserved,
Mathias was treated as a pariah and his story suppressed. A life-long
career in award-winning journalism concluded in disillusionment.

Mulroney may have sidestepped a public relations catastrophe,
but the respite was only temporary. I had learned of the payments,
and I wanted an explanation. I asked a series of questions, headed by
the most obvious one: What was the money for? I got different
answers from different people, but none of them was satisfactory.

Luc Lavoie, Mulroney's loyal spokesperson, told me that the
"money was paid to Mulroney to assist Schreiber with his pasta
business and to arrange a number of introductions and meetings with

international business executives." Mulroney himself would not give any details, but he did have an explanation – sort of. When he rejoined Ogilvy Renault, a leading Montreal law firm where he had first practised labour law after his call to the bar, he made it clear to the firm, he said, that, in addition to practising law, he would establish an independent international consultancy. The names of his clients would be confidential and would not be released without their permission. "If," and Mulroney emphasized the "if," clients paid for his services in cash, that would be reflected in the books of the company. All income would be declared and all taxes paid.

Fair enough. But had Mulroney been retained to lobby for Bearhead, at the very least he would have had to register as a lobbyist under legislation passed by Parliament under his government, which he did not. There might also have been conflict-of-interest issues, given that he had recently been prime minister and did not step down as a sitting MP until the general election on October 25, 1993. So perhaps, I thought, Mathias got that part of the story wrong, and the truth was that he received proper and appropriate payments for assisting Schreiber's other business interests in Canada and overseas.

That is exactly what happened, insisted Lavoie. Mulroney never lobbied for Schreiber, so he never had to register as a lobbyist. "All income was declared and all taxes paid." It was completely straightforward. "The truth is," Lavoie said in an interview with me, "Mr. Mulroney never had anything to do with Airbus, he had nothing to do with MBB, and he had nothing improper to do with Bearhead. Being hired as an international adviser after he left office was entirely consistent with the practice he was setting out to establish." It was certainly possible that Mulroney was only giving strategic advice. If so, registration would be unnecessary and no conflict-of-interest issue would arise. This explanation was a start, but not good enough.

What was the nature of the retainer? I asked. Was it for international introductions? Or was it for legal representation? Was it to help the pasta business? If so, exactly when did Schreiber begin that initiative? Was it as early as 1993? Schreiber laughed when I asked him if Mulroney helped him sell penne, but later, upon reflection, he told me that Mulroney did write him with some suggestions in 1994.[12] If the relationship was for legal advice, Mulroney would presumably have billed through his law firm, and any information about his activities on behalf of his client would have been privileged. The payment, if in cash, would have been recorded in the firm's records and books. If the money was paid to Mulroney as part of his international business consultancy, however, that would have been a different matter. In that case, what assignments were undertaken? How much time was put into the file? Was the fee proportionate to the service? And why cash? To be sure, Europeans frequently deal in cash – but North Americans generally do not. Former prime ministers operating international consultancies or practising law generally issue accounts, and then get paid in a more conventional way – by cheque or money transfer.

And on that point, why was Mulroney never asked any questions on the record while he was under oath about his relationship with Schreiber? He was examined by a number of government lawyers as part of his libel suit. Examination on discovery, as it is referred to in the province of Quebec, is a pre-trial procedure in which one side gets to ask the key witnesses for the other side, who swear under oath to tell the truth, any questions it has about the case. The purpose of the procedure is to save valuable court time by obtaining some of the evidence in advance. Mulroney spent two full days with his lawyers getting ready for his examination on discovery before his lawsuit. At the end of the first day of preparation, the lawyers said they were satisfied. Mulroney disagreed and did it all over again.

The real examination on discovery began on April 17, 1996, at the Montréal Palais de Justice. Before entering the courtroom, Mulroney turned to Lavoie and said, "Luc, do you know what [chief government lawyer Claude-Armand] Sheppard's problem is going to be today?"

"No, boss," Lavoie replied.

"He is going to ask me questions and he expects me to answer them."

This court appearance was the first time Mulroney had spoken publicly since he filed his lawsuit the previous November. He professed indignation and outrage. He seethed with anger against the RCMP, the Department of Justice, Jean Chrétien, Herb Gray, and Allan Rock, all of whom he believed were trying to destroy him and his place in history. Mulroney was well aware that the entire country was watching the heavily publicized proceeding. Every question became an opportunity for him to call the government to account, as he railed against the injustice of being called a criminal when he had not even been accused of a crime. In between his repeated condemnations of the wording of the 1995 Letter of Request, Mulroney was asked, and answered, a lot of questions about Schreiber and about his involvement with Schreiber's efforts, on behalf of Thyssen, to build light armoured vehicles in Cape Breton.

Obviously, Mulroney observed, any Canadian prime minister

would be interested in bringing manufacturing jobs to an area with one of the country's highest unemployment rates. Mulroney had a soft spot for Cape Bretoners; his alma mater, St Francis Xavier University, was located in nearby Antigonish. Mulroney was repeatedly asked about the Bearhead initiative, and he repeatedly made the point that it was his government that decided not to proceed with the project. The prospect that he had received any payment for this particular transaction, he insisted, was therefore unlikely.

Mulroney recalled that Schreiber was indefatigable. No matter how many times he was turned down, he would always come back with a different twist or spin to try to attract the government's interest. For example, when Ottawa said no to light armoured vehicles, he proposed building "peacekeeping vehicles" for use by Canadian and other troops on United Nations missions. But General Motors Canada already had a facility in London, Ontario, for building this kind of vehicle, and there was no way Mulroney's government was going to spend the $100 million required to help launch a second one.

Examinations on discovery provide each side in a legal action with wide scope to ask the other side questions – and this one was no exception. Government lawyers had the opportunity to put Mulroney's relationship with Schreiber under a microscope. But not once in the hundreds of questions they put to the former prime minister was he ever asked point-blank whether he had accepted money from Schreiber – even though the central claim made against Mulroney in the 1995 letter to the Swiss was that he'd been paid off. Had Mulroney been asked whether he'd taken a bribe, he obviously would have denied it. And there is no evidence, none whatsoever, that he had. But asking him whether he'd done business with Schreiber was a fairly logical place to start, along with a detailed inspection of every call, every letter, every visit – everything to do with all aspects of the relationship between the two men. When was the first time they met? Where? What did they discuss? When was the second time and the third time? Mulroney should have been asked, in detail, about each and every meeting and conversation they had ever held. He should have been asked about every letter they exchanged. Three days were scheduled for the discovery, but, as it turned out, the government lawyers called it quits after a day and a half. Mulroney was never questioned exactly how many times he had met Schreiber, in what circumstances, and where. Mulroney was asked very little about his relationship with Schreiber after he stopped being prime minister. But the topic was not avoided completely:

QUESTION: Did you maintain contact with Schreiber after you ceased being prime minister?

ANSWER: Well, from time to time, not very often. When he was going through Montreal, he would give me a call. We would have a cup of coffee, I think, once or twice. And he told me that he continued to work on his project, that he was pushing a new government ... the desirability at the time was to work with the provincial Government of Quebec and the federal government, the new federal government, to establish this new project in the east end of Montreal, where the jobs were badly required. And he told me that he had hired Marc Lalonde to represent his interests before the new Liberal government.

I wasn't really surprised because the word in Ottawa is that Schreiber and Lalonde had had a long relationship in the past. And so he also expressed dismay with me that my government had not agreed or could not include the contract that he liked. So, he said that he had hired Lalonde, and he hoped this would give rise to an agreement.

QUESTION: When he passes through Montreal and visits you, is it at your office or at your home?

ANSWER: Well, he doesn't pass through Montreal and visit me. He comes when he's on his way to Montreal. He called me and asked me, and I say perhaps once or twice, if I could come to a cup, have a cup of coffee with him at a hotel. I think I had one in the Queen Elizabeth Hotel with him.

QUESTION: Oh. So it's at his –

ANSWER: I had one in the –

QUESTION: Yeah

ANSWER: – in the coffee bar of the Queen Elizabeth Hotel.

Mulroney also was asked a number of times about his conversations with Schreiber after Schreiber informed him of the existence of the 1995 letter to Swiss authorities:

QUESTION: And the Canadian government alleges that very substantial sums were paid to Schreiber by Airbus Industries, and you didn't discuss with Schreiber whether it was true or not?

ANSWER: The document said, among other things, this: "This investigation is of serious concern to the Government of Canada, as it involves criminal activity on the part of a former prime minister." This is not an allegation, this is a statement of fact where the Government of Canada is judge, jury and executioner.

And what preoccupied me – inasmuch as I had never heard of the Airbus matter in my life – what preoccupied me were the extraordinary falsehoods and injustices as they involve me. And I wondered with my family and friends, quite frankly, how in the name of God could this come about? How can something like this actually take place?

And the fact that Mr. Schreiber may or may not have had any business dealings was not my principal ... my principal preoccupation. I had never had any dealings with him.

The statement "I had never had any dealings with him" was not quite correct. Mulroney had never had any dealings with Schreiber on Airbus. He had never had any dealings with him on the helicopter purchase. He had some prime ministerial dealings with him on Bearhead – he did not approve the project and the request for federal money. At the very least, he had dealings with him while in office – and he had had dealings with him since.

Later in the questioning of Mulroney, the following exchange occurred:

QUESTION: Perhaps I misunderstood. When you talked about having coffee with Schreiber at the Queen Elizabeth, it was in the period subsequent to November, 1995?
ANSWER: No, no, it was after I left office in 1993, and that's when he told me, as I indicated to you, that ... he was dismayed that my government had not allowed him to proceed with his desire to build this Thyssen project.

And that's when he told me that he had hired Marc Lalonde to represent him because he figured that Lalonde could prevail upon Chrétien and the government to have this done in the east end of Montreal. Which, by the way, had they been able to do it ... I thought it was a good project, and so I wouldn't have been critical of anything.

He told me he had hired Lalonde to do that; he told me he was contemplating legal action against my government; that he had hired a prominent law firm in Ottawa – I think Ian Scott's law firm, very distinguished lawyer – to take action against ... the bureaucrats in my government who, he alleged, had frustrated the fact that he was never able to get a deal through. This deal ... that was the kind of conversation we had.

He expressed the hope that Lalonde would be successful in

persuading the new Liberal government to agree to conditions that would enable him to proceed with the project. That was it.

But was that it? Mulroney had by then accepted a retainer of some kind from Schreiber. The questions to him were badly framed, and they were very, very carefully answered. Yet we should not, perhaps, be too critical of the government lawyers for not probing more deeply into Mulroney's commercial relationship with Schreiber. The impression his answers gave would not immediately lead them to conclude that there was any such relationship between the two men.

There are a number of reasons possibly explaining why Mulroney was not more forthcoming, given his commercial relationship with Schreiber. Before filing the lawsuit, he had, through his envoy, Roger Tassé, the distinguished former deputy minister of justice, offered to come to Ottawa and to make a complete financial disclosure – income-tax returns, business records, everything, including, presumably, details about his work for Schreiber – to government and RCMP officials. He was turned down flat.

Since then, the lawsuit had commenced and many months had passed. Mulroney was now facing at least nine government lawyers, and he had no intention of doing their job. He had, however, promised to respond to questions truthfully, and he kept his cards very close to his chest. "Ya gotta give something to get something," he once told me.

It is not unusual for witnesses to spin their testimony by avoiding embarrassing information or by giving half-answers or evasive responses. It is actually common for witnesses with a stake in the proceedings to do so. Yet Mulroney was no ordinary witness or litigant. He was suing his own country in a purported effort to defend his honour. More important, he was not only a lawyer, and that meant he was an officer of the court with special professional obligations for ethical conduct, but also the former prime minister of Canada, a person who would understand fully that questions are asked during an examination for discovery in order to uncover relevant information. While the law of perjury defined his legal obligations as a witness, his moral obligations were much more exacting. If he wanted to prove his honesty and integrity, rather than simply change perceptions about them, he would have to be completely forthright – he would have to give a full and frank response to questions, and not the selective, convenient responses a self-interested litigant in a private commercial lawsuit might offer.

Context is, of course, everything. Mulroney had ample opportunity to come clean about his professional relationship with Schreiber. Instead, he helped to create the impression that he carefully considered Schreiber's business proposal when he was prime minister but declined to give it the go-ahead after he determined it was not in the best interest of the Canadian people. He also left the impression that he subsequently maintained, at best, a cordial and infrequent acquaintance with Schreiber after he left office. Testifying that he and Schreiber simply had coffee together was intended to suggest that all contact between the two was trivial, when it clearly was not. The statement "I had never had any dealings with him" is even more problematical and oddly reminiscent of Bill Clinton's claim that he "did not have sexual relations with that woman, Miss Lewinsky."

In Canadian law, a successful perjury prosecution requires the Crown to establish four things – what the criminal law refers to as the elements of the offence. First, a person must make a false statement in a judicial proceeding or in a sworn affidavit for a judicial proceeding. Second, the person who makes the statement must know that the statement is false. Third, the person must make the statement with the intent to mislead. And fourth, there must be corroboration establishing that the accused knew that he or she was giving false evidence. With these hurdles to overcome, perjury charges are rare in Canada, and convictions rarer still. Whether the statement "I had never had any dealings with him" is perjury depends on many things – Mulroney's intention, for example, not to mention the tense in which he was speaking. In 1996, when Mulroney was examined under oath, he had had dealings with Schreiber – he took $300,000 in cash from him and had met with him on a number of occasions in different hotel rooms in order to do so. There were also innumerable telephone calls between the two after Schreiber informed Mulroney about the 1995 Letter of Request. Perhaps Mulroney's answer was confined, in his mind, to the Airbus period when he was in office. But the answer given, "I had never had any dealings with him," left the impression that he and Schreiber never did any business together – that they merely enjoyed a coffee from time to time.

Likewise, after giving a long answer during the discovery about Schreiber retaining Marc Lalonde to assist him in Bearhead, Mulroney said, "That was it." Again, Mulroney could and would claim that the answer relates entirely to the discussion of the Bearhead project. But the listener could be forgiven for concluding that "that was it" for the extent of Mulroney's relationship with Schreiber.

Only Mulroney can say whether these answers, given under oath, were framed in such a way as to mislead. He may very well not have had that intention, but they did mislead. They misled the government lawyers and they misled me (and explain why I readily accepted Mulroney's description at our first substantive interview of his limited relationship with Schreiber). They would cause any objective observer to conclude that things were other than they were – to believe that Schreiber was an unimportant character in Mulroney's life, not one of his employers and the source of a sum equivalent to more than five times the average Canadian family's before-tax income in 1996 of $56,629. Still, while his answers were slippery, evasive, calculated, they can be contextualized to suggest that they are not false. Mulroney could therefore successfully defend a perjury prosecution. What will be harder to defend is his reputation. This performance, given during a proceeding meant to reclaim his honour, will make it harder for him to sell himself as a man of honour. In his own self-interest, his answers buried an embarrassing truth. As a result, the Government of Canada was misled and the Canadian people were misled. He should have seized the opportunity to set out the entire story.

There were, Luc Lavoie points out, "nine lawyers sitting there on the government side and not one of them ever asked Mulroney whether he got money from Schreiber." And what if they'd done so? "If they had," Mulroney told me not long ago, "I would have answered the question." Not so, according to Lavoie: "They would have been told that the relationship was privileged."

The government lawyers, Mulroney counsel Jacques Jeansonne explains, had no entitlement to ask Mulroney any questions about these payments. Jeansonne has a technical explanation about the operation of the rules of civil procedure in Quebec and how those rules, properly applied to this case, would have disentitled the government lawyers to an answer. Now that would have been interesting. Surely in Quebec, as everywhere else in Canada, payments to Mulroney by the man alleged to have bribed him would be relevant and admissible, even if those payments were not related to Airbus and to the defamation lawsuit. That would have been, in any event, a matter for the judge to sort out later.

In any case, all these different explanations are inconsistent and do not add up. What kind of assistance could Mulroney offer in the promotion of pasta? While Mulroney is extremely well connected, it is doubtful that he knows either Mama Bravo or Chef Boyardee. Helping out on the purchase or sale of planes, helicopters, and light armoured vehicles makes much more sense for the former prime minister re-establishing himself in the world of international commerce.

Karlheinz Schreiber is a middleman and industrialist. He had a commission arrangement with Airbus Industrie, MBB, and Thyssen, the company behind the Bearhead project. Commissions were paid in all of these transactions. Schreiber kept some of the commission money for himself and distributed some of it to others, as was lawful in Germany.

According to documents unearthed by the *Fifth Estate*, half of the commissions earned on each Airbus sale were earmarked for distribution in Canada. Schreiber's German lawyer, Jan Olaf Leisner, in a major broadcasting coup by the investigative news show, went on air explaining what some of the commission money was for. Schreiber's role in the MBB transaction, he said, was to pass on *Schmiergelder*, lubrication money: "Mr. Schreiber's main role was to protect the recipients of the lubrication money ... by making every payment anonymous."[13] There is no evidence that Mulroney received any of these particular funds or any of the commissions paid in Airbus. Schreiber insists he has never bribed anyone in Canada. He has, however, been generous: "I was always generous my whole life," he says. Has he given a lot of money to a lot of people? "Sure," he replies.[14]

There are serious unanswered questions about the manner in which Schreiber paid Mulroney. Professionals in Canada are now, under the proceeds-of-crime legislation, required to report cash payments greater than $10,000, though at the time of Schreiber's payment to Mulroney this legislation was not yet in place. Why is this rule needed? Because cash payments are inherently suspicious. Moreover, where does someone get $100,000 in cash? Banks are required to report deposits of that amount. Where did Mulroney put his money? And where did he get the nerve to sue the RCMP and the Government of Canada for $50 million to refute a claim that he had been bribed by Schreiber, when the two had done business together in circumstances where Mulroney believed both the arrangement and the payments needed to be kept quiet? When Mulroney had been paid for those services, whatever they were for, in cash? When a more persistent questioner might have probed more deeply and possibly exposed the arrangement? And once exposed, Mulroney would have found it difficult to explain it away. His reputation would have been ruined forever. It was a very close call.

But, as fate would have it, it was not yet over. When I wrote my book on Airbus, I made many efforts to interview Karlheinz Schreiber but succeeded in speaking to him only once, briefly. "Bobby," Schreiber said, referring to his Edmonton attorney Robert Hladun, "says I should not speak with you." After hearing Philip Mathias's story, however, I renewed those earlier efforts for an interview and, after a long period of negotiations, he agreed to meet.

Schreiber is a very friendly fellow, naturally a bit of a rascal, smart and shrewd. The first thing he told me when we finally got together was that he was sorry he had never agreed to a proper interview before my book was published. He went on to say that he had asked various people about me and whether he should cooperate with me. Among those he talked to was Brian Mulroney. According to Schreiber, Mulroney advised him that under no circumstances should he consent to an interview with me because I was completely unreliable and likely hostile. Schreiber accepted the advice, having no idea until my book came out that Mulroney was cooperating completely, having agreed to make himself, his records, and his lawyers available without restriction. That, at least, was our agreement. I thought it was honoured. So until this meeting was arranged, I never had an opportunity to ask Schreiber about his relationship with Mulroney – the central question. Schreiber immediately began to provide some of the details. Without a doubt, if Luc Lavoie had not called him "the biggest fucking liar the world has ever seen," and suggested Mulroney held the same view, he would have kept quiet. But that was just too much for the man who had given Mulroney $300,000 – for the man who, like Mulroney, believes first and foremost in his own righteousness and honour.

In the midst of learning more about Schreiber's mysterious payments to Mulroney, I found out about a secret trial taking place at Toronto's Osgoode Hall. The details were sketchy. My sources skittish. To all appearances it was Airbus: The Sequel. One way or another, all the usual suspects had been invited or were in attendance: Brian Mulroney, Karlheinz Schreiber, Frank Moores, and, in a stunning starring role, their enemy number one: Canada's best-known investigative journalist, Stevie Cameron.

2 A Secret Trial

"What the fuck is this?" Eddie Greenspan asked out loud on April 9, 2001, when his assistant passed over a hand-delivered piece of paper advising him of a secret proceeding in progress at Toronto's Osgoode Hall courthouse. Greenspan sat down at the imposing desk in his oversized office in a restored bank building, around the corner from the St Lawrence Market, and eyed the huge tank filled with tropical fish. The secret trial, the document indicated, might be of interest to one of his clients.

Greenspan, the leading Canadian criminal defence lawyer of his generation, knew that, in certain rare circumstances, secret trials were permitted under the *Criminal Code*. But this, a letter dated April 9, 2001, from the Crown Attorney's Office in Toronto, was a first for him:

> I understand that you represent Karlheinz Schreiber. If this is not or no longer the case, please advise me immediately at the above number. Justice Then has asked me to convey to counsel for Karlheinz Schreiber the attached notice.[1]

On a second plain sheet of paper, the text read as follows:

Superior Court of Justice
Toronto Region

NOTICE TO POTENTIALLY INTERESTED PARTIES

PLEASE TAKE NOTICE that at 361 University Avenue, Toronto, on the 24th day of April 2001, at 10.00 a.m. or as soon thereafter as practicable, there shall be a hearing concerning the release of certain currently sealed search warrant information.

As your name is mentioned within that information, you

may consider attending to make any submission on your standing and interests concerning the release, public access and publication of this information beyond the access that the Court
may grant the subject of the search warrants in question.

You may appear in person or through counsel and you are
not obliged to attend or to be represented.

Greenspan reached for the telephone and called Schreiber, the man
at the centre of the Airbus scandal. For years, Greenspan had been
busy thwarting the Canadian government's efforts to extradite
Schreiber to Germany, where he was wanted on charges of tax evasion and bribery and for questioning about his role in a huge German fundraising scandal. Greenspan was also the lead lawyer on
Schreiber's $35 million lawsuit filed in Edmonton against the Cana-
dian government and the RCMP. And he had successfully represented Schreiber in his defamation action against Mulroney spokesperson Luc Lavoie.

Greenspan was the "go to" guy if you were in serious trouble.
For example, Gerald Regan, the former premier of Nova Scotia, beat
a path to his door when he was arrested by the police. More than
thirty women had claimed that Regan, who also served as a cabinet
minister under Pierre Trudeau (including, for a time, as minister
responsible for the status of women), had attacked them. In 1995,
he was charged with seventeen counts of rape, attempted rape,
forcible confinement, and indecent assault. The Crown proceeded
first with eight charges of sexual assault. Greenspan, in his trade-
mark "take no prisoners" approach, hammered at the memories and
motives of the complainants and, in the end, secured an acquittal in
a case many believed was a slam dunk for the Crown. Over the years
since his 1970 call to the bar, Greenspan defended mobsters, bikers,
rapists, murderers, police officers, celebrities, just about anyone in
trouble. Something of a media darling – he was always ready with a
colourful quote – Greenspan was a ferocious and talented gladiator
once he got into court. He always played by the rules, but in doing
so single-mindedly pursued the interests of his client. What in the
world, Greenspan now wondered, was going on?

What was going on was a secret legal proceeding in a country
where open courts are the general rule. It is a difficult and complicated story, but it is a critical one, important to everything that follows in this book.

Greenspan knew that the offices of Schreiber's Alberta accountants had been searched in December 1999. He had also heard that
Eurocopter, the successor company to MCL – Messerschmitt Canada

Edward Greenspan, Canada's leading criminal defence attorney, was not
pleased when he received official notification of the secret proceedings.

Limited, a subsidiary of MBB, the German helicopter manufacturer,
which had years earlier sold some helicopters to the Canadian Coast
Guard, had been searched around the same time. But, he thought,
that was it. Once he received this unusual notice, however, he had
lots of questions, which he began directing to the Crown attorneys on
the file, Michael Bernstein and Trevor Shaw. Bernstein was a 1979
McGill University Law School graduate with expertise in prosecuting complex commercial and stock fraud. He was the lead Crown on
the file. Extremely smart and highly conscientious, Bernstein, however, had a reputation for inflexibility, not to mention a tendency to
ask ten questions when one would do. Shaw was an academic super-
star. After graduating from Queen's Law School in 1992, he won a
coveted clerkship at the Supreme Court of Canada and then spent a
year at the University of Paris II (Pantheon-Assas), where he obtained

Crown prosecutors Trevor Shaw and Michael Bernstein

an advanced diploma in French criminal law. After he joined the Crown Law Office in 1996, he developed an extremely busy trial and appellate practice, focusing on criminal cases with an international or comparative dimension.

Under what authority, Greenspan asked, did the judge issue the notice to counsel? Was he to attend wearing his legal gown? Lawyers care about that sort of thing. Would the proceeding be held in open court or in chambers? Was his client a target of the search warrant or simply referred to in the Information to Obtain? The "Information" is the key background document the police present to a judge to get his or her approval for a search warrant. Other documents are often included to supplement the record. The purpose of this material is to satisfy the judge that there are reasonable and probable grounds justifying a search, because a very high standard must be met before the police are entitled to enter private premises, search, and remove what they wish.

Could he please, Greenspan asked, have a copy of the warrant? Who else was getting notice? Could he meet with Justice Then before April 24 to review these and other issues? Edward Then was a 1970 graduate of the University of Toronto Law School, with an MA in political science. He spent his entire career before his appointment to

Mr Justice Edward Then – a fair but
not especially speedy jurist

the bench as a lawyer in the Crown Law Office, handling special
prosecutions, high-profile long trials, murder cases, and important
criminal appeals. He looks like a gentle giant and is extremely good-
natured. In 1989 he was appointed to the bench, incidentally by Mulroney, and has since earned an excellent reputation as a fair-minded
judge.

Wear a gown, Crown Counsel Trevor Shaw replied, and the matter will proceed in a courtroom. In the meantime, there could be no
"pre-emptive" meetings with the judge. "I am not in a position,"
Shaw wrote on April 20, "to provide more information than that contained in the Superior Court Notice and accompanying letter. This is
because of two circumstances: The *in camera* nature of previous proceedings and existing sealing orders." *In camera* means that the proceedings were being held behind closed doors only for invited guests.
No spectators were allowed.

Greenspan knew from the notice that there was a search warrant
and that his client's name was in the Information. The notice also
indicated that this background document had been ordered sealed –
in other words, access to it was also restricted. The April 20 letter
informed Greenspan that the case was not just beginning but was
already under way. What Greenspan did not know, but would soon
learn, was that it was at the suggestion of the Crown attorneys, in an

April 4, 2001, letter to Justice Then, that Karlheinz Schreiber, Frank Moores, Brian Mulroney, and Harvey Cashore and the Canadian Broadcasting Corporation were getting an identical notice of the proceeding. Only one conclusion could be drawn: Schreiber, Mulroney, and Moores were all mentioned in the search warrant Information. But why were Cashore and the CBC being invited to the party?

Harvey Cashore first became interested in Brian Mulroney when he worked for John Sawatsky on his critical biography of Mulroney, *The Politics of Ambition*, after graduating with a degree in journalism from Carleton University. Later, Cashore joined the CBC's *Fifth Estate*, first as a researcher and then as a producer. Intellectually rigorous and extremely fair-minded, he has won, or been nominated for, just about every journalism award given in Canada. He had been following the Airbus story for years, and, together with Stevie Cameron, had written a book called *The Last Amigo*. It was mostly about Karlheinz Schreiber, but Mulroney played a strong supporting role. Cashore and the CBC were now being notified because they were already aware of the legal proceedings. Cashore had, in fact, made an earlier attempt to cover the case. Now, a year later, Justice Then believed they should be told about its resumption, if only to make representations about their entitlement to attend. Judges take the *Charter of Rights and Freedoms* seriously, and Justice Then was no exception. He believed that Cashore and the CBC, at the very least, deserved notification so they could argue in favour of their constitutional right to report on the proceedings.

For Schreiber, Mulroney, and Moores, it was a different matter. They did not have a clue about the closed-door proceeding. Greenspan did not have much experience with secret trials – few Canadian lawyers do – but he did not need a road map to conclude that, whatever was going on at the University Avenue courtroom, it was probably bad news for his client. Schreiber was wanted by the authorities overseas, and he had been heavily implicated in the earlier and still ongoing Airbus investigation, when the RCMP had accused him of paying bribes to Mulroney. Greenspan was well aware that, whatever was taking place, his client was almost certainly a target. But of what? The answer to that question would be found in Justice Then's courtroom when the case continued on April 24, 2001.

As part of the settlement of Mulroney's lawsuit, the RCMP had made it clear that it would continue its investigation into wrongdoing. Mulroney encouraged the police to do so, in his words, "until the cows come home." That is the way it must be in a democracy. It is the police who decide whom to investigate, when to investigate,

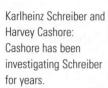

Karlheinz Schreiber and Harvey Cashore: Cashore has been investigating Schreiber for years.

and when to stop investigating. In the aftermath of Mulroney's settlement, the RCMP preserved these fundamental principles. Litigation is often a tactic, and if it had been employed by Mulroney to intimidate the RCMP into calling the whole thing off, it failed. If anything, it had the opposite effect, as even more resources were directed to the investigation.

By December 1999 the Mounties were ready to move. On December 8 Ottawa Superior Court Justice James A. Fontana signed five search warrants for five searches: the offices of Eurocopter in Fort Erie, Ontario; the Department of Fisheries and Oceans in Ottawa; the main branch of the Bank of Nova Scotia in Calgary; the offices of accountants Buchanan, Barry & Co., also in Calgary; and the offices of John Verhey, another chartered accountant, in Nepean, Ontario, just outside Ottawa. These warrants were unusual because, at the same time that he gave his judicial authorization to the various searches, Justice Fontana directed that just about every document associated with the case be placed under seal. Not only that, even the application to seal the background documents was ordered sealed, as were the actual search warrants. Justice Fontana did not give detailed reasons for his decision other than noting "that overriding circumstances justify the issuance of the present order." The judicial direction was authorized by section 487 of the *Criminal Code*.

Section 487.3(1) of the *Criminal Code* provides that a judge issuing a search warrant may make an order "prohibiting access to and the disclosure of any information relating to the warrant or authorization" if the following grounds are met:

(a) the ends of justice would be subverted by the disclosure for one of the reasons referred to in subsection (2) or the information might be used for improper purpose; and

(b) the ground referred to in paragraph (a) outweighs in importance the access to the information.

Subsection (2) sets out the circumstances in which the ends of justice would be subverted:

(a) if disclosure of the Information would
     (i) compromise the identity of a confidential informant
     (ii) compromise the nature and extent of an ongoing investigation
     (iii) endanger a person engaged in particular intelligence gathering techniques and thereby prejudice future investigations in which similar techniques would be used, or
     (iv) prejudice the interests of an innocent person; and

(b) for any other sufficient reason.

Under subsection (3), a judge is given broad discretion in making such an order to impose terms, including terms related to the length of the prohibition on disclosure, providing, where appropriate, for partial disclosure, and so on. Under subsection (4), an application can be made to the justice or judge who made the order, or to a justice or judge of the court before whom any proceedings arising out of the investigation may be held, to terminate the order or to vary any of its terms or conditions.

In the usual course of events, after a search warrant is executed and after the objects found as a result of the search are brought before a judge, any member of the public is entitled to inspect the warrant and the background documents on which it is based, unless it has been established that the ends of justice would be subverted by disclosure or that the judicial documents might be used for some improper purpose. In fact, even if nothing is seized during the search, an accused who was the target of the search is generally entitled to inspect the Information, the warrant, and any related documentation. Targets of search warrants usually have a keen interest in knowing what evidence the police have amassed against them.

The leading case interpreting this part of the *Criminal Code* is called *Attorney General of Nova Scotia v. MacIntyre*. In that instance, Linden MacIntyre, a well-known CBC journalist pursuing a story on political patronage in Nova Scotia, sought a declaration that he was entitled to inspect particular search warrants and the background documents used to obtain them. When the justice of the peace refused to hand over the materials, the CBC went to court, and the case went all the way to the Supreme Court of Canada. MacIntyre took the position throughout that, although he was a journalist, his right to the court file was no different from that of any other member of the public.

On behalf of the majority, Justice Brian Dickson, later the Chief Justice of Canada, held that a member of the public is entitled, after the search warrant has been executed, to inspect a warrant and the Information on which it was based. Search warrants, obviously, are granted in secret and on the application of the police. Surprise is necessary. Search warrants legalize what would otherwise be illegal – entry and seizure of private property. "As is often the case in a free society," Justice Dickson wrote, "there are at work two conflicting public interests. The one has to do with civil liberties and the protection of the individual from interference with the enjoyment of his property. There is a clear and important social value in avoidance of arbitrary searches and unlawful seizures. The other competing interest lies in the effective detection and proof of crime and the prompt apprehension and conviction of offenders. Public protection, afforded by efficient and effective law enforcement, is enhanced through the proper use of search warrants."[2]

In balancing these interests, Parliament made a choice. Notwithstanding the need for openness in judicial proceedings, that objective had to give way to secrecy in the granting and execution of search warrants. It all made eminent sense. If targets could find out in advance of a planned search, the whole initiative would become pointless.

Before the *MacIntyre* case, there was little law on the rights of the public to inspect warrants and Informations. It was well established that interested persons, usually the targets, could have a look after the search. An interested party has always had the right to apply to set aside or quash a search warrant. This right can be exercised only if the applicant is entitled to inspect the warrant and the background documents immediately after the warrant is executed.[3] This right is subject to the various exemptions for extenuating circumstances provided in the *Criminal Code*.

Linden MacIntyre was pushing the envelope by seeking to extend these rights to members of the public. He wanted the same disclosure entitlements after a warrant was executed as the targets and other interested persons enjoyed. "The question," as Justice Dickson framed it, "is whether, in law, any distinction can be drawn in respect of accessibility, between those persons who might be termed 'interested parties' and those members of the public who are unable to show any special interest in the proceedings."4 The answer to that question, he continued, "should be guided by several broad policy considerations, namely, respect for the privacy of the individual, protection of the administration of justice, implementation of the will of Parliament that a search warrant be an effective aid in the investigation of crime, and finally, a strong public policy in favour of 'openness' in respect to judicial acts ... In short, what should be sought is maximum accountability and accessibility but not to the extent of harming the innocent or of impairing the efficiency of the search warrant as a weapon in society's never-ending fight against crime."5

"In my view," Justice Dickson continued, "curtailment of public accessibility can only be justified where there is ... the need to pro-tect social values of superordinate importance." One of the values that Justice Dickson identified was protection of the innocent. Many search warrants are issued and executed, and nothing is found. In these circumstances, he said, there is little justification for the in-evitable sullying of name and reputation that would follow publi-cation of the search: "The public right to know must yield to the protection of the innocent." The situation was completely different, however, if the warrant was executed and something was seized.6

There was nothing wrong, the Supreme Court found, in approv-ing the warrant behind closed doors: "The effective administration of justice does justify the exclusion of the public from proceedings attending the actual issuance of the warrant."7 Nonetheless, the interests served by secrecy at the approval stage disappear once the warrant has been executed. "There is thereafter a 'diminished inter-est in confidentiality' as the purposes of the policy of secrecy are largely, if not entirely, accomplished."8

Where did these deliberations leave Linden MacIntyre? If inter-ested parties could see the warrants and the background documents once the warrants were executed, there was no reason, the court held, that members of the public should not be placed in that same situa-tion. After all, once the search took place, members of the public were in no position to frustrate the administration of justice. In those cir-cumstances where there was a risk, the court could act: "Undoubted-ly every court has a supervisory and protecting power over its own records. Access can be denied when the ends of justice would be sub-verted by disclosure or the judicial documents might be used for an improper purpose. The presumption, however, is in favour of public access and the burden of contrary proof lies upon the person who would deny the exercise of the right."⁹

Simply put, the court ruled that it was proper to obtain judicial approval for warrants behind closed doors. Once that was done, and after the warrant had been executed, the public should not, except in exceptional circumstances, be precluded from learning about the reasons advanced by the police and accepted by the judge as justification for what was, after all, an invasion of private property. Our system requires checks and balances. Public scrutiny of state behaviour is a democratic mainstay.

The warrants Justice Fontana approved were directed to a number of different targets. One was Eurocopter, which had sold twelve helicopters to the Canadian Coast Guard for $26.7 million in 1988. Schreiber received commissions in that sale, having been appointed a middleman for the company by Franz Josef Strauss. Frank Moores also got commissions; moreover, his company, Government Consultants International (GCI), had registered as the firm's lobbyist. The transaction had, at the time, attracted some mild criticism from internal auditors at Transport Canada: "Traditionally, comprehensive program needs assessment of cost-benefits analyses have not been conducted to justify helicopter acquisitions." It was the usual government jargon, but what was significant was that the auditors were not taking issue with the brand chosen or the cost, but with whether the Coast Guard needed any helicopters at all.

As it turned out, the product was tested across the country and introduced into the Coast Guard fleet with "exemplary smoothness." MBB established a joint venture with Fort Erie's Fleet Industries, where much of the manufacturing work for the new helicopters took place. That meant Canadian jobs, as well as an important transfer of technology. The Ontario government also came on board, and, ultimately, about $30 million of taxpayers' money was poured into the manufacturing facility. As with most other large government acquisitions between 1984 and 1993, rumours swirled around this one, particularly given the background presence of Schreiber and Moores. In the 1995 Letter of Request, the RCMP asserted that Mulroney had directed the contract to MBB in return for a financial benefit.

By December 1999, more than four years after the Letter of Request was sent to Switzerland, and some two years after the government and the RCMP settled with Mulroney and apologized to him, the Mounties had enough information to convince a judge to authorize a search. That search warrant was executed on December 13, 14,

Inspector Allan Mathews – he took charge of the investigation but learned only late in the game that there was a confidential informant.

and 15, 1999 (with the other locations being searched several days later). For three days, eighteen RCMP officers, led by Inspector Allan Mathews, descended on Eurocopter's Gilmore Road offices in Fort Erie. The investigators targeted four areas in the plant: the corporate offices, information technology, the finance department, and the archives storage area.

Mathews was a thirty-year veteran of the force. Unlike many RCMP recruits, he arrived at the "Depot Division" training college in Regina with a BA from Montreal's Sir George Williams University. His first posting was in southeastern Saskatchewan, in Weyburn, former home of CCF founder Tommy Douglas. Assignments in Balcarres, Buffalo Narrows, and Kamsack, all in rural Saskatchewan, followed, where Mathews learned the ins and outs of town, rural, and aboriginal policing. After being promoted to the rank of corporal, he was one of a handful of officers sent by the RCMP to the University of Ottawa to attend law school. Mathews and I first met when he was a student in a class I taught (as a law professor there between 1986 and 2000). He graduated in 1989, *magnum cum laude*. Six months later he was promoted to staff sergeant. Promotion to inspector came in 1997. In 1998, he was assigned to the Special Projects Department of the Commercial Crime Section, where, among other duties, he worked on the Airbus file, assuming responsibility for it in November 2000. In 2002 he was promoted to superintendent, one of the highest ranks in the force. He had been preparing for this raid for months. And when he got to the Eurocopter plant, company officials cooperated completely.

The RCMP was given the use of its boardroom and accorded all the information technology assistance it requested to enter the system and access the electronic files. The search went on from one day to the next, and the boardroom, used by the team as its central depository, was placed under twenty-four-hour armed guard. After a couple of days a Quonset hut and sea container outside the office began to attract attention, and a warrant was obtained to search them as well. In the meantime, advised that the first warrant had been served and that a search was in progress, Eurocopter's legal counsel, Paul B. Schabas, an experienced litigator from the Blakes law firm in Toronto, got Mathews on the telephone and asked him for a copy of the Information.

"No way," was the response, "the Information is sealed." What about a copy of the sealing order? Forget it, the Bay Street lawyer was told. Schabas, without a doubt one of Canada's top media lawyers, had started out his career as a criminal defence attorney, and he knew his way around the criminal courts. He graduated with his law degree from the University of Toronto and was called to the Ontario Bar in 1986. Over the years he racked up extensive experience as a trial and appellate counsel with expertise in a number of other areas, including constitutional and human rights law as well as corporate and commercial litigation. Schabas sent an articling student from the firm's Ottawa office to the main courthouse at Laurier and Elgin to obtain copies of any documents in the public domain. It was a dead end. Everything connected with the search was under seal.

What Schabas did not know, but would learn later, were the reasons first given for all the secrecy. It was essential, Inspector Mathews swore in his affidavit, that the Information remain under seal. Disclosure, he explained to the judge, would subvert the ends of justice by prejudicing the interests of innocent persons. Who did the RCMP have in mind? The indirect answer was Brian Mulroney, "persons of considerable public stature or who are engaged in public service and whose reputation is their significant asset." Mathews noted that the investigation had already "experienced the consequences of the disclosure of a 1995 Letter of Request to Switzerland."[10] In case Justice Fontana missed the point, the RCMP inspector elaborated at

Tony Wong and Paul Schabas – Schabas was on the case from the beginning, assisted by his promising associate, Tony Wong.

length, concluding that: "An order restricting disclosure of the Information ... in this case until the conclusion of the investigation and a final decision on any charges would best protect the interest of all those presumed innocent."

The RCMP was looking out for Mulroney's reputation – and that was certainly a twist on an old story. It was also, it claimed, concerned about compromising the nature and extent of the investigation, one of the other grounds listed for sealing in the *Criminal Code*. That seemed reasonable enough. The aircraft industry operated in secrecy. Many of the people the Mounties had sought assistance from had been reluctant to participate. If the information became public, the chances of securing their cooperation, and the cooperation of others, would be substantially reduced by the publicity. "This difficulty," Mathews wrote, "is compounded by the relatively early stage of the MBB investigation."[11]

Now that was interesting. A search warrant had been granted and tens of thousands of pieces of paper seized, among other records. And the investigation was in its early stages? Where had we heard that before? When Mulroney first learned about the 1995 Letter of

Request, he retained Roger Tassé and sent him to see the RCMP. Tassé, who knew the system from the inside out, having served as deputy solicitor general (1972–77) and deputy minister of justice (1977–85), advised the RCMP that Mulroney was ready to come to Ottawa at a moment's notice, to answer any questions and to provide any records – including all his personal financial records – that the RCMP wished to examine. That was not necessary, Tassé was told by a senior RCMP officer: "We are just beginning our investigation." After several more years and thousands of investigatory hours by more than a dozen RCMP officers, forensic accountants, and support staff, another investigation remained in its early stages.

According to Inspector Mathews, simply banning publication was not enough. Journalistic inquiries were inevitable. No kidding. The execution of the search would inevitably come to the attention of the press. Eighteen RCMP officers had arrived at Eurocopter's Canadian headquarters in Fort Erie and had stayed there, around the clock, for three weekdays. The search was sure to become public. Yet among the grounds set out in Mathews's affidavit advanced in support of the sealing was the argument that potential witnesses might be scared off if details of the investigation leaked out.

It would be a long time before Schabas got to see this affidavit. An affidavit is a written statement of fact, voluntarily made, and the person making it takes an oath that the contents are true. Affidavits are a convenient method of bringing sworn evidence to the attention of the court. In this case the evidence in the affidavits, all supplied by Inspector Mathews, gave the judge – and eventually the other parties – the various rationales being advanced in support of the Crown's position on secrecy. Paradoxically, however, even when this particular affidavit and others were disclosed, large portions were blacked out or, in the language of the criminal courts, redacted. In the meantime, Schabas knew from experience that when Justice Fontana signed the warrants, and then sealed everything in sight, he would have relied on a supporting affidavit of some kind. Accordingly, Schabas wrote to Justice Fontana and asked for further details. "As I am sure you are aware," Schabas elaborated, "once a search warrant has been executed, the usual need for secrecy regarding its issuance no longer applies, and in most cases the subject of the search (and the public) is entitled to review the Information."[12] The matter was of some urgency: "I am writing to you as a last resort requesting any details or information which the Court can provide regarding the issuance of the warrant and the basis for it and the basis for and terms of any sealing order. As you can appreciate, as matters cur-

Mr Justice James Fontana –
he wrote the book on search
and seizure.

rently stand, my client has been subjected to a search, the basis for which is unknown to it, and its efforts to obtain information through the Court have been completely unsuccessful. At the very least, my client should be provided with information regarding the basis for the sealing order and its terms, including the duration of the sealing order."[13]

The request seemed reasonable enough. Schabas was clearly acting properly, but Justice Fontana thought otherwise: "Your letter to me," he wrote, "is unorthodox and inappropriate. Contact the local crown if you like," he continued, suggesting that any requests for assistance be made through channels other than him. "If you are not content," he concluded, "you have remedies."[14] Fontana was a no-nonsense judge. An Osgoode Hall Law School graduate, Fontana was called to the bar in 1966, beginning his legal career as an Assistant Crown Attorney in Ottawa, before moving into private practice. In 1984, he was appointed to the Ontario Court of Justice (Criminal) by Attorney General Roy McMurtry. Not only had he written a best-selling book (into four editions) titled *The Law of Search and Seizure*, he had also published a novel. A judge of the old school, he had taken obvious umbrage at being directly approached on a matter before him by the Toronto lawyer.

Schabas, who was just trying to find out what was going on, did as suggested, and the local Crown put him in touch with the two Crown counsel assigned to the case, Michael Bernstein and Trevor Shaw. Schabas decided to appeal to them for assistance: "My client," he wrote on December 17, 1999, "has been subjected to a three-day search, in which many documents were seized. Yet my client is unable to obtain any details of the basis for the search, in order to assess whether the search was reasonable or justified in any manner. Further, my client is unable to even obtain information as to why it cannot review the Information, as the sealing order and any evidence supporting the sealing order is also sealed. Indeed, because the sealing order is apparently indefinite in length, my client has no idea when, if ever, the grounds for the sealing order, let alone the search itself, will be disclosed or reviewed by a judicial officer." This situation, Schabas suggested, was "intolerable." On December 22, 1999, it seemed that Schabas was getting through. The first sealing order was made public in Ottawa, while the second sealing order was released the next day. Schabas was not allowed, of course, to see any affidavit material justifying the sealing.

That was a good start, but Schabas needed to know more because both orders told him very little he did not already know. He asked Shaw to advise when the Crown expected the sealing order to be vacated – meaning, when the background documents and the Information would become available to the public. Schabas also asked Shaw to arrange for copies to be made of some of the business records that had been seized, since Eurocopter needed them for day-to-day operations.

The company also took strong objection to the scope of the search. Many of the documents the RCMP took away were government documents or were already available in the public domain. Other records, Schabas argued, had nothing to do with anything the RCMP could have any legitimate interest in knowing about. Those documents should be returned. Perhaps most important of all, Eurocopter wanted the sealing orders set aside – immediately. Schabas knew that the Crown would, periodically, be required to justify the continued detention of all the documents that had been seized. In the normal course, that would take place every four months. But the sealing was a different matter. There was nothing in the *Criminal Code* that put time limits on that. Unless a judge ruled otherwise, the background documents and the Information, the affidavits – everything – might stay sealed forever. When these representations got nowhere, Schabas decided to make an application to the court

– an application to the same Justice Fontana he had previously annoyed. He had no choice, for the *Criminal Code* provision, and it was a new one, indicated that any application to vary or terminate a sealing order should go back before the judge who issued it. If Schabas had no success in convincing Justice Fontana to change his mind, his only recourse was to appeal to a higher court.

3 In Court

The unusual hearing into Eurocopter's request to unseal the Information to Obtain, the key background document used by the RCMP to persuade Justice Fontana to approve the search, along with various supporting documents, including affidavits filed by Inspector Allan Mathews explaining to the judge why there was a continued need for secrecy after the warrant was executed, began on January 28, 2000, in Ottawa. Several days earlier, Inspector Mathews had, as required by the *Criminal Code*, reported to Justice Fontana, providing the judge, in a document called a "return," with a lengthy inventory of everything the RCMP had seized. Over 1,700 documents had been taken away – and a copy of the list was sent to Eurocopter lawyer Paul Schabas. At the same time, Inspector Mathews applied, again under the *Criminal Code*, for an order to detain everything he had seized. He provided another affidavit setting out the reasons why. As is the practice, only the judge got to see it.

Mathews privately reported to the court that he was in the process of completing a Letter of Request to Germany for assistance in the Eurocopter investigation. There was obviously an overlap between the contents of the various background documents placed before Justice Fontana and the contents of this new Letter of Request. The RCMP inspector expressed the concern that, if any details were made public about either the contents of the Information or the new Letter of Request, or even if only a description of the records seized by the RCMP and listed in the return was made public, all these documents could give someone under investigation an insight into the police theory of the case and place the investigation in jeopardy. The RCMP wished to avoid any such result.

It was bad enough, Mathews swore in his affidavit, that Karlheinz Schreiber had learned about the Eurocopter search. Surely, however, Mathews did not expect that the RCMP could search the offices of

Schreiber's accountants without his becoming aware that the investigation had moved to a new phase. In fact, even though nothing was reported in Canada, an account had been published in *Der Spiegel*, the leading German newsmagazine. Indeed, German media interest in all matters related to Schreiber was accelerating. Schreiber was wanted in Germany to face outstanding tax evasion and bribery charges. German investigations had already been thwarted by disappearing evidence, and Schreiber was not the only fugitive from German justice. To the extent possible, the RCMP wanted to keep the investigation under wraps. Still, it was hardly surprising that word quickly leaked, especially to people who had an interest in knowing about this sort of thing. It would be even worse, Mathews suggested, if, through further disclosure, Schreiber got wind of any future police investigative actions. Clearly, other investigations were in progress – and Schreiber was one of the targets.

When Eurocopter lawyer Paul Schabas arrived at the Ottawa courthouse, his first challenge was figuring out where the proceedings were being held. No information about the case was posted anywhere, and court officials could provide no assistance. Schabas began to wander around. Eventually Crown attorney Trevor Shaw approached and introduced himself. He then led Schabas to a small motions courtroom on the completely deserted fifth floor.

When the proceedings eventually began, Schabas asked the judge to unseal the court file. "I know," Schabas began, "Your Honour is very knowledgeable of the search and seizure law, but I think it's fair to say that my client is in a somewhat unusual, if not extraordinary position." Schabas spelled it out: Eurocopter had been subject to a search of its premises over the course of three days. A large number of documents and records had been seized. But the company was not even allowed to know the basis for the search: "Not only is it denied the right to know why it has been searched, it is denied the right to know why it can't be told why it can be searched." Schabas freely acknowledged that it was within the discretion of the judge to determine the extent of any sealing, but he suggested that this discretion be exercised in a manner that did not run roughshod over his client's rights.[1]

The Eurocopter lawyer was, obviously, at a major disadvantage. All he had was the warrant and the sealing order. He had not seen any of the background materials, nor had he seen any of the affidavits filed by Inspector Mathews in support of the initial and continued sealing. But Schabas knew, of course, why the search had taken place. The 1995 Letter of Request to Switzerland had asserted major criminal conduct on the part of his client, not just Brian

Mulroney, Karlheinz Schreiber, and Frank Moores. In its most blunt terms, the Letter of Request claimed that bribes had been paid to Mulroney in return for directing Air Canada to buy planes from Airbus Industrie, and the Coast Guard to buy helicopters from Messerschmitt Bolkow Blohm (MBB). The RCMP claimed that Schreiber and Moores were also involved in the criminal conspiracy to steal from the Canadian people. Moreover, the search warrant itself, which Schabas and his client did get to see, identified some of the targets and listed the offences under investigation. So while Schabas did not need a compass to figure out in which direction the RCMP was going, he did want to know what, exactly, the police believed his client had done wrong. But he had no details, none whatsoever. At the very least, he pleaded with the judge, would he please "embark on some review of the Information itself to determine what can be provided to my client and me in order to have an understanding of why the material is sealed."[2] In simple terms, Schabas was asking the judge to look carefully at the sealed materials and fully satisfy himself that nothing at all could be released. If that were the case, he asked Justice Fontana to consider providing a judicial summary that would not threaten any of the interests being protected but, at the same time, give Eurocopter some information about the basis for the search.

An outstanding lawyer and a master of the spoken word, Schabas had an arsenal of arguments. One good starting point, he knew, was the unanimous decision of the Supreme Court of Canada in *MacIntyre*. Schabas quoted from the decision at length and suggested that Justice Fontana pay heed to it, particularly the former Chief Justice's conclusion that, after a search had been conducted, there would rarely be occasions in which continued secrecy was justified.

In this case, the existence of the investigation was not a secret. When the RCMP and the Government of Canada settled the Mulroney lawsuit, they made it clear that the investigation into the Airbus and MBB transactions would continue. Nevertheless, the search was a surprise – Eurocopter had no idea it was coming until the police came calling. It had been carried out in an extremely public fashion over a number of days. It was now, Schabas asserted, time to justify the search by making the background materials public. Eurocopter needed to know the grounds for the search so it could decide whether to challenge them. The company also wanted to determine whether the seized documents fell within the terms of the search warrant or whether, in the vocabulary of the criminal courts, there had been an "overseizure." In that case, Schabas wanted any documents that had been wrongfully taken to be returned.

To be sure, the Eurocopter lawyer acknowledged, the Crown might have some legitimate interest in keeping the supporting documents secret, along with the application to keep them secret. But the interests of Eurocopter also deserved protection. The *Charter of Rights and Freedoms*, Canada's supreme law, applied. There were important constitutional interests at stake. Schabas argued that any balancing favoured the protection of Eurocopter's rights and the prevention of any possible continuing violation of the company's *Charter* rights. What Schabas was referring to was section 8 of the *Charter*, which provided that "everyone has the right to be secure against unreasonable search and seizure." That included Eurocopter. Under section 24(2) of the *Charter*, a judge has the power to exclude unconstitutionally obtained evidence in some circumstances where it has been established, having regard to all the circumstances, that the admission of the evidence would bring the administration of justice into disrepute. Exactly that, Schabas argued, might have happened here.

The Crown argued otherwise. In Crown counsel Trevor Shaw's view, the sealing in this case more than met the legal test set out in the *Criminal Code*. Section 487, he pointed out, listed a number of grounds for sealing an Information: where disclosing it would compromise the identity of informants, adversely affect the nature and extent of an ongoing investigation, endanger intelligence-gathering techniques, or prejudice the interests of innocent persons. "There is nothing," Shaw wrote in his legal pleadings, "to indicate that the sealing order was improperly granted in the first place or that one or more of the criteria no longer apply. There was nothing to establish that the mere execution of the warrant has vacated the grounds in favour of sealing."[3] It was an accepted principle of criminal law, Shaw submitted, that any variation or recession of a sealing order required a material change in circumstance. The mere execution of a search warrant, he submitted to Justice Fontana, did not meet that test. The courts had recognized many situations in which access to court documents could be denied in the interests of the administration of justice. This case, Shaw suggested, was one of those situations where the balancing act favoured continued sealing.

None of these denials meant that Eurocopter was completely without a remedy, Shaw continued. The *Criminal Code* provided a mechanism for the return of seized items. Moreover, Eurocopter knew from the search warrant what offences were under investigation, what transactions were in issue, who some of the suspects were, what documents were considered relevant, and what documents had been seized. It was very well aware of its own history and actions.

Canadian courts had, Shaw observed, repeatedly upheld sealing orders on the basis that the litigation of search warrant issues was generally best left for eventual trial. Once charges are laid and a trial begins, the interest in investigative secrecy has generally diminished, so much so that there is usually no further interest in sealing. By that time, accused persons are most at jeopardy and they generally have full rights to all the evidence gathered against them. Originating judges, like Justice Fontana, were purposefully given a broad discretion in deciding what to make public and what to keep secret. The judge who eventually presided over the criminal trial, assuming charges were ever laid, would be in the best position to review that decision. In the meantime, Shaw argued, Justice Fontana's ruling should not be disturbed.

After hearing all these submissions, Justice Fontana had a number of different options available. One possible starting point was revisiting his decision ordering a publication ban at the start of the hearing on January 28. As Schabas pointed out, the only matter of importance from that day's proceedings was that he argued in favour of unsealing the documents, and the Crown argued for continued sealing. Nothing of a confidential nature was raised during the case. Why should the proceedings be secret? Why should the transcript of the proceedings be placed under lock and key? On what basis was the public being deprived of knowledge of the proceeding?

These are important questions and they raise issues that transcend this case. We live in a free country with open courts. This is not a utopian ideal but an essential requirement of democracy. It is so important that it is guaranteed by the *Charter of Rights and Freedoms*. As much as we admire the judiciary and respect the police, their actions must be subject to public scrutiny. There must be very strong reasons in favour of a publication ban, such as the protection of the identity of a child, the name of a victim in a sexual assault case, or the rights of an accused to a fair trial. None of these interests could be raised in this case. What was the reason, therefore, for the order preventing publication of a hearing in one of Her Majesty's courts?

The judge also had to decide what, if anything – the sealing orders, the Information, the documents appended to the Information, and the numerous affidavits filed in support of the sealing orders – Eurocopter could see. Justice Fontana could have directed the release of all the materials, some of the materials, or none of the materials. He could have provided a judicial summary. Or he could have maintained the status quo. Justice Fontana opted for the last of these options – and in a roundabout way. On January 31, 2000, he dismissed Eurocopter's request for the return of documents that the company claimed had been overseized. On February 7 he heard some more submissions and, about one week later, he dismissed Eurocopter's motion to unseal the background documents. Judge Fontana rejected the application on the basis that continued sealing of everything was necessary to protect two interests. First, to prevent innocent parties from damaging speculation or publicity. And, second, to protect the ongoing investigation. Moreover, in light of the overall breadth and scope of the investigation, the police needed additional time before everything could be made public.

The investigation, the judge ruled, involved an inquiry into complex corporate and commercial transactions, calling for the scrutiny of experts and time-consuming analysis. "In refusing the motion," Justice Fontana concluded, "it is useful however to remind the investigative authorities acting on behalf of the Respondent that despite the magnitude and complexity of the investigation the sealing order ... should not be viewed as open-ended. It is not a case of 'seize at large, examine at leisure.' The Crown must continue its inquiries with dispatch."4 The admonition was hardly comforting to Eurocopter. Though the *Criminal Code* provided for periodic review if the Crown wished to hold on to seized documents, the sealing order was not subject to any statutory revisiting and rejustification.

On March 15, 2000, the matter came back before Judge Fontana, two days after he received yet another affidavit from Inspector Mathews – again one not shared with Eurocopter. Mathews dutifully reported, using language he now knew was sure to appeal to this judge, that the investigation was not only ongoing but extremely complicated. He urged that the records seized continue to be detained and that the Information stay sealed. After another hearing, Justice Fontana extended the detention order until the middle of June and ordered that all the materials filed in support of that detention order continue to remain sealed. Again, however, he admonished the Crown to proceed with dispatch. There was little that Schabas could do, practically, about the detention order. However, Justice Fontana's decision denying his client access to the various documents in the bulging court file, such as Inspector Mathews's expanding body of affidavits, was a different matter. On February 28, 2000, Eurocopter served notice that it would seek a judicial review of Justice Fontana's decision. And that is how the case ended up before Mr. Justice Edward Then.

A closed-door hearing was held in Toronto on March 20, 22, and 23, 2000. The issue before the court was whether Justice Fontana had committed a jurisdictional error in continuing the sealing. Schabas's objective was straightforward: set aside Justice Fontana's order and open everything up. Then, without warning, an unexpected and not entirely welcome ally turned up in court.

Despite all the secrecy about this process, and the fact that Eurocopter had done nothing to bring its efforts to the attention of the press, the CBC's Harvey Cashore was present at the courthouse when the proceeding commenced on March 20. Cashore had been following Airbus/MBB/Bearhead for years and, together with the *Fifth Estate*, was responsible for just about every new revelation in the developing story. In the process, he had cultivated excellent contacts and sources in Canada and around the world. He had heard about the Eurocopter search and, like all good investigative reporters, began asking questions. He quickly learned that Schabas was on the file. Schabas, who regularly acts for the *Toronto Star* in media cases, refused comment when Cashore called, asking him what was going on. A courthouse clerk in Ottawa told Cashore that the case had been moved to Toronto. He began digging some more and eventually discovered that the matter was set down for a hearing. On the appointed day, Cashore arrived at the University Avenue courthouse, where no one in charge knew, or would say, anything about the case. After a few detours, Cashore made his way to the right courtroom and took a seat in the third row. Immediately he attracted the attention of the judge.

Who is he? Justice Then asked Trevor Shaw. The Crown attorney had no idea, and the judge finally asked Cashore to stand up and identify himself. Cashore did, and the judge sighed before asking whether Cashore wished to remain in the room. The answer, of course, was yes. Justice Then advised Cashore to call his lawyer, which he did. In the meantime, at Justice Then's request, Cashore stepped outside so the matter could proceed. When Inspector Mathews asked him how he knew about the proceeding, Cashore replied that he just happened by the court on his way to work. That was a joke, but Mathews did not get it and he reported the explanation verbatim in his files. Soon enough, Cashore was knocking on the courtroom door with CBC lawyer Michael Hughes in tow. In the meantime, acting as a friend of the court, Paul Schabas educated the judge in the line of cases dealing with open courts. He made sure that Justice Then was aware of the range of options available other than a completely closed court. Nevertheless, the public and the press were excluded, as Justice Then directed that the case take place *in camera*. He also issued an extraordinary order prohibiting the parties and their lawyers from even mentioning the proceedings to anyone. Cashore might have been kicked out of the courtroom – this was one very secret trial – but he kept on top of the case as much as he could, regularly calling Justice Then's office for an update.

Eurocopter's lawyer had a difficult job ahead of him. Schabas was not being given a second chance at arguing for disclosure, at least not directly. Rather, his application sought judicial review, called *certiorari*, where the task of the reviewing court is extremely limited. The *Criminal Code* gave Justice Fontana broad discretion in deciding whether to make a sealing order. A reviewing court should intervene in cases of this kind, legal precedent held, only when it was of the view that the originating judge had made a serious error that could not be corrected by any existing remedies available at law. In effect, Justice Then was being asked to exercise a prerogative – an exclusive discretionary power. According to received wisdom, that power should be exercised rarely.

In reaching a conclusion, it was important for Justice Then to bear in mind that Eurocopter had twice appealed to Justice Fontana for relief, and it could continue to do so when that judge's latest detention order expired, on June 30. Moreover, after one year had elapsed, it would be up to the Crown to justify the continued detention of the records taken by the RCMP. The transcript indicated that Justice Fontana had considered the arguments that were made, had taken into account the respective interests of the parties, and had exercised the discretion given to him under the *Criminal Code*. Furthermore, Justice Fontana, as the author of a leading text, *The Law of Search and Seizure in Canada*, was an acknowledged expert in this area of the law. In these circumstances, what possible basis was there for setting aside his order?

Yet there were still some strong arguments to muster, and Schabas was up to the task. Any decision to seal, he argued, had to be in accordance with *Charter* values – those constitutional values recognized by the courts as upholding the principle of open courts and open court documents. Any exercise of judicial discretion to close courts or court documents had to be based, given these fundamental values, on a conclusion that the interests protected in the *Criminal Code* outweighed both these *Charter* values and his client's entitlement to know the basis on which a judge had authorized a search. The Eurocopter lawyer also argued that the judge had made a serious mistake. Under the *Criminal Code*, sealing was justified where the ends of justice "would be subverted by the disclosure" for one of several reasons such as that disclosure would compromise the nature and extent of an ongoing investigation, or, for instance, prejudice the interests of an innocent person, or reveal the identity of a confidential informant. Did Justice Fontana's ruling meet the requirements of that provision? Schabas asked.

Justice Fontana had concluded that disclosure "might" compromise or frustrate the investigation, Schabas pointed out. This misstatement of the criteria, the Eurocopter lawyer believed, gave rise to a reasonable inference that the judge erred in law in exercising his discretion under the provision that required him to be satisfied that there "would" be a subversion of justice unless the information was sealed. As Justice Fontana had misapprehended and then misapplied the relevant criteria, he could not be said to have acted judicially. Schabas argued, therefore, that Justice Fontana lost jurisdiction by making a legal mistake. It was a pretty good argument, especially when a balancing of interests involving the rights of the target and the principle of open courts in an open society were added to the mix.

But there is almost always another way of looking at things. Justice Fontana, Crown attorney Shaw pointed out in reply, was so expert in this area of the law that it was inconceivable that he would have or could have misapprehended the relevant criteria.[5] Eurocopter had not been criminally charged (that would come later), so it was a "non-accused target." The company was not in immediate jeopardy. Investigative interests and those of innocent third parties therefore prevailed. This did not mean that the *Charter* was being ignored. There are all sorts of *Charter* values: protecting the innocent was one of them; ensuring that police investigations "reach their logical conclusion unmolested" was another.[6] The list went on and on, and it was clear, at least to the Crown, that Justice Fontana had considered these interests. In a measured response, he had upheld, not once, but twice, the sealing of the court record.

In Shaw's opinion, Eurocopter had hardly been shortchanged. It had already received substantial information, details that could be usefully deployed to challenge the warrant and the basis for granting the search. Moreover, while the search was clearly a surprise, the company surely knew that the MBB commissions to Schreiber and Moores had been under police investigation for years. In addition, there was nothing stopping Schabas from arguing overseizure without unsealing: all he had to do was compare the fruits of the seizure to the search warrant. If and when someone was charged, that person would have all the rights accruing to an accused person. That meant disclosure to a criminally accused of all the evidence the police had collected, required as a matter of law. There were, Shaw observed, many cases in which these disclosure rights trumped those of the Crown, and in which all the background documents were ordered unsealed. But that was a matter for the future, not for today.

Schabas got the last word. "Your Lordship," he concluded, should not "lose sight of the fact we are in an absolutely extraordinary situation in this case." Eurocopter had "been searched, can't challenge the search and can't find out why they can't challenge the search ... Why can't we know in this case? ... I go to Justice Fontana and say, tell me, and I'm not told and we're three and a half months later and we're in exactly the same situation ... for my friend to say, well, I am not hampered" is false; "without any facts, I am unable to make effective submissions." Justice Then listened to Schabas's impassioned argument but did not buy it, at least not completely. "I must say that the ingenuity of counsel meets no bounds without any ammunition, and I may say so quite effectively."[7] This comment was a compliment, of sorts, but Schabas had to do a lot better. He went on to make submissions tackling, one after another, the points Shaw had made.

First, simply because Justice Fontana had written a book and was an acknowledged expert in this particular area of the law did not mean that he made the right call in this case. Second, just because Eurocopter was not necessarily the target did not mean that the police could infringe its *Charter* rights. Third, it was unreasonable to be subjected to a search warrant and not be told why. Finally, it was not reasonable, in all the circumstances, to maintain secrecy. That was perhaps the most ludicrous part of all, Schabas charged: "It is not a secret investigation as my friend says." Quite clearly, "the CBC is aware of something, the issue of the investigation of the helicopter sales, of Airbus, of armoured vehicles and Cape Breton ... and indeed after the search took place, the *Time* magazine of Germany, *Der Spiegel*, said Eurocopter Canada has been subjected to a search ... It's not a secret at all. And when 18 officers walk into a big factory, they're not attempting to keep it secret." At the very least, Schabas pleaded in conclusion, he should be allowed to see the key documents placed before Justice Fontana, and some senior Eurocopter executive resident in Canada and subject to Canadian laws should see them too, after giving an undertaking that they will not be disclosed. "That would give effect to my client's right to know why it's been searched and give effect to its ability to seek a remedy."[8] Judges generally respond positively, and are appreciative, when they are offered a reasonable way out that comes somewhere between the positions of the parties – and the compromise that Schabas proposed would also ensure that whatever investigatory interests the RCMP was attempting to protect would not be endangered by public disclosure.

Justice Then decided, however, to consider the submissions he had received and reserved on his ruling. The parties began to wait … and wait.

The weeks turned into months, with no decision coming down from the court. The different lawyers began to focus their attention on June 13, 2000, the date when the detention order was scheduled to expire. On that day, the RCMP brought an application before Justice Then for the continued detention of the seized documents. It filed yet another affidavit in support, setting out reasons why the Mountie request should be granted. Again, the affidavit was shared only with the judge.

Inspector Mathews drew the judge's attention to the volume of documents: tens of thousands of pages, many of which required translation. A core group of up to ten RCMP members, three forensic accountants, a computer specialist, and support staff, supplemented as needed by additional personnel, were engaged in investigating this matter, along with "GCI/IAL related matters generally."[9] GCI, Government Consultants International, belonged to Frank Moores, while IAL, International Aircraft Leasing, belonged to Karlheinz Schreiber. At least one more letter of request had been sent to a foreign jurisdiction – clearly, the Letter of Request to Germany that he had earlier drawn to the attention of the court. Thousands more pages of related documents had been identified overseas, Inspector Mathews noted, and efforts had been initiated to bring them to Canada. The RCMP considered it noteworthy that the Munich Tax Court had, at least according to a newspaper article in *Berliner Zeitung*, accepted Schreiber's explanation that some of the money that had moved through his accounts was not taxable to him because he had only facilitated the transfer to third parties – it was *Schmiergelder*, grease money, or *nutzliche Aufwendungen*, the German term meaning "beneficial expenditures" or "useful contributions." No matter what term was used, Mathews insisted, these were payments to foreigners for business promotions, including paying bribes and commissions. Before 1996 both bribes and commissions were lawful in Germany and tax-deductible for export business, provided those receiving the payments were in a position to exercise influence on the decision-making process that was beneficial to the

party making the payment. This influence could be exercised directly or indirectly. The RCMP believed that these bribes and commissions
had been used in the helicopter purchase.

Inspector Mathews also highlighted the CBC's presence in court
way back on March 20, 2000, when Justice Then began hearing
argument on the continued sealing. The RCMP was concerned that
the ongoing investigation, including the overseas activities, would be
discovered and publicized, to the detriment of the interests enumer-
ated in the *Criminal Code* – the interests that, only months earlier,
Justice Fontana had concluded deserved protection.

This argument was bizarre. Eighteen RCMP officers had searched
one of the biggest industrial enterprises in Fort Erie over the course
of three workdays. Everyone in Fort Erie who worked at Eurocopter
knew about the search. Schreiber knew about it. The CBC knew
about it. A story about it had appeared in a leading German newsmagazine. Still Inspector Mathews insisted that there was a legitimate interest in keeping all the background materials secret.

Justice Then decided to reserve his decision about the detention
application until after he had decided the earlier application for judicial review. This judge gave extremely careful consideration to every
matter put before him. Eventually, on December 19, 2000, he issued
a bottom-line decision, called an "endorsement," retroactively granting the detention order sought six months earlier, in June 2000, and
making it effective for another half year, and also denying the application for judicial review: "I am satisfied, having reviewed the affidavit in support of sealing ... that it is appropriate ... to make an
order prohibiting access to and disclosure of any information relating to the warrant on the ground that the ends of justice would be
subverted by the disclosure for the reasons that the disclosure ... of
the Information would a) compromise the nature and extent of an
ongoing investigation and b) would prejudice the interests of an
innocent person. I am further satisfied that the reasons above ... outweigh in importance the access to the Information. I have exercised
my discretion mindful of the high onus on the Crown to justify sealing and in accordance with *Charter* values ... *Charter* values of
access to the administration of justice based on freedom of the press
and the principle of openness of the courts." This endorsement was
later supplemented with more detailed reasons for decision released
on January 10 and 15, 2001.

Under the *Criminal Code*, the Crown and the police could make
more than one application for the continuing detention of any documents seized, but the statute had a fail-safe, limiting detention to

one year. Where an extension was requested beyond one year, a judge had to be satisfied, "having regard to the complex nature of the investigation," that "further detention of the thing seized" was warranted. Based on yet another affidavit from Inspector Mathews, which Eurocopter and its lawyer were not allowed to see, Justice Then ordered continued detention for another nine months – until September 2001, when the Crown would, once again, be called upon to make its case.

With that matter taken care of, the judge had to supplement his earlier endorsement dismissing Eurocopter's application for judicial review. After setting out some of the background facts and citing the relevant provision of the *Criminal Code*, Justice Then reviewed some of the principles governing judicial review. Having disposed of that task, he turned to his main job, deciding whether Justice Fontana had made a mistake. Schabas had argued that the Ottawa jurist got it wrong, badly wrong, when he justified his decision on the basis that unsealing *might* compromise the ongoing investigation. The *Criminal Code* was much more strict than that: it required the reviewing judge to be satisfied that the ends of justice *would* be subverted by disclosure. There was a big difference between the two.

Schabas's appealing argument did not carry the day. Justice Then completely agreed with the Crown that it was inconceivable "that a judge with the experience of Justice Fontana would have misapprehended the criteria."[10] Judges do what they can, exercising "curial deference," to avoid reviewing and reversing each other except in the clearest of cases. Justice Then had also had the benefit of reading everything under seal. He simply declared that there was "ample evidentiary basis" in the affidavits and in the other background documents to support the sealing. The ends of justice, he concluded without explaining in any detail, would be subverted by disclosure.[11]

Eurocopter immediately filed an appeal, and the Crown grappled with how to conduct it in secret. Schabas said no way, and the likelihood of the Court of Appeal agreeing to go *in camera* was slim. Days before the appeal was scheduled to be heard in early March 2001, Crown attorney Michael Bernstein indicated that disclosure was forthcoming and that just about everything would soon be made public. Schabas held his thunder and the appeal was put off. The armour was clearly beginning to crack as the Crown faced the daunting task of justifying what was apparently unjustifiable – the continued sealing of everything associated with this case. While preparing the various documents for disclosure, the decision was made to notify several potentially interested parties.

And so it was that, in April 2001, the players would assemble again before Justice Then, but this time the courtroom would be more crowded. Summoned by the mysterious notice from the Crown, lawyers for Mulroney, Schreiber, and Cashore and the CBC would be there too. Mulroney did not personally attend, but Schreiber and Cashore did just about every time the proceedings reconvened. They would all, as the first order of business, get to see much of the court file, as Schabas had been demanding for sixteen months. The hearing, however, would continue *in camera*, and a new publication ban was imposed. Most extraordinary of all, the judge reconfirmed his earlier order directing that none of the parties or their lawyers inform anyone, anyone at all, about anything that had taken place, or was about to take place, in the courtroom.

4 The Theory of the Case

Secret trials and democracy do not mix well. Secrecy is the instrument of the enemies of freedom, while an open judicial system is a prerequisite of a free and democratic country. The police and other prosecutorial authorities wield huge power, and it is through open courts, accessible to the public and to a free press, that state power is checked. Secret trials have huge potential for injustice and oppression, which explains why tyrants like them so much.

There are exceptions, of course. There have to be. In 1946, following revelations by Igor Gouzenko, the government appointed the Kellock-Taschereau Royal Commission on Espionage to look into the existence of a Russian spy ring operating in Canada. This brave Soviet cipher clerk fled the USSR Embassy in Ottawa with papers documenting the treachery of a number of Canadians, including a Communist member of parliament named Fred Rose, who was later deported to his native Poland. In some of its activities, critics claimed, the Kellock-Taschereau Commission aped some of the tactics and methods of the Soviet government and its secret police. Still, no serious commentator ever doubted the fundamental fact that secrecy was necessary – not to apprehend the accused agents and bring them to justice, but, once they were locked up, to investigate fully the extent of Soviet subversion.

Although rarely resorted to, secret proceedings were permissible under the old *Official Secrets Act*. During the Cold War, the struggle between freedom and democracy on the one hand and Communist totalitarianism on the other, secrecy was considered necessary to apprehend what was, often correctly, perceived as a threat to the continued existence of the state. From time to time, persons charged with offences were tried behind closed doors. Many of the abuses under the *Official Secrets Act* were eventually corrected, but the need for some secret proceedings continued. Even if the proceedings took place *in camera*, however, sentencing was always public.

In recent years, as the west was forced to face a new set of national security challenges, the law has been changed so that refugees and permanent residents can be declared a security threat, arrested, held without bail, and, at trial, denied the opportunity to see the evidence against them. Safeguards against the arbitrary use of this authority, and there are a few, include the fact that the security certificate justifying the detention, based on information provided by the Canadian Security and Intelligence Service, must be signed off by the minister of public safety. The proceedings largely take place *in camera*, with the evidence presented by the Crown attorney directly to the judge in the absence of the accused and his or her lawyer. Only a summary of the evidence is provided to the accused, who is then faced with the difficult challenge of meeting, at least in part, an unstated case. Critics, and there are many, complain that the safeguards are completely inadequate. If the judges are doing their job, however, they will demand evidence that satisfies the most stringent standards. What is missing is the glare of public scrutiny on all aspects of the process, including the adequacy and reasonableness of the decision of the presiding judge. There is nothing like a public process to bring out the best in people, including judges.

In Canada, the general rule is no secret trials. There can be publication bans. The judge can also order that the names of juveniles accused of crimes or victims of sexual assault not be published. But the courtroom is open to everyone, with limited exceptions, such as witnesses who might be excluded until called on to give their evidence. The various witnesses in a proceeding are often not allowed to listen to the evidence of others because of concern they may then tailor their own testimony to complement, or rebut, the witnesses who have already told their stories. Yet, even when there is a publication ban or an order excluding witnesses, the public and the press can attend. Everything comes out at the end except, possibly, the name of the complainant in a sexual assault case or information that could lead to the identification of the complainant. At worst, all that happens is that reporting on the proceedings is delayed. The principle of open courts is preserved.

Not in the Eurocopter case, however. Those secret proceedings lurched from month to month and year to year. The CBC was there but unable to say anything: Justice Then's earlier order precluded any discussion whatsoever about the case. The rest of the media were completely oblivious to the proceeding. So, too, for the longest time, were Brian Mulroney and Karlheinz Schreiber.

The two men had not seen each other for years. They had, through their lawyers and others, kept in touch. Moreover, Elmer MacKay, the Nova Scotia MP who had stepped down to open the way for Mulroney to first enter Parliament, continued his intermediary role. The Eurocopter case almost continued without them.

While the Crown believed it had an obligation to notify these "interested persons," Eurocopter's lawyer did not agree. Paul Schabas was willing to concede that the CBC, as a matter of courtesy to counsel who attended during the first round, should get notice. But insofar as Mulroney and Schreiber were concerned, Schabas argued against it. Surely, he pointed out to the judge, they had been entitled to notice a long time ago or not at all. Non-media third parties had no constitutional right to attend. Telling them about the case, he added, would be unprecedented and would only delay the proceedings. Inviting Mulroney and Schreiber to the party would, more likely than not, further complicate an already complicated case. Any legal proceeding involving Mulroney and Schreiber, and particularly the two of them together, was bound to attract attention. Eurocopter, anxious to secure government procurement orders, particularly the mother of all Canadian helicopter deals, the Sea King replacement contract, wanted to ensure that the proceedings stayed below radar. Besides, Schabas had no idea why the Crown believed that Mulroney and Schreiber should receive notice of the proceeding. How were they implicated, and how would that affect his client? Put another way, were they friends or foes? That would take some time to sort out.

In the meantime, the judge, who had the benefit of having read the complete court file, directed that both Mulroney and Schreiber receive notification, and that Moores be told as well. Soon enough, Eddie Greenspan, Schreiber's high-profile attorney, was not the only lawyer looking for answers to questions. Mulroney received notice through Gérald Tremblay, a leading Montreal lawyer and Mulroney's chief legal counsel in the Airbus lawsuit. Tremblay referred the matter to Mulroney's long-time friend and "fixer" – they had been classmates at St Francis Xavier University – Toronto lawyer Sam Wakim, who immediately put two other lawyers from his firm, Weir Foulds, on the file: Kenneth Prehogan and Nicholas D.C. Holland. Wakim would faithfully attend all the hearings, and he kept Mulroney, who was taking a keen interest in the case, current on developments, but he left the actual legal work to his partners. Like Greenspan, Prehogan, when he received notification of the proceeding, wanted an immediate meeting with the judge. He, too, was refused. His only option was to attend at court.

Before the hearing, all the lawyers were served notice of an application, which the Crown intended to make on April 24, 2001. The

Sam Wakim with Eddie Greenspan – Wakim was Mulroney's eyes and ears at the secret trial.

Crown wanted to unseal most of the Information, the key background document presented to Justice Fontana to persuade him to approve the search. The government had no choice. Under Justice Then's January ruling, the Crown was required, every four months, to justify the continued sealing. Crown attorneys Michael Bernstein and Trevor Shaw are lawyers who take their responsibilities seriously. They work hard to secure convictions, but they understand that the system depends on them, as on all Crown attorneys, to ensure that everyone's rights are respected. When Bernstein and Shaw sat down and took a second look at the key background document and the supporting affidavits, they realized that much of the initial justification both for the sealing and for the publication ban had disappeared. Also influential was Eurocopter's scheduled appeal of Justice Then's earlier decision. Could Bernstein and Shaw justify the continued sealing to the Court of Appeal? Apparently not, and it was noteworthy that the entire document had been sealed from the outset. Was it conceivable that none of it could have been released at an earlier date? In any event, by signalling to Schabas the intention to disclose, the Crown did an end run around any appellate oversight.

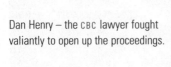
Dan Henry – the CBC lawyer fought valiantly to open up the proceedings.

Much had happened since the December 1999 search of Eurocopter headquarters in Fort Erie. Most important of all, the CBC's *Fifth Estate* had broadcast a new show at the end of March 2001, a program all about Eurocopter, beginning with a dramatization of the RCMP's December 1999 search of the Fort Erie headquarters, and it then detailed the secret commissions that had been paid. Names, dates, places, documents, and an explanation were all provided for the secret commissions, which led, in turn, to the Eurocopter search. Despite the cone of silence imposed on the proceedings, the CBC had continued its work.

Initially, the lawyers eyed each other suspiciously, not yet knowing who was allied with whom. After Justice Then called the court to order, the lawyers discussed at length whether the proceedings should be open or closed. Dan Henry, the CBC's longtime in-house lawyer, argued in favour of unsealing all the documents and opening up the proceedings. Henry, the president of Ad IDEM, Advocates in Defence of Expression in Media, usually spent his days advising *As It Happens, The Fifth Estate, Disclosure, Marketplace, The National,* and *The Royal Canadian Air Farce,* all flagship CBC shows, how to avoid defamation writs. His entire professional life has been devoted to advancing the cause of press freedom by attack-

ing publication bans in a number of celebrated cases, defending lawsuits brought against the CBC and its reporters, and intervening
when necessary in other court proceedings to advance the overall
cause of press freedom. Temperamentally unable to believe anything
bad about a journalist, he was in court on behalf of his client. He
had hung around the CBC long enough, however, to smell a good
story, and this one, he thought, had the potential to be among the
great. Schreiber, Mulroney, Moores, the RCMP, and the Crown – all
gathered in a Toronto courtroom for Airbus: The Sequel. That was
something CBC viewers would be interested in.

Eddie Greenspan, Schreiber's lawyer, did not agree. How could
he? He had no idea what the proceedings were about, and which,
if any, of his client's interests might be affected. Kenneth Prehogan,
the senior Mulroney counsel on the file, was a member of both the
Ontario and the Quebec bars, with extensive trial and appellate
experience. Mr Mulroney, Prehogan told the judge, had been notified of this matter but did not know the reason why. Until he knew
what the RCMP and the Crown attorneys were saying about him, if
anything, he wanted the case closed to the public and to the press.
Prehogan knew that if Mulroney was publicly associated with
Schreiber and Moores in a criminal investigation, a large part of the
Canadian public would conclude that he had been up to no good.
There was, he argued, an overwhelming need for the proceedings to
continue *in camera*, at least for the time being.

The case, Justice Then observed late in the afternoon of the first
day, was like no other: it was "fraught with difficulty." That was putting it mildly. A long, repetitive, and generally unproductive discussion ensued. Should the CBC alone attend, or the CBC with other
media interests? Should there be some access to the background documents for the targets, and less or no access for everyone else? On
and on it went, as the judge attempted through discussion to negotiate a resolution. "What can you live with, Mr Greenspan?" the judge
asked at one point. "Kick the CBC out," he replied. At the very least,
Harvey Cashore and his co-author, Stevie Cameron, should not have
any access to the proceedings, Greenspan argued. Cameron had not
asked to attend, although she later reported that she knew about the
case and had tried to get in. That was news to the other participants,
who never saw her anywhere near the courtroom. In any event,
Greenspan linked her, Cashore, and the CBC, as he would continue
to do throughout the proceeding. The inconclusive discussions went
on, it seemed, forever. But at the end of the day, as promised, the
Crown made its disclosure.

Large sections of the Information and supporting documents had been redacted, but the lawyers now knew exactly what crimes the Mounties were trying to prove, for this background material spelled out, in detail, the theory of the police case. The Information was almost two hundred pages in length, not counting the hundreds of appended supporting documents and exhibits. The initial objective of the massive paperwork had been to satisfy Justice Fontana that there were reasonable and probable grounds to believe that the police would find evidence establishing the commission of crimes – in this case fraud and conspiracy to commit fraud, both crimes contrary to Canada's *Criminal Code*.

Overall, the package was impressive. It was hardly surprising that Justice Fontana had given the search his approval. With pages of particulars and references to hundreds of documents apparently supporting those particulars, the overall impact created the impression that serious criminal wrongdoing had been, or soon would be, established. The police surely had reasonable and probable grounds to go out and search. At least that is the way the information was pitched.

Different types of records were identified – government records, business records, banking records, accountants' records, company documents, personal records, invoices, and requests for proposals. The list was extremely detailed. The RCMP wanted everything in any way related to the Canadian Coast Guard's decision to buy helicopters from MCL, Messerschmitt Canada Limited, a subsidiary of MBB, which later became Eurocopter Canada. What the Mounties were especially interested in were any records of commissions or payments to Frank Moores's former company, Government Consultants International (GCI), or to Moores himself; to Karlheinz Schreiber and his company International Aircraft Leasing (IAL); and to two other Schreiber companies, Bitucan Holdings and Kensington Anstalt.

The Mounties had a pretty good idea what had happened, or at least what they believed had happened. They theorized that MCL, or its corporate parent MBB, later Eurocopter Germany, and two of its senior officials, German residents Heinz Pluckthun and Kurt Pfleiderer, defrauded the Canadian government and the Canadian people by paying commissions on the Coast Guard sale. Pluckthun was the former chairman of the board of MCL, the former vice-president of finance for MBB Helicopter, and the former president of MBB Helicopter. Pfleiderer was a member of the board of MCL and had also been, at one time, president of MBB. When Pluckthun became president in 1986, Pfleiderer assumed the position of vice-president of sales.

In 1986, the RCMP explained, the Canadian Coast Guard, then under the direction of the Department of Transport, contracted, through the Department of Supply and Services, for twelve light utility helicopters from MBB's Canadian subsidiary, MCL of Fort Erie. The $27 million contract had been awarded without tender – "sole sourced," in government parlance – and approved by the deputy minister of the Department of Supply and Services. There was nothing unusual about this sale. The Coast Guard was already using MBB helicopters, was completely satisfied with them, and only MBB helicopters met the department's technical requirements. The helicopters were manufactured in Germany and finished in Canada. The contract was unexceptional. It was between MCL, the contractor, and the Department of Supply and Services, the purchaser, and contained the usual clause found in government contracts:

22. *No Bribe Etc.*
The contractor warrants,
(*a*) that no bribe, gift or other inducement has been paid, given, promised or offered to any official or employee of Her Majesty for, or with a view to, the obtaining of the contract by the Contractor, and
(*b*) that it has not employed any person to solicit or secure the contract upon any agreement for a commission, percentage, brokerage or contingent fee.

Commissions were prohibited for an obvious reason. The negotiations had been held directly between the vendor and the purchaser. No commission had been earned by anyone. If a commission was paid, that could mean only one thing: the people of Canada were being cheated because the price was too high and there had been a departure from the "most favoured customer" status that the Government of Canada routinely demands from all its contracting partners. In fact, the vendor MCL had promised as much, confirming to the Department of Supply and Services that the price quoted was "not in excess of the lowest price charged anyone else, including our most favoured customer ... [and] does not include an element of profit on the sale in excess of that normally obtained by us on the sale of products of like quality and quantity."[1]

It is fair to say that under no circumstances would the Canadian government have agreed to a contract for the purchase of these helicopters had it known that commissions were to be paid. It would have been unjustifiable in the circumstances. No commissions could legitimately be paid because no commissions could have been earned on this transaction. As Raymond Hession, the deputy minister of supply and services at the time of the purchase, told Inspector Allan Mathews, the senior RCMP officer on the case: "If the contract had been signed and the delivery of the helicopters was not at that point completed, it likely would have been cancelled. If we were in mid-delivery say, then practicalities would likely lead to some negotiated sanction, financial in that example." Hession also observed that commissions could easily lead to a blacklisting of the company. "That latter is perhaps the most significant sanction, because not only does it affect them in this market, but given the international-ization of markets, that would be known everywhere, and it would-n't wear well in the company."[2] Even if the commissions did not mean that the government paid more money for the helicopters than it should have, the answer would still have been no. Any commis-sions, the former deputy minister insisted, were "a flat misrepresen-tation ... in complete contravention of the clause."[3]

That was also the view of the senior MBB man in Canada. Court documents indicated that when Helge Wittholz, the president of the Canadian subsidiary, MCL, learned about the behind-the-scenes arrangements, he was furious – and fearful. The helicopters were supposed to be sold by the German parent company to its Canadian subsidiary for just over $1 million each. When Wittholz received an invoice from MBB for the cost of the goods, however, he realized that the price had increased by almost $100,000 per unit. He asked for an explanation. Wittholz was told by head office that the increase in "pricing was necessary to meet commission requirements."[4] He knew that the additional amounts could not be passed on to the Coast Guard, so, inevitably, it would have to be absorbed by the Canadian subsidiary.

When the contract was first being negotiated, Wittholz told the RCMP, he became concerned that Schreiber and Moores seemed to be hanging around every time there was a meeting with his German superiors. He therefore sought and obtained assurances that the Coast Guard contract, between MCL and the Department of Supply and Services, complied with Canadian laws, in particular the "no commissions, no bribes" provision. He was given that assurance, and, in a note to file, he recorded his conversation with MBB's legal adviser in Germany that "there were no connections between the agreements between MBB and Frank Moores, and MBB and Karl-heinz Schreiber."[5] Wittholz could, therefore, with a clean conscience, sign the contract with the government on behalf of MCL.

However, he soon learned that he had been lied to. Wittholz was provided with a copy of the IAL sales representation agreement. He had been completely blindsided, and he raised an objection. Wittholz told Pluckthun that the extra transfer cost of approximately $100,000 per helicopter would not only eliminate MCL's net profit of some $30,000 per unit on the transaction but cause a significant loss. He also informed Pluckthun that there was only one North American price for these aircraft. That price was the amount set out in the contract, and it could not be changed. He brought to the German's attention the "no bribes, no commissions" term of the agreement. Making matters worse, if that were possible, he pointed out that MCL and MBB owed a duty to its minority shareholder, Fleet Aerospace Ltd., which, obviously, was not in this particular loop. According to Inspector Mathews, Wittholz got nowhere with Pluckthun. Concerned about the commission document and appreciating the dangers it raised, Wittholz destroyed it. Later, having second thoughts and realizing that it might be in his long-term interest to have a copy, he arranged to get another one, which he held on to and, years later, provided to the RCMP.

In the meantime, Wittholz continued to raise a fuss, especially after the invoice arrived from MBB with the inflated helicopter price. The loss, he continued, could not be kept from the Canadian board of directors, and the MCL president asked Pluckthun to change the invoice. Instead, Pluckthun, in December 1986, summoned Wittholz to Germany for a meeting. Wittholz told Pluckthun, who attended along with Pfleiderer and another MBB official, that the commission arrangement was unlawful. Pluckthun and Pfleiderer disagreed. In fact, Pluckthun claimed that there was no North American price list and that commissions in the 5–7 per cent range were appropriate in the United States. When Wittholz sought confirmation of this fact from the head of the American subsidiary, he learned that Pluckthun was either mistaken or lying. Regardless, head office had its way. Wittholz was instructed, in future, to price any new business in accordance with the IAL agreement. The commission price would be built into future sales.

Wittholz did not believe this arrangement was in the interest of the company, and he told Pluckthun and Pfleiderer as much at a breakfast meeting held in the private dining room on the Gold Key floor at the Château Laurier in Ottawa in October 1987. James Grant, MCL's vice-president of marketing at the time, accompanied his boss to the meeting and was even more forceful. "This is not the way you do business in Canada," he told the two German officials, adding that Canada was not a corrupt country. Wittholz had spent years working for MBB in Europe and so was familiar with its corporate culture and commission-paying practices. The situation here was different, however. The politicians were not crooked, nor were the civil servants. "It was," Grant continued, "just a big waste of money." The visitors were not used to being spoken to this way and made it clear that they did not care for it. It was, Grant recalled, "like a lower-level Indian telling them that they were out to lunch."[6]

Grant could be easily ignored. All Pfleiderer and Pluckthun had to do was begin speaking German, which they soon did. When Wittholz tried another tack, he was also shut down. Pfleiderer told him that he was an "idealist" who would be "better off selling ball point pens" if he was not able to "accept common business practices." The common business practices Pfleiderer was referring to were *nutzliche Aufwendungen*, "useful contributions." These were the commissions or, less politely put, the possible bribes that the RCMP would later begin investigating.

What made the payments especially problematic, from Wittholz's point of view, was that neither Schreiber nor Moores had done anything to facilitate the sale. Yet both had profited from it. (Moores readily admitted receiving MBB money, telling the *National Post* on September 25, 1999, "I have never denied receiving commissions from the sale of 12 helicopters to the Canadian Coast Guard.") The paper trail conclusively established that Schreiber was the paymaster. On what basis could Moores and Schreiber have received commissions? Pfleiderer, nevertheless, defended the payments, advising Wittholz that it "needed to be done" and pointing out that Schreiber had "good connections with the Canadian government." It was well known that Schreiber also had excellent connections with the late Bavarian politician and strongman Franz Josef Strauss and his political party, the CSU in Bavaria, where MBB had its central offices and production facilities. Pfleiderer, intimating that Wittholz had better start reading between the lines, advised his Canadian subordinate to "wake up."[7]

In fact, Wittholz was having trouble sleeping at night, and he suggested to his superiors in Germany that MBB's relationship with Schreiber and Moores, whatever it was, be terminated. Also on his hit list was Robert Shea, yet another Mulroney classmate from St Francis Xavier University, who had, despite his American citizenship and Boston residence, made his way onto the MCL board of directors. But Wittholz got nowhere.

Schreiber and Moores remained in the background, present but with no apparent official role, and Shea stayed on the board until 1993, coincidentally the year Mulroney exited public life. For some reason – the refusal of local management to obey overseas orders may have been one of them – MCL was restructured soon after Wittholz tried to get his superiors to cut the connections with Schreiber and Moores. The company was brought under the overall direction of its American sister subsidiary. Opposed to the restructuring, Grant resigned but made it clear, in a letter to the American president, that corporate reorganization was only part of the explanation for his departure. "Behind the scenes, as you are well aware, are a number of political factors that are extremely significant ... They are serious and provide the basis to bring down a Government or cause a major international problem. I need say no more."[8] And he did not say any more until the RCMP came to interview him. Wittholz resigned from MCL in 1989.

Most of the directors of MBB's Canadian subsidiary knew nothing about the overseas deal. Given the way the Canadian subsidiary was run, this ignorance was not out of the ordinary. Just about all of the key decisions were made overseas: the biggest contract in the history of the Fort Erie–based company had not even gone to the Canadian board for approval, although it was in the company's business plan. Heinz Pluckthun and Kurt Pfleiderer, the senior MBB executives who were also Canadian directors of MCL, had clearly kept the commission agreement between MBB and IAL to themselves. They had to: the contract could not have been clearer – no commissions and no bribes were allowed.

Giorgio Pelossi, Schreiber's former bookkeeper, was not inclined towards discretion, however. Together with Stevie Cameron, he was Schreiber's almost full-time nemesis. A resident of Lugano, Switzerland, Pelossi worked as an accountant of sorts: his expertise was in creating paper companies in tax havens for people who wanted to move money around quietly and quickly. A longtime Schreiber employee, he was not exactly a straight shooter. He had endured more than his share of encounters with the law, spending time in Swiss, Italian, and American prisons. In the early 1990s he and Schreiber had a falling-out about money. The dispute was over Pelossi's supposed share of the spoils – in particular, the money coming Schreiber's way from the 1988 sale of Airbus aircraft to Air Canada. When Schreiber refused to give Pelossi 20 per cent of the profits, Pelossi diverted some of the Airbus commission flow to his own account. Once Schreiber discovered what his lieutenant had done, he terminated Pelossi's employment. The two then exchanged

Stevie Cameron – Canada's most
celebrated investigatory journalist

lawsuits and, in due course, Pelossi went public. Pelossi had been in
charge of the books and he had retained some of the records. These
he made freely available to anyone who asked, including, eventually, Stevie Cameron.

Cameron was a Canadian publishing sensation. She was also the
best-known investigative journalist in Canada, with a reputation
that went from coast to coast to coast. According to the CBC's Larry
Zolf, Cameron was "Canada's greatest and most truthful investigative reporter ever."[9] Her 1994 book, *On the Take: Crime, Corruption and Greed in the Mulroney Years*, was a runaway bestseller. She
had spent years of her life trying to implicate Mulroney in wrongdoing. Cameron nailed a handful of his colleagues and his associates
in her book, but not once in the five hundred pages did she come
close to establishing that Mulroney had broken the law or behaved
dishonestly in any way. What she did do, extremely effectively, was
paint a very unflattering portrait of the man and his wife, Mila, both
of whom were depicted as mean-spirited, grasping, social-climbing
arrivistes, ostentatiously wallowing in luxury at someone else's expense, usually the Canadian public's. Much of what Cameron wrote
was undeserved, and all of it was unfair because it was completely
devoid of even the pretence of journalistic balance. But she touched
a truly Canadian nerve, one that responded enthusiastically to her
unproven assertion that Mulroney was "on the take," his govern-

ment populated principally with scuzballs, crooks, and thugs. The hardcover sold more than 100,000 copies – and it became required reading at the RCMP.

Without a doubt, Cameron was the international expert on wrongdoing in the Mulroney government, both real and imagined. Moreover, Cameron was a truly marketable brand with huge name recognition. She knew everyone – journalists, judges, politicians, and the Canadian elite – and had worked at leading newspapers and magazines in Ottawa and Toronto, impressing colleagues not just with her professional dedication but with her warmth and generosity. A Cordon Bleu–trained chef, Cameron was an early volunteer at St Andrew's Church in downtown Toronto, preparing and serving meals to the homeless.

While a number of Mounties carefully studied *On the Take* looking for clues, the force soon concluded that Cameron had uncovered absolutely nothing that would warrant opening a criminal investigation. A statement to that effect was issued on November 4, 1994.[10] In early 1995 the situation changed. Giorgio Pelossi started talking. His allegations began to attract the attention of the media in Europe and the *Fifth Estate* and Stevie Cameron in Canada. The *Fifth Estate* would broadcast a series of newsbreaking shows, while Cameron would soon publish the paperback edition of her book. While clearly a disreputable individual, Pelossi was also a regularly used police source, always anxious to please investigating authorities if they, in turn, could make life difficult for his former employer, Karlheinz Schreiber. Another way of hurting Schreiber was by hurting his friends – and they included Mulroney and Moores. At the end of June 1995 RCMP Staff Sergeant Fraser Fiegenwald – the lead Airbus/MBB/Bearhead investigator at the time – travelled to Switzerland to meet with Pelossi.

As an ex-felon with an axe to grind, Pelossi was hardly a disinterested witness. The RCMP had to be concerned about his low level of credibility. And they had to bring their concerns to the attention of Justice Fontana. Accordingly, the search warrant materials reviewed some of his background, including his criminal convictions and his extended prison sojourns. "I am," Inspector Mathews wrote, "cognizant of Pelossi's criminal history and recognize the risks associated in relying on unsupported information provided by persons of this background." Mathews observed, moreover, that while Pelossi clearly had an interest in causing trouble for Schreiber, it was possible that Schreiber had welched on the deal to share the Airbus spoils (although, the Information noted, before the "appropriation," there had been "little profit sharing," casting some doubt on the accuracy of Pelossi's account of an arrangement). It was not the Airbus commissions that concerned the RCMP in 1999 but the MBB commission arrangements – and with good reason too. The facts, at least the ones asserted this time around, appeared to line up.

In February 1985, and then again the next month, Pelossi, on behalf of Schreiber and his company, IAL, entered into a Sales Representation Agreement with MBB. Pelossi passed on a copy of the agreement to the RCMP. It appointed IAL as the sales representative for MBB helicopters to the Canadian government. MBB agreed to compensate IAL with a commission fee of 8 per cent on each sale, and 15 per cent for spare parts and ground-support components. The agreement noted that the commission was in recognition of a "retainer fee" paid by IAL to Alta Nova, a consulting company owned by Frank Moores and others that later transmogrified into Government Consultants International. When that happened, the agreement was amended to substitute GCI for Alta Nova. There was, Mathews pointed out, evidence indicating that GCI, and before it, Alta Nova, received a monthly retainer of $6,000.

The money could have been for anything, and MBB sold a lot more in Canada than helicopters. Yet the commission agreement was specifically for helicopters, and there was no evidence whatsoever that Schreiber, Moores, Alta Nova, or GCI had ever had anything to do with the Coast Guard deal. A link had to be established between this money and other payments and commissions on the helicopter sale to the Coast Guard to establish a breach of the *Criminal Code*.

The RCMP claimed to have this evidence. Originating with Pelossi, it had a document indicating an agent fee payable from MBB to IAL in the amount of $1,122,072 – precisely twelve times the almost $100,000 added by MBB to the price of each helicopter to be sold to the Canadian Coast Guard. There was clear evidence indicating that substantial MBB money made its way to GCI, as well as to one of Moores's two Swiss bank accounts, and to yet another account opened to channel funds to various "Canadian friends."[11] Some of the money probably contributed to the cost of the Jupiter, Florida, condominium where Moores wintered, while substantial other funds, although perhaps not MBB-source funds, were directly and indirectly transferred in the late 1980s to one of Schreiber's Canadian companies, Bitucan, and from there, according to Pelossi, to a variety of interesting destinations.

Pelossi had much information and many documents detailing the complicated web of MBB payments. Unfortunately, Fiegenwald's investigatory efforts had turned up nothing but smoke. Fortunately, however, he had an informer who had been promised secrecy in return for working with the police. This informer had been passing on information for years and was more than willing – anxious, as it turned out – to give the RCMP a hand. "Vast information," as the RCMP later described it, arrived in Ottawa. Courtesy of his informer, and now knowing exactly what to look for, Fiegenwald embarked on a European jaunt in June 1995.

The law is very clear. The permission of the foreign state is required before a member of a police force of another country can come to that state to pursue a criminal investigation. The RCMP liaison officer in Berne had received approval from his Swiss counterpart for an informal interview, provided no statements were taken and no documents passed over. By obtaining approval for an informal meeting, the law was respected. Still, one condition of the approval stipulated that the interviewer could take no statements or documents. Staff Sergeant Fiegenwald, notwithstanding this understanding, may, according to an RCMP report, "have brought back several documents just in case Pelossi lost some before they could be sent to Canada via official channels."[12] Fiegenwald was obviously thinking ahead. In addition to supplying some documents, Pelossi confirmed that MBB had an agreement with Schreiber and his company, IAL, to pay commissions on the sale of MBB helicopters to the Government of Canada. Pelossi had signed on behalf of IAL and Schreiber, and Pfleiderer signed for MBB.

According to the RCMP, Pelossi also informed Fiegenwald that the commissions were to pay off Canadian officials for their help in obtaining the helicopter contract. If that was true, it was an extremely serious charge: Canadian officials taking bribes. Pelossi told Fiegenwald that Schreiber enjoyed a similar commission arrangement with Thyssen Industries for the Bearhead project, and with Airbus Industries for the sale of Airbus aircraft. Fiegenwald returned to Canada and accelerated his investigatory efforts, all of which were now directed at securing a Letter of Request to Switzerland asking for Swiss assistance in opening up several numbered accounts that Pelossi advised were holding, among other things, Brian Mulroney's proceeds of crime. What happened instead was that Mulroney, in the fall of 1995, got wind of the Letter of Request and its overheated, unsubstantiated, and untrue allegations, filed suit, and put the RCMP on the defensive. It took years for the Mounties to recover. By 1999 the investigation was much more modest in scope.

This investigation was now about only the helicopter sale. The

RCMP believed it had been fraudulent because MCL promised that no commissions would be paid. While the payment of the commissions, at best, constituted a breach of contract (and even that was far from clear, as the commission arrangement had been agreed on between corporate parent MBB and IAL, without the knowledge of the Canadian subsidiary), the RCMP believed that these payments were evidence of a crime. The Mounties also believed that the monies went to both Schreiber and Moores, using "a scheme of bank transfers and corporate exchanges from one company to another to conceal the origin and purpose." The whole arrangement, according to the RCMP report, "put the economic interest of the Government of Canada at risk of deprivation by causing Canada to enter into a contract it would not otherwise have entered into."[13] At the same time, the Mounties went out of their way to avoid attracting another lawsuit from Mulroney by stating that no public official, past or present, was under investigation for conduct that might be the subject of a charge under section 120 or 121 of the *Criminal Code* – paying a bribe to a public official or receiving one.

Obviously, a large part of the RCMP case originated with Pelossi. It was important to demonstrate to the judge who would be asked to approve the different search warrants that this source was a credible one. After all, the Mounties wanted to search the offices of Eurocopter and the Department of Fisheries and Oceans for documents relating to the Coast Guard helicopter purchase, as well as the Bank of Nova Scotia in Calgary and accountants Buchanan, Barry & Co. for Bitucan financial and banking records – all to track the commission trail. It began with the Department of Supply and Services and the Canadian Coast Guard, led to MBB, and then to IAL, GCI, Schreiber, and Moores. Inspector Mathews and his team of investigators also wanted to look at some old GCI records stored in Ottawa. The whole purpose of the Information was to satisfy a judge that there were good reasons to believe that these searches would uncover evidence of the crime that the lengthy document laid out so carefully.

Inspector Mathews was convinced that Pelossi was telling the truth. "I have reviewed the information provided by Pelossi extremely carefully. I consider it to be generally reliable for the following reason, namely that events over which he claims personal knowledge or participation in, as set out herein, have been repeatedly confirmed by way of documentary evidence provided by Pelossi, or by the accounts and documentary evidence of independent witnesses unconnected to Pelossi ... without significant contradiction."[14] Moreover, in February 1998 a trained and certified polygraphist, Sergeant G.W. Taker, travelled to Milan and examined Pelossi, who, in his opinion, answered all the questions he was asked truthfully. In only one instance that Inspector Mathews knew of, involving the purpose of one of Moores's Swiss bank accounts, was Pelossi's information contradicted by other evidence. Even convicted felons like Pelossi sometimes tell the truth – and maybe he was too, this time. At least his documents seemed genuine.

With respect to everyone else whom he had interviewed, Inspector Mathews "observed nothing in the demeanour or answers of the individuals involved to cause him to question their sincerity of conduct towards myself or the completeness of their recollection."[15] Twenty-eight "relevant" interviews were conducted. The full names, dates, and places of these interviews were set out in the documents released in April 2001. One name was blacked out: "#xix." This person, who had been interviewed twice, had a last name beginning with an A, B, C, D, or E, for the RCMP had listed all its sources in alphabetical order. The blacked-out source fit somewhere between Susan Allison, a clerk in the Registry Office in Palm Beach who provided information about Moores's Florida condominium, and Karl Elsner, a Calgary accountant. When Eddie Greenspan first read the Information after the search warrant materials finally began to be disclosed, he wrote in the margin on his copy: "Who?" Could it possibly be the same person who had provided documents to Fiegenwald, reigniting an investigation that had otherwise run out of gas?

That was a very good question.

5 Open or Shut?

Giving someone notice that his or her interests may be affected by a legal proceeding is just a first step, one designed to ensure that a person's legal rights are protected – assuming, for the sake of argument, that the person does have interests recognized by the law that may be affected by the proceeding. Notice does not mean standing, however. Standing, in legal parlance, means that the person given notice actually has the right to participate in the proceeding as if he or she were a party to the proceeding. In order to assist Mulroney, Schreiber, and the CBC in making submissions on whether they were entitled to standing, now that the matter of notice had been determined, Justice Then, in April 2001, disclosed just about the entire court file, reasoning they could make informed submissions about standing only if they knew what the key document used to obtain the search warrant said and in what way it pertained to them. The disclosure was not, however, complete. First, some of the documents in the court file continued to be withheld. Second, parts of the materials that were disclosed came in redacted form: significant sections were blacked out. Third, because of Justice Then's earlier order, only a short list of lawyers and, of course, their clients were allowed access to this material, and any discussion of it with others was strictly forbidden.

Dealing with the issue of standing was, therefore, the first order of business when the court reconvened the following month, May 2001. The new players and the old ones were back, but this time the CBC was represented by different counsel, the high-profile criminal lawyer John Rosen.

Rosen is best known for his spirited defence of multiple murderer and sex predator Paul Bernardo. There was no saving Bernardo, of course – the evidence against him was too compelling. What Rosen

John Rosen – the CBC called out the heavy ammunition to blow the lid off the secret trial.

succeeded in doing, however, was shifting the public's perception of the case, leaving many believing that Bernardo's partner in crime, Karla Homolka, was at least as guilty as he was of the murder and torture of two young girls. There were important criminal law issues at stake in the Eurocopter case, and the CBC rightly reasoned that expert criminal counsel was required.

The CBC was in a difficult spot. It knew about a secret trial in progress at Osgoode Hall. And it knew that the RCMP, Brian Mulroney, Karlheinz Schreiber, and Eurocopter were all involved. But because of Justice Then's order, it was precluded from broadcasting that the proceedings were taking place, even if it went no further than simply reporting the existence of a secret trial somewhere in Canada. Justice Then's prohibition on discussion was airtight. Only the lawyers and the clients got to know. The situation was intolerable and Rosen made all the expected submissions in a straightforward manner. The media were entitled not only to be there but to report that they were there. One corollary was the right of access to all the transcripts of the proceedings to date, the unabridged Information (the key document advanced by the RCMP before Justice

Fontana to secure his approval for the search), and the affidavits Inspector Mathews, and perhaps others, had filed in support of the search warrant application and the sealing of almost everything in sight. The CBC wanted standing – and it wanted full disclosure of the complete court file.

Open courts, Rosen argued, are the rule – repeating the submissions that Eurocopter lawyer Paul Schabas had been making for a year and a half to no avail. The press must be free to comment and report on court proceedings to ensure that the courts are, in fact, seen to operate openly, subject to the light of public scrutiny. This was no mere aspiration. It was the law of the land, provided for in the *Charter of Rights and Freedoms* and its guarantee of freedom of expression, including freedom of the press. Free access to the courts was an indispensable corollary of that right, recognized repeatedly by the Supreme Court of Canada.

In a different case involving the CBC, Rosen pointed out, the Supreme Court of Canada had set out the test to be followed where an order was sought to exclude the public from court proceedings:

... the trial judge should ... be guided by the following:

(a) the judge must consider the available options and consider whether there are any reasonable and effective alternatives available;

(b) the judge must consider whether the order is limited as much as possible; and

(c) the judge must weigh the importance of the objectives of the particular order and its probable effects against the importance of openness and the particular expression that will be limited in order to ensure that the positive and negative effects of the order are proportionate.[1]

As far as the CBC was concerned, Rosen said, a continuing basis for the exclusion of the public had never been established in this case. Even if it did exist at one time, that time had come and gone.

Secret trials, Rosen pointed out, were a rare exception. He cited the *MacIntyre* decision. It was, after all, one of the leading cases supporting the principle of open courts and open access to legal documents. But there were other important authorities, including *Dagenais v. CBC*.[2] In that important decision, the Supreme Court of Canada set out the standards that had to be met before a publication ban could be maintained:

(a) Such a ban is necessary in order to prevent a real and substantial risk to the fairness of the trial, because reasonably
available measures will not prevent the risk; and

(b) The salutary effects of the publication ban outweigh the
deleterious effects to the free expression of those affected by
the ban.

The court concluded in *Dagenais* that "the objective of a publication
ban authorized under the rule is to prevent real and substantial risks
of trial unfairness – publication bans are not available as protection
against remote and speculative dangers."

Rosen noted that the Crown had conceded that there had been a
significant change in circumstances. It could no longer satisfy the
legal onus it had to meet to keep all the court documents completely sealed. That is why some materials, redacted and unredacted, had
already been disclosed. It was now time, the public broadcaster
argued, to unseal everything else. If any of the other parties to the
proceedings wanted the remaining sealing orders to continue, Rosen
suggested it was up to them to persuade the judge that continued
sealing, in light of the *Charter* and the case law, was justified. Making matters worse was the monumental cone of silence imposed by
judicial order over the entire proceeding. No one could say anything
to anyone about any matter related to the case without getting into
serious trouble with the judge.

Before the CBC's submissions could be addressed, Justice Then
had to decide who else would be allowed to participate. Until Mulroney and Schreiber's legal status in the case had been addressed, he
could not make any proper decisions on the CBC's motion on secrecy and sealing. He therefore scheduled a hearing for July 25 and 26,
2001, to deal with this issue. Mulroney and Schreiber had received
notice only because they were potentially interested persons. That
merely got them in the door. If they wanted to stay, they had to convince the judge that their rights and interests could be affected by the
proceeding, or that there was some other valid reason in favour of
their attendance. Mulroney's lawyers were up first thing in the morning on July 25, asking for an order that the former prime minister be
granted "limited standing as an intervenor." An intervenor is someone who asserts an interest in a particular legal proceeding because,
for instance, he or she may be affected by it, and so he or she seeks
leave from the court to participate voluntarily in it, subject to limits
imposed by the court.

Since the release of some documents on April 24, 2001, Mulroney and his lawyers, like Schreiber and his lawyer, had learned more about the case. Mulroney now knew two key facts. The Minutes of Settlement resolving his $50 million lawsuit against the Government of Canada were included in the court file. Mulroney was also referred to in an affidavit that had been filed in support of the sealing under the heading "Interests of Innocent Persons." Mulroney was being protected. Inspector Mathews explained in detail:

> Disclosure would prejudice the interests of innocent persons in several respects. Many of the names found in the Information to Obtain are those of innocent persons, and of persons of considerable public stature, or who are engaged in public service whose reputation is their significant asset. The names of those persons can be found in the Information to Obtain that forms part of this application. In particular, this investigation has already experienced the consequences of disclosure of a 1995 Letter of Request to Switzerland as set out more fully in the Information to Obtain. This resulted in public attention and speculation to the highest degree on an international scale that continues to this day and in the initiation of civil action for damages. Although the Information to Obtain in this case is careful to circumscribe the allegations in question, it is inevitable that their disclosure would attract an unusually high level of publicity and might result in potentially damaging speculation on matters beyond the intended scope of the Information to Obtain. I believe it is also inevitable that as part of any renewed media attention, reference would again be made to the 1995 request whose disclosure led to claims of damaged reputation even though there are no allegations or suggestions by the Informant in this exhibit or the related Information to Obtain that any government officials did anything wrong in connection with the dealings of MBB/MCL. To the extent that the investigation of MBB/MCL may make reference by way of disclosure or otherwise, to Airbus-related matters, similar levels of attention may be expected if the investigation is publicized. An order restricting disclosure of the Information to Obtain in this case until the conclusion of the investigation and a final decision on any charges would best protect the interests of all those presumed innocent, subject to the Court's power to vary.

In the most simple terms, the RCMP was going out of its way to safeguard Mulroney's reputation – or, at least, that is what it claimed when it initially argued in favour of secrecy. Once burned, twice shy:

the Mounties were not going to be accused this time around of doing anything to harm Mulroney's most "significant asset."

Mulroney also knew now that the reason he got notice was because the Crown could no longer justify many, if not most, of the background documents remaining sealed – at any rate, at least not completely. In bringing this important fact to the attention of Justice Then, Crown attorney Trevor Shaw had earlier advised the court that "Mr. Mulroney's position as a presumptively innocent party was invoked in favour of the sealing order sought. This position has not changed, though the time may have come – subject to some editing – for the sealing to end, at least in relation to Eurocopter. However this does not mean that Mr. Mulroney might not seek to articulate a continued interest in restricting access or publication beyond Eurocopter."[3] In lay terms, the Crown believed that there was no further justification for any sealing of any of the materials, at least insofar as Eurocopter was concerned. On Mulroney, the Crown recognized that he might have a personal interest in the proceedings continuing behind closed doors. Mulroney could take the position that his reputation might be unfairly damaged merely because of his association with this case and that, as a presumptively innocent person, he was entitled to protection under the *Criminal Code*.

While Mulroney and his attorneys learned much by reading the Crown's April disclosures, they were not yet in a position to make any submissions on this issue. They needed to know more. Mulroney wanted to be allowed to attend the proceedings, to review any documents that were disclosed, and to make submissions, if need be, with respect to his rights of privacy. He was extremely curious about the proceedings – he sensed something was up – and so he wanted his lawyers, at least two at a time, to maintain a watching brief. Mulroney's instincts told him that it would probably be worthwhile to stick around, at least for a while. Accordingly, he asked for limited standing as an intervenor.

Schreiber was also in attendance. He wanted standing to attend, to participate, and to receive disclosure. He was, as his lawyer Eddie Greenspan pointed out, extensively referred to in the court file. He was characterized as a "participant in the commission scheme." While not the direct target of the search warrant, he was, without a doubt, an indirect target, implicated in alleged wrongdoing. Paying bribes and illegal commissions is as much a crime as receiving them. If Eurocopter went down, Schreiber might follow.

Accordingly, Greenspan argued, the public disclosure of the information and the affidavits would, in these circumstances, result in irreparable damage to Schreiber's integrity, privacy, and reputation.

It would also infringe his right to privacy. For good measure, Greenspan suggested that the court take a closer look at the activities of Harvey Cashore. This was the oldest trick in the book, but a good one. Go on the attack. Create a diversion. Throw a wrench in the works. Provoke a delay and then another one. Cashore, Greenspan now knew, had shown up uninvited at the University Avenue courthouse the very first day the proceedings moved to Toronto. He had done so because he was a reporter following a story. But that just gave Greenspan an opportunity to do his job – to distract attention from one inquiry and perhaps persuade the judge to embark on another one with a better upside for his client, especially if, as Greenspan was beginning to suspect, the RCMP's handling of the case was not in accordance with the proper administration of justice. This theme would be further developed as the proceedings continued. In the meantime, Cashore, Greenspan pointed out, together with his colleague Stevie Cameron, had since published a book replete with details of the Eurocopter search. Someone might have violated the sealing order, and Greenspan suggested that the court enter into an inquiry to find out who that was.

Eurocopter no longer objected to the court's granting status to Mulroney and Schreiber. "These individuals clearly have an interest in the materials, as recognized by the Crown, and as is apparent from the subject matter of the materials under seal," Schabas agreed on behalf of the helicopter company.[4] Eurocopter did not even take a position with respect to the CBC's application to intervene. What it wanted to know was the basis for the Crown's change of position with respect to the sealing orders, the turnaround that led to notification for both Mulroney and Schreiber and to the disclosure of a number of the important search warrant documents. The Crown had filed another affidavit, which only the judge got to see, at the same time as it made its disclosure in April 2001. Presumably this affidavit explained the switch in position, and Eurocopter wanted to know what had made the government change its mind. Until then, Eurocopter did not want any variation of the overall order directing the *in camera* proceedings. Like the Crown, however, it had completely reversed course. Everyone was switching positions, and it was all a little hard to follow.

At first the Crown wanted everything sealed as well as a publication ban. Eurocopter wanted everything unsealed and no ban. Later, in April 2001, avoiding a trip to the Court of Appeal, the Crown made significant disclosure. Now, the next month, it wanted to vary the sealing order in a number of different ways. If the judge agreed, there would be public access to some of the previously sealed materials, while other documents would remain under seal. Schabas was visibly incensed. There was an affidavit explaining the switch, but Eurocopter did not get to see it. As Schabas complained to the court, Eurocopter "has not been informed of grounds for varying the sealing orders which the Crown has otherwise so vigorously pressed to maintain for the past eighteen months." In these circumstances, the company was "unable" to make any "meaningful submissions on the issue," one that might "have a serious detrimental impact on it."[5] Actually, Schabas was more than able to take the government lawyers to task, severely criticizing the manner in which Michael Bernstein and Trevor Shaw were conducting the case, and he was doing so to their evident discomfort.

The Crown's latest position, Schabas continued, was inconsistent with the stance it had taken for eighteen months: that "an order restricting disclosure of the Information to Obtain in this case until the conclusion of the investigation and a final decision on any charges would best protect the interests of all those presumed innocent."[6] How could it be fair, Schabas asked, for the Crown to fail to justify the sealing for all this time and then, without any explanation, announce that the situation had changed?[7] Schabas expressed the view that such a change could not happen: "In the absence of disclosing the grounds for varying the sealing order, which would permit meaningful submissions being made to the Court, the Crown has not met the onus on it to justify a variation of the sealing Orders." Moreover, he argued, the lifting of the sealing Orders and publication ban would cause Eurocopter "serious and irreparable harm" for two reasons: an innocent person would be prejudiced by damaging publicity; and Eurocopter, if eventually charged, would be prejudiced in its ability to mount a defence.[8]

What, then, did Eurocopter hope to achieve? It wanted *exclusive* access to everything, to the entire court record, including all the grounds for continued non-disclosure of any of the documents, or any part of any of the documents, and it wanted these materials in advance of the court's dealing with the request for a broader variation of the *in camera* order and publication ban. In other words, Eurocopter wanted to know why the Crown had changed its mind about the sealing order. It wanted to see everything before the court began hearing submissions on whether the hearing should be opened to the public and, if it was opened up, whether there should be a publication ban.

Schabas pointed out that Justice Then had already accepted, as had Justice Fontana in the earlier proceeding, that the sealing was justified by the need, first, to prevent prejudice to the interests of presumptively innocent parties and, second, to protect the ongoing investigation. What had changed since January 2000? Even if certain steps relating to the investigation had been completed, there were still the interests of the presumptively innocent. Protection of the innocent, Schabas argued, was a social value recognized by Canadian courts. Eurocopter was in pretty much the same position as the innocent persons whose interests justified the initial sealing. It had not been charged with an offence. It was merely the subject of an investigation. It was, therefore, like Mulroney and others, entitled to the presumption of innocence. As a supplier to the Canadian government, and to governments around the world, Eurocopter's reputation was one of its significant assets. The mere allegation of impropriety would almost certainly damage the company in the marketplace.

Although only an edited version of the key background document presented to Justice Fontana in support of the search had, so far, been disclosed, it contained substantial detail of the evidence the Crown would be relying on should charges be laid. Witnesses were identified, and while "will-says" – summaries of evidence expected to be tendered – were not exactly provided, it was abundantly clear what each of the identified witnesses would say if summoned to court. Credibility was likely to be in issue, and Eurocopter's interests could be adversely affected if all the evidence of all the expected witnesses was in the public domain.

Why give everyone the opportunity to get their stories straight, Schabas asked? That would surely jeopardize the helicopter manufacturer's right to a fair trial. Besides, what was the rush? The investigation was continuing. No charges had even been laid. At the very least, even if the sealing order was lifted, Schabas urged the court to impose a publication ban. Such a ban was necessary to protect the interests of an innocent third party and to ensure Eurocopter's right to a fair trial. "While a publication ban may result in limiting freedom of expression, the salutary effects of such a ban outweigh the deleterious effects that would result from the non-disclosure, at this time, of the sealed information."[9]

The Crown had to acknowledge that Eurocopter had the right to make submissions on the sealing and unsealing issue. In the same way, given the *Charter* guarantees, it had to agree that the CBC was entitled to make submissions about lifting the publication ban and permitting public access. Where Schreiber was concerned, the Crown had little interest in allowing his participation. He had, Michael Bernstein suggested, no direct interest in either the premises that were searched or the documents that were seized. This may have been technically correct, but Schreiber was obviously an interested party, identified in the Information as a key player in the commission arrangements – the very act the Crown and the RCMP were asserting constituted a crime.

At the same time, Bernstein argued, Schreiber had not been charged. His privacy rights and right to a fair trial were not implicated. The argument that he should be given access to the proceedings because his rights to privacy and reputation were at issue was, Bernstein suggested, "novel." That was a polite way of saying that Greenspan was asserting an entitlement not recognized in law. If, Bernstein continued, Schreiber was one day charged with an offence, there was a possibility that unsealing the remaining documents and setting aside the publication ban might impinge on his right to a fair trial. There were, Bernstein pointed out, a variety of remedies for any such unfairness, including a change of venue. The publicity would have to be so adverse that there was a reasonable likelihood that prospective jurors could not be impartial, or that the accused could not receive a fair trial in the local venue for judicial intervention. The presiding judge would have to be satisfied that the adverse publicity could not be cured with proper instructions from the bench about what the jurors could and could not take into account. All these events, if they were to come to pass, were not only contingent and far in the future but could be dealt with in a proper way at the appropriate time. In contrast to the position taken on Schreiber, however, the Crown raised no objection to Mulroney's request to attend.

Many months later, on October 4, 2001 – this judge certainly liked to consider matters carefully – Justice Then issued his reasons for decision. He revealed, for the first time, that it was not just Mulroney, Schreiber, and the CBC who were given notice of the proceedings back in early April. "Another person" was also notified as a "potentially interested party."[10] That person, Justice Then wrote in his decision, "did not attend and has received no further notice of these proceedings." This item was not news to either Mulroney or Schreiber. They were well aware that Frank Moores had been notified about the proceeding. With that out of the way, the next issue to be decided was whether Mulroney and Schreiber would get standing. Not only did Justice Then have the discretion to grant them standing, but he believed this case was an appropriate one in which to exercise it.

The judge dealt with Mulroney first. It was significant, he said, that neither the Crown nor Eurocopter opposed standing for Mulroney. Both recognized that the former prime minister ought, "on the basis of information disclosed to date," to be "viewed without qualification as an 'innocent person.'"[11] Indeed, even the RCMP had realized as much, advancing this ground in its initial application for sealing. In somewhat of an understatement, Justice Then, referring to the 1995 Letter of Request to Switzerland, observed that it "is unnecessary to detail the nature of the publicity surrounding [Mulroney] which has already attended the previous disclosure in this investigation."[12]

One of the critical interests identified by the Supreme Court of Canada in the *MacIntyre* decision was the protection of the innocent. While the Supreme Court had, in that case, concerned itself with the protection of innocent persons who were subject to a search – which Mulroney was not – "there is no obstacle in law or policy that I can discern," according to Justice Then, "to extending that protection to innocent persons mentioned in the Information supporting the search warrant where there is a reasonable prospect of stigmatization to name and reputation by the publication of the search or the Information giving rise to it." Justice Then reasoned that if the target of the search is entitled to protection because he or she is presumed innocent, a non-target should be entitled to similar treatment. "I cannot accept that Dickson J. in *MacIntyre* could have differentiated between the innocence of the subject of the warrant and that of others mentioned in the warrant if there was a reasonable prospect that an innocent person would be unfairly stigmatized by disclosure. I do not mean to imply that public access will automatically be curtailed with respect to demonstrably innocent persons but only that it is just, based on *MacIntyre*, that the court be vested with discretion to extend standing to appropriate interested and potentially innocent persons whose names and reputations may be damaged, whether they are the direct subject of the warrant or not, by the publication of the search and the Information upon which it is based."[13] As the proceedings presented a potential threat to his name and reputation, Mulroney was entitled, at a minimum, Justice Then concluded, to make submissions. His application for limited standing as an intervenor was, therefore, granted.

Justice Then turned next to Schreiber's application. The judge accepted that Schreiber was an interested party, entitled to fully participate in the proceeding. His name, and allegations of his misconduct, were all over the Information that detailed his alleged extensive involvement in the commission arrangement. While the Crown had argued otherwise, Justice Then granted that application.

"It would seem obvious to me," Justice Then reasoned, "that if the subject of the search and the target of the charges is deemed innocent, and if nothing is found during the search, and [if the subject of the search or target of the charges is] deserving of protection from disclosure because of the unjust possibility of stigmatization, then a non-target, who is nevertheless implicated but deemed innocent because the search yields nothing to advance his complicity, equally deserves protection." The judge was not pre-determining whether Schreiber would succeed in any future applications – for example, to keep the proceedings *in camera* or the documents sealed – but deciding only that he should have the opportunity now to make submissions.[14]

Deciding on the CBC's application for standing was the least difficult matter before Justice Then. The *Charter* guaranteed both open courts and the freedom of the press, and the news organization was granted standing – an almost preordained result. These rulings on standing were just another step on a long journey. After discussion among counsel, two days, December 14 and 18, 2001 – this case moved at a snail's pace – were set aside for hearing the Crown's application to determine whether future proceedings would be held in open court. The CBC made it clear that, when the case reconvened, it intended to seek an order lifting both the remaining sealing and the publication ban.

Schabas decided on a decisive pre-emptive strike. At the end of November 2001, Eurocopter served a notice on everyone involved: the judge, the Crown, the CBC, Mulroney, and Schreiber. When the case next convened, in mid-December, the company intended to make a motion to quash the search warrant. It also wanted to obtain exclusive access to the remainder of the documents, disclosed and redacted, and undisclosed, and to cross-examine Inspector Mathews about the RCMP theory of the case. Schabas wished to know the identity of the witness whose name was blacked out, that person whose last name began with an A, B, C, D, or E, and he was especially interested in learning how Staff Sergeant Fiegenwald had obtained certain key documents in the spring and early summer of 1995. Something did not smell right. Schabas took the position that his motion had to be addressed before the court considered whether there should be any further unsealing of the court file or whether the proceedings should be opened to the public and the publication ban rescinded. He insisted that his motion move to the top of the agenda.

The case was definitely getting interesting. The unsealed documents appeared to indicate that Staff Sergeant Fiegenwald had been provided with materials originating from Giorgio Pelossi in May and June 1995, well before the Letter of Request had been sent to Switzerland. Schabas did not yet know that the RCMP had received permission for an informal visit, provided that no statements or documents were taken. As it happened, the visit was a proper one, though documents may have been improperly received. But that revelation would not come until much later and, in the interim, Schabas could work only with what he knew. If some of the assertions in the material put before Justice Fontana in support of the application for the search warrant were based on illegally and unconstitutionally obtained evidence, he asserted, then the warrant itself, and its fruits – the thousands of pages of documents – would have to be returned.

Eurocopter was also concerned that most of the two hundred and more appendices had not been disclosed. These documents were specifically referred to in the Information as supporting Inspector Mathews's "ground for belief." But where were the interview transcripts of Pelossi, identified by the RCMP as a "credible witness"? The weight of this paperwork, directly or indirectly, undoubtedly influenced Justice Fontana in concluding that there were reasonable and probable grounds to justify the search. That being the situation, Schabas insisted on his client's right to have a look.

The legal onus was on the Crown to justify non-disclosure, and it could do so only by establishing that the material was beyond its control, clearly irrelevant, or privileged. No such claim had been made about the appendices. They ought to be released. Unless and until Eurocopter got all this information, it was prevented, Schabas continued, from seeking relief under the *Charter* to be free from unreasonable search and seizure. Simply put, Eurocopter needed more facts, more documents, more details to understand the justification for the search. Without being able to scrutinize the entire grounds for belief, and the reliability of those grounds, particularly when it was clear that the principal witness was an ex-convict with a known grudge and more than ample motives to lie, it could not mount a proper case.

Arguably, by failing to provide Eurocopter with full disclosure, the Crown was prejudicing the company's constitutional right to make full answer and defence. If Eurocopter were ever charged, it would normally be immediately entitled to the full, unexpurgated court file. What principled basis was there, two years after the search, for denying Eurocopter the documents it needed to assert its right against unreasonable search and seizure? To the extent that the justification was, as advanced, to protect the rights of innocent persons, that justification would disappear the day the company was charged. The Crown would then be required to make full disclosure.

There was another possible explanation for the continued secrecy. In a December 14, 2001, sworn affidavit – after Schabas in his November motion openly questioned why one witness name was blacked out and demanded to know who it was – Inspector Mathews revealed another reason for the sealing: there was a confidential informant.

To this point in the case, the sealing, the publication ban, and the limited disclosure of documents – with significant sections blacked out – had been justified in court on two grounds: to protect the presumptively innocent, now known to be Mulroney, and to maintain the integrity of an ongoing investigation. These grounds are recognized in the *Criminal Code*. These were the grounds advanced by the RCMP through the Crown as justification for the initial sealing and publication ban. These were the grounds accepted by Justice Fontana way back when justifying the sealing. These same grounds were accepted by Justice Then. Now the RCMP through the Crown was saying something new, something different, something surprising – at least to Eurocopter, Mulroney, and Schreiber.

Another ground recognized in the *Criminal Code* for justifying sealing and publication bans is to protect confidential informants, police informers, in other words. This justification had not been raised in this case before. Yet the key background document, the Information, the way it was written and organized, led the experienced criminal lawyers on the case to believe that none of the assembled evidence had come from a confidential informant. Normally, when the police rely on an informer, they make that fact crystal clear. They almost never tell even the judge the actual identity of the source, so secret is the identity of the informer. They almost never include the informer in the witness list, as was done here. But now this justification for the sealing of documents was being advanced.

The RCMP was asserting, years into the case, that at least partial sealing was justified to protect the identity of a police informer. None of the lawyers could understand how this claim could be raised so late in the day, given the architecture of the Information to Obtain. If there was an informer, he or she should have been identified, not by name but by number, at the outset. Initially, it was thought that maybe the blacked-out name on the witness list was an innocent person being protected. Once Mulroney was identified as the innocent person, that possibility fell by the wayside. It was now clear that the RCMP was asserting that the name being protected was that of a police informer. Inspector Mathews was an experienced and senior police officer. He had been working on the file for years. He had drafted the Information to Obtain. Was it credible that he did not know the name of the police informer? Was it possible that he learned about a police informer only years into the investigation? Was it conceivable that he knew there was a police informer, but still listed his or her name in the Information when that is almost never done? Might he have been aware of a police informer but decided, for some reason, to keep that information from the judge? And what did the Crown attorneys know and when? What in the world was going on?

Under Canadian law, a police officer has the power to promise informers secrecy, expressly or by implication, with a guarantee sanctioned by the law that this promise will be kept, even in court. For instance, when Fiegenwald obtained "vast information" from someone in early 1995, he could have offered his source informer status. In exchange for this promise, the police officer can secure information that otherwise would be difficult, if not impossible, to obtain.

Informers come in many different guises and operate within different arrangements. Sometimes they sign an informer agreement. Sometimes they are paid. There are casual informers and coded informers. Informers often get special or preferred treatment from the courts in exchange for the information they have provided to the police. One thing they always get is peace of mind: they know that the information they have provided will never be traced back to them. At least, that is the theory.

Not long after Schabas filed his various motions at the end of November 2001, the legal proceedings – still secret, still subject to Justice Then's blanket prohibition order – resumed. Schabas took the position before Justice Then that the very act of naming a confidential informer in the Information – if this is indeed what happened – meant that the RCMP and the Crown had waived any of the privilege that attached to the status. Alternatively, it meant that there was no confidential informant who might be entitled to protection from disclosure, but merely a witness who had no such rights. In either case, Schabas wanted to know a name. He insisted that the "who" not be used as justification for depriving him and his client of the information that was sought – access to all the documents so he could convince the judge to toss out the warrant. A police informer justification would, he argued, be bogus and should not sway the judge.

As the target, Eurocopter was presumptively entitled, Schabas argued, to inspect the unexpurgated Information, and all its appendices, to determine the validity of the search conducted on it. The Supreme Court of Canada had recognized that this was a broad right that had, as its purpose, the protection of individuals from unjustified state intrusions on their privacy. It was true enough that Justice Then had, less than a year earlier, upheld the sealing when Eurocopter brought its first motion for judicial review. But much had happened since that time, including the limited disclosure that had subsequently taken place, not to mention the startling revelation, long after the proceedings commenced, to Eurocopter and the other parties at least (although possibly not to the judge) that sealing was justified to protect a police informer – a police informer entitled to privilege. But police informer privilege was asserted only when Schabas demanded that the Crown reveal the identity of a mystery person on the Information's witness list. While Mulroney's and Schreiber's disclosure entitlements depended on their status, a matter not determined until October, Eurocopter was a different matter: normally it would have been told about the informer exemption in a proceeding of this kind at the outset.

Although hardly complete, the disclosure had provided Eurocopter's lawyer with some factual foundations to take issue with the entire process. The RCMP and the Crown were then forced to make a new and, given its timing, especially disturbing disclosure. There was a police informer entitled to protection.[15]

Eurocopter was also seeking leave of the court to cross-examine Inspector Mathews. After all, the search warrant had been granted on his sworn affirmation that there were reasonable and proper grounds for the search, and now there were questions about some of the documents he had provided. For example, had he accurately described the two hundred and more appendices in the Information? It seemed clear that a significant part of the inspector's grounds for belief was based on these materials. If so, why had he not attached them to the Information? If there was a good reason for not attaching them, Schabas invited the inspector to give it. Schabas was determined to get to his real objective: quashing the warrant and, in doing so, bringing the proceeding to an end.

There were some compelling arguments. The Information, Schabas suggested, did not support reasonable and proper grounds to believe that an offence had been committed, as had been alleged. There was no evidence that the management of MCL in Canada knew of any of the alleged commission payments between MBB and IAL. In fact, Schabas noted, the evidence was explicitly to the contrary. The RCMP narrative established that Pluckthun and Pfleiderer deliberately withheld information on the commissions. If the RCMP theory of the case was correct, they had committed a crime – against MCL. Neither Pluckthun nor Pfleiderer was in charge of MCL. To the extent that MBB may have paid commissions at their direction, that had nothing to do with MCL. Any arrangement between MBB and IAL also had nothing to do with MCL, and it could not constitute a crime against the Government of Canada. At the very best, all that the Crown would ever be able to prove was a breach of contract, and there was no guarantee that it could succeed even in doing that. There was no evidence that the commission was, or even could have been, added to the sale price for the contract between MCL and the Coast Guard. There was, in summary, no evidence of any criminal wrongdoing by MCL, and no basis to search its premises. Schabas concluded by asking the judge to give all appropriate orders and directions.

Now it was Eddie Greenspan's turn to speak. For the one and only time in this entire proceeding, Greenspan was brief. Schreiber's lawyer was happy to quash the warrant, and he supported the Eurocopter motion. That would end an investigation that was clearly not in the interest of his client.

The Crown, however, disagreed. Standing had been granted to interested parties so they could make submissions about release, public access, and publication of the documents in this case. Those were the issues scheduled for a hearing, and they should be dealt with first, not the Eurocopter motion to quash. Besides, Crown attorney Bernstein argued, Schabas had let too much time go by. He had held the materials he was relying on for months – since April 2001 – and could have made his motion at any time. This new motion was not served in compliance with procedural rules, since it failed to provide all the parties to the court proceeding with a reasonable opportunity to prepare and respond. Furthermore, there was no justification for allowing Eurocopter to disrupt the order of proceedings – to jump the queue and sidetrack, for who knew how long, the question of access and publication. And there were other issues too.

Initially, Bernstein continued, Eurocopter had demanded that the Information be unsealed and that the public have an unrestricted right

of access to everything. Time after time, Schabas had zealously asserted the primacy of the right of access to both courtrooms and public
documents. Over and over again, the lawyer had insisted that important constitutional values, such as an open court and the public's right
to know, be put in place. In keeping with those important values,
Bernstein observed, the Crown had, in April 2001, made many of the
documents available to the parties. Now the Crown sought the continued sealing of only a small part of the material that remained protected by the *Criminal Code*. It was also important to remember that
Justice Fontana, in granting the sealing application, went out of his
way to remind the Crown that he was not providing it with the opportunity to "seize at large, examine at leisure." Similarly, Justice Then
repeated this admonition when he upheld the continued sealing in his
January 2001 reasons for decision but provided for periodic review.
The Crown, Bernstein insisted, had taken these directions seriously
and had released significant portions of the materials. More materials had followed, and still more would follow. If anything, the evidence established that the Crown had acted carefully, prudently, and,
as was its obligation, it was now updating its sealing request so that
even more of the Mounties' materials could be disclosed.

Eurocopter had been fighting for public access from the beginning and was now taking a different line. How could it switch positions and argue that public access was wrong? It would have to persuade Justice Then that, when it was arguing for public access, it was
doing so in a different context: to obtain access to the documents so
as to challenge the validity of the warrant. Now that it had obtained
more access, it was still interested in having the warrant set aside and
the seized documents returned. Alternatively, it wanted to restrict
any further access to itself, in order to limit any unnecessary damage
to the company's reputation or, should charges eventually be laid, to
its rights to a fair trial. The Crown was not, however, buying any of
this and, in effect, suggested that Justice Then tell Schabas and Eurocopter to get real.

It was an unholy mess, a legal proceeding that had gone off the
rails, lurching from month to month with no end in sight. By the time
the proceedings were concluded for the year, in December 2001, the
judge had six motions under review:

1   The Crown's application to vary the existing sealing order and al-
    low general access to material presently disclosed only to counsel.

2   The Crown's application to have some material continue to re-
    main sealed, in part justified by the belated disclosure that there
    was a police informer whose identity had to be protected.
3   Eurocopter's application for limited access to documents that
    remained sealed and blacked out.
4   Eurocopter's application for exclusive access to the documents
    referred to in the Information.
5   Eurocopter's application to cross-examine Inspector Mathews.
6   Eurocopter's application to quash the search warrants.

As things transpired, when the proceedings reconvened in February 2002, some two years after Eurocopter first sought judicial
review of Justice Fontana's decision, these motions would remain
undecided. Eddie Greenspan used the intervening weeks to study
everything that had been disclosed and everything that had ever been
written by anyone about Airbus, MBB, and Bearhead. He knew he
was sitting on a bomb. This time, Greenspan would speak at length.
When he was finished, everything would have changed.

6 Police Informer

Police informers play a critical role in the fight against crime. Usually in return for something, they give police information they would not otherwise obtain. One thing all informers receive is a legally binding promise: the right never to be called to account for the information they have provided to the police. If the identity of police informers became known, people with information would cease to come forward; moreover, the safety of those who had performed that function would be put into jeopardy. As a result, a legal privilege attaches to the status of informer. Once you become a police informer, nobody is allowed to ask you even if you are a police informer. The asking alone could lead to discovery of this privileged and confidential relationship.

In *Leipert v. The Queen*,[1] the Supreme Court of Canada was called on to define the contours of informer privilege. In that case, an anonymous source had provided the police, through Crime Stoppers, with information that Richard Leipert, a Vancouver resident, was growing marijuana in his basement. This tip led to the police conducting their own investigation. A police officer and a police dog named Bruno walked in front of Leipert's house. Bruno gave a bark, indicating the presence of illicit drugs inside. The officer also observed that the basement windows were covered and that there was a smell of marijuana in the air. On the basis of these facts, a search warrant was obtained. One of the background documents filed in support of that warrant mentioned the Crime Stoppers tip. The paperwork made clear, however, that the main grounds for the warrant were the observations of the police officer and the reactions of Bruno, obtained at the site. When the search warrant was executed, the police found marijuana growing in the basement and seized it. Leipert was charged with two counts: cultivation of marijuana, and possession for the purpose of trafficking.

At trial, Leipert asked to see a copy of the Crime Stoppers document forwarding the tip to the police. The Crown objected. The trial judge viewed the document, attempted to edit out any references to the informer, and disclosed what was left. What happened next was unusual. The Crown asked to rely on the warrant without any reference to the tip. The trial judge refused this request because the accused did not consent. The Crown ceased to tender any evidence, the defence elected to call no evidence, and the trial judge entered an acquittal. This verdict sent the case to the Court of Appeal.

The Court of Appeal reversed the decision of the trial judge and ordered a new trial. Madam Justice Mary Southin found that the tip, while part of the background to the case, was irrelevant because the Crown did not rely on it either to justify the issuing of the warrant or for establishing guilt. British Columbia Chief Justice Allen McEachern, who was also sitting on the panel hearing the appeal, agreed, but added that the document recording the tip was privileged. Trial judges, he suggested, should be cautious in ordering the production of even carefully edited tip sheets or reports for which informant privilege is claimed, given the possibility that seemingly innocuous details may lead to identification of the informant. The case then made its way to the Supreme Court of Canada, as Leipert, having no interest in being retried and probably convicted, attempted to get his acquittal restored.

Justice was ultimately served in February 1997 when the court ruled that the Crime Stoppers tip was privileged and need not be disclosed. Leipert's case went back on the docket for a new trial. In reaching this conclusion, the court examined at length some of the key principles underlying the promise of confidentiality and the privilege given to police informers: "A court considering this issue must begin from the proposition that informer privilege is an ancient and hallowed protection which plays a vital role in law enforcement. It is premised on [the] duty of all citizens to aid in enforcing the law. The discharge of this duty carries with it the risk of retribution from those involved in crime. The rule of informer privilege was developed to protect citizens who assist in law enforcement and to encourage others to do the same."[2]

The system generally works this way. A police officer has the power to promise informers secrecy, with a guarantee sanctioned by law that this promise will be kept. Information obtained from informers assists police officers in carrying out their duty: ensuring that the law is obeyed and enforced. Police informers are used in all sorts of investigations, and their value has been repeatedly and properly recognized. Successful prosecutions of drug trafficking operations and organized crime, in particular, depend heavily on informers.

Many privileges are recognized in law: solicitor-client, husband-wife, and Crown privilege, invoked by the government to keep its documents secret, to name just three. The last type of privilege involves a careful balancing between the interests of the Crown in maintaining secrecy and the interests of doing justice. There is, however, no balancing in informer privilege. It is, arguably, the most important privilege of all: "Informer privilege is of such importance that it cannot be balanced against other interests. Once established, neither the police nor the court possesses discretion to abridge it."[3]

The privilege belongs to the Crown, but, in a sense, it also belongs to the informer. Without the informer's consent, the Crown cannot waive the privilege either expressly or by implication by not raising it. Very simply, once informer privilege has been conferred, the Crown must take every possible step to protect the identity of the informer and prevent its detection. "This follows," the Supreme Court of Canada ruled in *Leipert*, "from the purpose of the privilege, being the protection of those who provide information to the police and the encouragement of others to do the same."[4] To ensure that this principle is given effect, the courts have developed a series of rules outlining how the informer privilege works in action. In deciding what documents an interested party – Eurocopter and Karlheinz Schreiber, for instance – would be entitled to see, the court must, if the police are relying on a confidential informant, take great care to ensure that nothing is released that could possibly lead, directly or indirectly, to unmasking the identity of the individual involved. In many cases the Crown contacts the informer to review what evidence may be released without compromising the informer's identity. It is not permissible to compel a witness on the stand to disclose whether he or she is an informer. The question cannot even be asked.

There is only one exception to these strict rules: the "innocence at stake exception." That exception applies where the informer's identity is needed to demonstrate the innocence of the accused. An innocent person may not be sent to jail in order to safeguard the identity of a police informer. Obviously, to allow otherwise would be to implicate the authorities knowingly in a miscarriage of justice.

Not surprisingly, informers come forward for different reasons. In some cases, a target or some other interested person has reason to question the motives of the suspected confidential source. In *Leipert*, the Supreme Court of Canada considered the relationship between informer privilege and challenges to search warrants: "Where the accused seeks to establish that a search warrant was not supported by reasonable grounds, the accused may be entitled to information which may reveal the identity of an informer notwithstanding informer privilege in circumstances where it is absolutely essential." "Essential circumstances," the court added, "exist where the accused establishes the 'innocence at stake' exception to informer privilege. Such a case might arise, for example, where there is evidence suggesting that the goods seized in execution of the warrant were planted. To establish that the informer planted the goods or had information as to how they came to be planted, the accused might properly seek disclosure of information that might incidentally reveal the identity of the informer."[5] Without extremely strong grounds indicating that the disclosure of the identity of the informer will establish the innocence of the accused, the identity of the informer will remain privileged. In short, this privilege is zealously protected. The obligation on the Crown and on the presiding judge to ensure that the identity of the informer is not revealed cannot be overstated.

Late in the day in the Eurocopter case, as we have seen, the RCMP and the Crown asserted that some of the documents had to remain under seal to protect a confidential informant. The timing of that disclosure was strange. Normally, the confidential informant privilege is claimed at the outset. In this case, there was no reason to believe that the revelation of the name of a police informer would establish anyone's innocence. There was, nevertheless, considerable suspicion about the timing of the disclosure and the identity of the person being protected.

On February 12, 2002, it was Greenspan's turn to make submissions when the court proceedings reconvened. His primary legal objective was to get the warrant justifying the search on the Eurocopter plant in Fort Erie quashed. If it was set aside, the Eurocopter investigation would return to square one. His client, Karlheinz Schreiber, would not be out of trouble, but, at least temporarily, two immediate dangers would have been dealt with. There would likely be no charges against Schreiber without the search warrant evidence for his role, if any, in the Eurocopter case. Perhaps more important, if Eurocopter or any of its officers were eventually charged – the most likely scenario considering the police theory of the case – Schreiber could, and almost certainly would, be called to give evidence. If he was, and if Greenspan was unable to quash that subpoena, his testimony could be used against him – not in Canada, but overseas. The best defence is often a good offence, and sending the Eurocopter case back to the drawing board would serve several purposes. Accord-

Eddie Greenspan with his client, dealmaker Karlheinz Schreiber

ingly, Greenspan's main objective was to get the warrant quashed. If that failed, he wanted, alternatively, to keep the publication ban in place because his client could only suffer from the publicity of association with the Eurocopter proceedings.

Greenspan, therefore, had one objective: nullification of the search warrant. The judge had to be persuaded to agree. Greenspan determined that the judge could reach the desired result only if he understood the case in its full context.

The context that Greenspan was referring to was a matter of widespread public interest set out in several books, numerous episodes of the *Fifth Estate*, and countless newspaper and other media reports following September 29, 1995, when the Canadian government sent the Letter of Request to Switzerland – the letter that became public. That letter had asserted in its very first paragraph that Mulroney, Schreiber, and Moores were criminals, even though they had not been charged, much less convicted, of any crime. Since that time, the Airbus affair had been a subject of intense public and media scrutiny. This public interest, Greenspan argued, could not be ignored. Yet these Eurocopter proceedings, in contrast, had been under a "monumental cone of silence." The secrecy had been going on for almost two years. "The search warrants were executed in December of 1999. That's two years and two months ago. And all of this silence."[6]

Now, Greenspan said, the Crown had changed its mind and disclosed virtually all of the Information to Obtain, the key background document used to justify the search, along with a number of supporting affidavits. "So the Crown says to you, 'Look, with the greatest of respect, My Lord, I don't owe you any justification for why I'm changing. And you may imply it, that I don't think it's necessary any more, in terms of protecting the investigation. You may imply it, that there's no longer any need for the protection of the innocent. You may imply it, but I'm not going to tell you, (a), I don't have an onus; and (b), I don't owe you any explanation. And you know what? You can't even ask me for it.'"

But, Greenspan continued, it was not good enough. Looking up at Justice Then, he urged him to exercise his discretion carefully and judicially. It was just not right, he suggested, for the Crown to come forward several years into the case and say: "No more, don't need it." An explanation was required. You must, he said, addressing Justice Then, insist on knowing what has happened that made the Crown change its mind. "If there was a material change, what was it? The Crown was simply not entitled to say, at this late date, 'We control the case. We now decide it's not necessary.'"

Equally unsatisfactory, in Greenspan's view, were some of the other unsavoury aspects to the case. How did Stevie Cameron and Harvey Cashore, the authors of The Last Amigo, get hold of the details of the Eurocopter warrant and other pertinent details: place, offences under investigation, and the names of the individuals believed to be involved? How did Cashore know what courtroom to attend in Toronto and on what day? What was going on between the press and the police? Greenspan made sure that the judge got the full picture.

The paperback version of On the Take had come out in the early fall of 1995. Cameron claimed at that time to have "dramatic new material" on Airbus, Bearhead, and the helicopter purchase from MBB. "Where did she get that information?" Greenspan asked. He would return to that subject shortly. First, he had other points to make.

It was now clear, he argued, referring regularly to the material Justice Then had ordered disclosed, including several affidavits from Inspector Mathews, that the RCMP went to Switzerland and interviewed Pelossi on June 28, 1995, and that Staff Sergeant Fiegen-wald, the interviewing officer, obtained documents from him. The Supreme Court of Canada, Greenspan reminded the judge, has ruled that, when peace officers go abroad, they must take the *Charter* with them and also act in compliance with the law of the country where they go. Swiss law prohibits police officers from foreign jurisdictions conducting investigations on Swiss soil. It requires authorization, which is obtained only through a Letter of Request. Like Schabas, Greenspan had no idea that the Swiss had pre-approved a meeting, provided no statements or documents were taken. The RCMP had not, therefore, violated the law by travelling to Switzerland before obtaining formal authority to do so. However, Fiegen-wald quite possibly took possession of some documents for safe-keeping. Although he was unaware that the meeting was lawful, Greenspan now suggested that the RCMP, in the aftermath, attempted something of a cover-up. The RCMP, he argued, tried to cleanse all of this illegality by submitting the September 1995 Letter of Request and obtaining the information lawfully. It was an extremely serious charge of police misconduct.

Greenspan did not mince his words. "My suggestion is this: That not only did they breach the law in order to achieve their end, but they purposely deceived the Swiss in the Letter of Request, because they wouldn't have got the Letter of Request if they had said, 'We went over illegally and interviewed somebody there.' They wouldn't have got it. And there'd be nothing here. There'd be nothing." The Eurocopter search warrant, Greenspan argued, did not stand "a snowball's chance in hell" of surviving the motion to quash. It was based on illegal information from the outset. All the lawyers were clearly paying careful attention as Greenspan spoke. So, too, was the presiding judge.

Was Greenspan saying, the judge asked, that the Letter of Request was necessary to obtain "that which they already had, because they realized that what they had obtained was illegally obtained?" Though often extremely informal in manner, Justice Then is both sharp and very well versed in the criminal law. He is known for his excellent ability to summarize the submissions of counsel, as he had just done for Greenspan. "Precisely," was the response. Greenspan, echoing Schabas's request, then asked the judge to postpone hearing submissions on public access. After all, one day everything would come out. It was merely a question of when. Greenspan moved directly to the heart of the matter: the legality of the search. On that topic, he had more submissions to make. But it was time to adjourn. They would all be back the next day, Wednesday, February 13, 2002.

Crown attorney Michael Bernstein never seems happy, but he was particularly unhappy when the proceedings reconvened. "There are," he said, addressing Justice Then, "very serious allegations directed at the RCMP... [Greenspan] alleges police misconduct in connection with an interview conducted on Mr. Pelossi by Staff Sergeant Fiegenwald in June of 1995. And my submission is, there's not evidence of police misconduct." Greenspan agreed that the allegations were "very, very serious." Bernstein concurred: "It's very, very, very, very serious." That's "four verys," Greenspan retorted. The judge, although visibly amused, interjected. "The other way to look at it is as a ... potentially serious allegation of misconduct that might, in some distant future, lead to consequences vis-à-vis the warrant. But what to do, in terms of the point we find ourselves at now?"

Bernstein was clear about what the judge should do. Put Greenspan back on track. If he wanted, at some later date, to argue about police impropriety, he could do so. This proceeding was about lifting the sealing and the publication ban – and Greenspan, the Crown attorney suggested, should focus his attention on that.

Greenspan never likes being pushed around, and he liked it even less when Bernstein was doing the pushing. "Understand, Mr. Bernstein, with the greatest of respect, that I do not say this lightly ... this is unbelievable." After more unproductive discussion, Greenspan finally got to make his submissions, uninterrupted by Bernstein or anyone else.

"You are," Greenspan told Justice Then, "sitting on ... what is an historical case." It was important that the judge understand some of the background. A good place to start, he suggested, was my book *Presumed Guilty: Brian Mulroney, the Airbus Affair and the Government of Canada*. "You are not suggesting," Bernstein interjected, "that that book is evidence?" Greenspan ignored the interruption. "The book is interesting in terms of laying it all out. He obviously had access to a lot of people. They are getting ready for trial ... Harvey Strosberg is counsel to the Minister of Justice, Allan Rock, and deeply involved in the case. And at pages 278 and 279 it says this: 'At the end of November ... Fiegenwald had told a journalist known to be highly antagonistic to Brian Mulroney that Mulroney was named in the letter of request to Switzerland.'"

What Greenspan was referring to was the revelation, not long before Mulroney's $50 million civil suit against the Government of Canada was scheduled to start, that Staff Sergeant Fraser Fiegenwald, the RCMP officer in charge of the Airbus investigation, had earlier told Stevie Cameron that Mulroney was named in the Letter of Request. The main plank of the government's defence to the Mulroney lawsuit had always been that it acted in scrupulous good faith in writing and sending the Letter of Request. The Swiss required these letters to be strongly worded, and the RCMP had merely complied with that requirement, taking all necessary steps to keep the letter confidential. Belated news of the unauthorized disclosure from Fiegenwald supposedly blew apart the government's good-faith defence and laid the groundwork, although Mulroney did not know it at the time, for the settlement discussions leading to the apology and the payment of his costs.

Greenspan continued: "We have, at least in this book, a reference to the fact that the admission was that the leak was a government leak, and it was Fiegenwald to Stevie Cameron. That's what we have ... they settled, because he had leaked to Stevie Cameron. Now that's the first thing that I want to bring your attention to. Now, the next thing that I want to bring your attention to is that – "

Bernstein again leapt to his feet, a bit like a jack-in-the-box: Greenspan could push him down for a moment or two, but he would quickly pop up again. "Why," he asked, "are you reviewing these parts of the book? Surely it was not for the truth." It was, he added, somewhat unusual for counsel to read books in court. Greenspan agreed but insisted on having his way. Eventually, the judge made Bernstein sit down: "So go ahead and do that, Mr. Greenspan."

Greenspan then guided the judge to page 300 of *Presumed Guilty*, where it was reported that Cameron instructed Quebec City lawyer Michel Jolin to call Jacques Jeansonne, one of Mulroney's attorneys. Jolin asked Jeansonne whether Mulroney would insist when the case came to trial that Cameron, subpoenaed by Mulroney to give evidence, disclose her source in the RCMP. The answer was "absolutely." At that point, Cameron had her lawyer, Peter M. Jacobsen, call Strosberg with the news that Fiegenwald had leaked, thereby "scuttling the government's good-faith defence."

Still leafing through *Presumed Guilty*, Greenspan took the judge to page 301, where there was a reference to a briefing note from the RCMP to Solicitor General Herb Gray. According to the book, the journalist Stevie Cameron had been referred to in a briefing note to the solicitor general reporting on the Airbus investigation and referencing information she had supposedly obtained. "What," Greenspan asked, "was that all about?" Greenspan knew only half of it, but what he knew was extremely disturbing: "a journalist ... a major political enemy of the Right Honourable Brian Mulroney ... It's hard to even imagine how she can hate somebody as much as she does.

But she does, and she's somehow in bed with the RCMP, somehow to the point where it's mentioned in a briefing note." Bernstein stood up. "Are you putting all of this in for its truth?" he asked Schreiber's lawyer. "I didn't mean that in a concrete way," Greenspan replied, "that she's in bed. I'm not making that suggestion. That's a metaphor," he patiently explained to the Crown attorney, as if he were speaking to a young child, "for getting close to people" – and then he resumed addressing the judge.

"A journalist who hates him, who hates his guts, and she's talking to the RCMP. And it's significant enough that it's put into a briefing note to the Solicitor General of Canada. It's in there. I'd sure love to see that briefing note ... I think we might have a fairly quick resolution of this and go to a motion to quash ... because the briefing note, in my submission, is very interesting, in terms of what leads to the following, and here's what I want to put to you. I'm not going to read the book, because my friend will get up and say, 'Oh, he's reading the book, he's reading the book.' So what I'm going to do is say this. As a result of this, life did not go well for Mr. Fiegenwald, as you might imagine." Even Cameron and Cashore, Greenspan pointed out, said so on page 291 of *The Last Amigo*: "For the Mounties, these were the darkest days of the Airbus investigation, though the effort continued despite setbacks. Fraser Fiegenwald was pulled off the Airbus file, assigned to 'administrative duties' and placed under investigation for allegedly leaking information to Stevie Cameron. Although the internal review cleared him of any wrongdoing, RCMP brass had him charged anyway with disobeying the force's code of conduct. His colleagues held a barbecue on the grounds of RCMP headquarters in Ottawa to help raise money for his legal fees, but a disciplinary hearing on the charges was eventually abandoned."

Fiegenwald, Greenspan continued, had asserted that he wanted an open hearing, and a court application to open up the hearing by the Southam media chain succeeded. But rather than face public exposure, the Mounties quietly negotiated an agreement with the staff sergeant who, on the eve of the disciplinary hearing, retired from service. Greenspan again quoted from Cameron and Cashore's *Last Amigo*: "Fellow officers believed he had been thrown to the wolves by those who would protect the politicians' careers above all else. Fiegenwald decided to leave the force for a forensic accounting job in the private sector and received a generous financial package from the government. The contradiction seemed enormous. An honest cop's RCMP career was destroyed, and the deal-maker who hid those commissions received an apology." It was a good story, but

Greenspan was not buying it. He had a different theory about what had happened, a more complicated theory.

"So Stevie Cameron," he continued, "who, thanks to her indiscretion, because she's got to write about it, says that Fiegenwald is an honest cop. Now I read that and I say to myself, if Fiegenwald leaked to her, which seems to be what we can gather from these books ... he breached the RCMP Act. He breached it. There's no question about that, unless he didn't breach it. If he breached it, he's not an honest cop." But maybe he was an honest cop? Maybe there was a different explanation?

"But if he ... didn't breach it, and he's an honest cop, then how does he not breach it? Well, one of the ways that he doesn't breach it if he tells her, is if she's an informant. He could tell an informant. That wouldn't be a breach. And why was there no hearing on this? Why? Why did they settle with him? Why did they bury it? I mean it was out. It wasn't like it wasn't public. It wasn't like it wasn't public in Kaplan's book that Fiegenwald leaked to her. That's not news ... it's a matter of public domain that Fiegenwald leaked to Cameron. So why are they not having a hearing? Why are they burying it? Why is Stevie Cameron saying he's an honest cop?

"And all I can say to myself is, if he did not breach the RCMP Act, according to Cameron, it means she was in a category of persons that could be told, and that's an informant."

Stevie Cameron, Greenspan was suggesting to the judge, was a police informer. Justice Then knew this was true; he had known since April 2001, when Inspector Mathews advised him, but none of the parties to the proceeding knew until much later that there was an additional ground supporting redaction: protection of a police informer. There was one name on the Information that was blacked out for everyone but the judge and the Crown.

There were many reasons to wonder about Cameron's relationship with the RCMP. Greenspan had been thinking about it for months. There was Cameron's speech to students at the University of Saskatchewan in February 1995 when, after expressing the view that the Mulroney government was not just corrupt but infested throughout by organized crime (although never going so far as to suggest that Mulroney himself was a made man), she went on to boast about her contacts with the RCMP: "I talked to the Mounties about this last week in Ottawa," she told her rapt audience.

The speech was a thin reed on which to base a charge of major misconduct, but there were other clues. Approximately one year earlier, in early April 2001, Greenspan had decided to put the question directly to Cameron in a letter faxed and delivered to her Toronto home. "It is imperative," he wrote, "that you respond to the following questions as soon as possible. It is also essential that you answer these questions truthfully. You may wish to seek legal advice before you answer these questions, but," Greenspan insisted, "I require answers to all of the questions."

First, in 1995, he asked Cameron, were you a confidential informant of the RCMP? If so, were you paid? How much were you paid? Could you provide me with a copy of your contract? If there was no contract, could you please explain why not? Have you been a police informer since 1995? How much in total have you received, if you were paid? On and on, the questions continued, although Greenspan made it clear that he did not require any information about any informing activities that did not involve Schreiber. He concluded his letter by instructing Cameron to produce all documents in her possession that related to Schreiber. The tone was aggressive and the letter was presumptuous. Greenspan had no legal right to make the demand. Cameron, whatever her actual status, was more than justified to tell the high-profile lawyer where to go.

Just over one week later, Greenspan received a reply from Peter M. Jacobsen, Cameron's longtime libel lawyer. Jacobsen was a McGill Unversity graduate, called to the Ontario Bar in 1978. He is one of Canada's best-known media lawyers, and Cameron relied heavily on him for "his wise and affectionate counsel."7 "Ms. Cameron," Jacobsen wrote, "is not prepared to answer your questions ... It would not be appropriate for her to be seen to be assisting any party in the litigation as it would compromise her objectivity as a journalist. Also, with respect to your request for documents, it is Ms. Cameron's position that these are her confidential, journalistic work product to which you and your client have no right of access."8 This statement was, as it turned out, pretty rich. Cameron, through her lawyer, was asserting her journalistic objectivity in order to avoid answering questions that would prove she had none.

Now, almost one year later, Greenspan was back on topic, increasingly dubious about Cameron's objectivity. "How," he asked the judge, "does a reporter or writer put into a book called *On the Take*, a book against Brian Mulroney, a scandalous book, adding to the paperback 'dramatic new material about MBB,' if she doesn't have some source for it? How does she write a book called *The Last Amigo*, and talk about all the stuff she talks about, unless she doesn't have some source for it? And why is she defending Fiegenwald ... unless he is an honest cop. And he may well be an honest cop. And how does a man called Cashore walk into this room when ... you think that between Mr. Mulroney and Mr. Schreiber, we might have heard of it. And we didn't, just didn't. We were about as astounded by the letter we got to come as we could be. But early on, Mr. Cashore is here. How did they hear about it? What's going on, in terms of this ... is there some kind of relationship? How do you get books ... by Stevie Cameron, and Stevie Cameron and Cashore, on ongoing investigations that are supposed to be the subject of secret, sealed material?"

It was, Greenspan asserted, absolutely scandalous. "If Stevie Cameron, Cashore, either one of them or both of them, were somehow getting very close to the police in either giving them or getting from them and getting from other people [information], if this investigation kind of gets jump started by them ... if she co-opted a national police force, if she has a relationship with the RCMP ... that's why we come to this question now of informant."

Confidential informants, Greenspan explained, are often relied upon and referred to in search warrant applications. In general, the background documents put before the judge will say that the confidential informant is reliable because he or she has been used in the past. Often the warrant will refer to the confidential informant by number, as numbers are often, but not always, assigned by the police to informants. "But one thing you know when you look at the search warrant is that they go out of their way to let the Court that has to make the judicial determination about granting the search warrant – they let that judicial officer know this is a confidential informant."

Greenspan then turned to the written materials relied on by the RCMP to convince Justice Fontana back in December 1999 to authorize the Eurocopter search. A name, just a name. No reference to confidential informant. No reference to reliability of the confidential informant. No number. No code. No initials. The name of someone in the alphabetical list of witnesses, but that name blacked out when some of the materials were finally disclosed. As the RCMP helpfully listed all the witnesses in alphabetical order, the confidential informant had a last name beginning with an A, B, C, D, or E.

"And the one thing that I would submit is, is that if Mr. Bernstein were involved in this in the beginning and knew that there was a confidential informant, we would have gotten from him what you traditionally see, because I believe him to be that kind of lawyer, and he is. There's nothing, nothing. Just a name. And a claim advanced well into the proceeding that the person named is a confidential informer, providing legal grounds for keeping the name secret.

"Now we fast forward to just about a month or two ago." Greenspan was referring to the Crown disclosure at the end of 2001 or early in 2002 that there was a police informer being protected. "And lo and behold, they tell us this is a confidential informant. Are you to accept that? Is that something that should be tested by way of Inspector Mathews getting into the stand and letting us cross-examine, not on who the informant is, but on this business of surrounding the confidentiality, to determine whether this is some kind of afterthought, that this person is some kind of informant, confidential informant?" What was interesting about this case was that there was no number, no initials, and no assertion that the informant was reliable. Those details were always found in search warrants. But not this time. All they were trying to protect was a name, just a name. "Why?" Greenspan asked.

No one was suggesting, Greenspan pointed out, that this informant needed protection. "I can't imagine that anybody's suggesting that this informant has to be protected from possible harm, that somehow Eurocopter is going to go out and shoot him or her." There was also no suggestion of a need to protect any ongoing investigation. It was the Crown, after all, that wanted to unseal the Information leading to the earlier disclosure to counsel of nearly all that document, and many of the supporting affidavits too. Why was it, Greenspan continued, that he had to read books to find out about the case? How did Stevie Cameron get some of her information? "You'd think there's a leak somewhere ... This is rare. This is so rare in Canada. Let Mr. Mathews get on the stand and swear under oath that he's never met Stevie Cameron ... Let him – let him do that.

"Because if that's the name, okay – and you know it – if it's ... Stevie Cameron, that's the name you've seen, then in my respectful submission ... this would be an unbelievable scandal.

"And we know from the [Kaplan] book that her name is mentioned in a briefing memo of the RCMP that goes up to the Solicitor General. And if she's some kind of confidential informant, if it's her name, if it's Cashore's name, political enemies of the former Prime Minister, involved as confidential informants so that they can flog books and make money ... where is the reliability in anything that they said?

"And the RCMP would never want that to come out. They would never want that to come out, because if that came out, you've got ... a scandal on your hands ... because if the Solicitor General and anybody else in the government knew that the source for the RCMP was Cashore and Cameron, and that they would launch this whole thing on that, or in part on that, that they go and seek a letter of request based on this, that there's some kind of protection going on of a writer who's the unbelievable political enemy of the prime minister, in my respectful submission, you'd have ... an enormous scandal.

"So you know, they're protecting a name ... Tell me who it isn't, not who it is. Why can't my friend just say to me, it's not – underneath that black, is not Stevie Cameron, is not Harvey Cashore, is not a journalist. Tell me. Just tell me that.

"But – and if my friend won't tell me who it isn't – ... you know who it is – you can draw the adverse inference, not because you know who it is, but because he's not prepared to tell me. Tell me that Stevie Cameron was not part of some kind of ... police investigation. Tell me that she wasn't. Tell me that she has no status with the police. Tell me that. Just tell me that, that she doesn't."

Greenspan had been speaking for hours. Because he was in court he was allowed to make certain submissions that, if made outside court, would attract a lawsuit – such as the suggestion, entirely without merit, that Cashore had violated the sealing order and, making matters worse, was working with the RCMP. Nevertheless, the judge had been listening carefully – and so were Mulroney's lawyers. Wakim and Prehogan could not believe their ears. What they had long suspected, what had been hinted at and privately talked about, was apparently true. Stevie Cameron had supplied information to the RCMP, information that the RCMP and the Government of Canada later admitted did not establish any wrongdoing on Mulroney's part. But that information either initiated or gave a great boost to the entire investigation against him and poisoned the reputation of the former prime minister among the Canadian people. This information was implicitly repudiated when the RCMP and the Government of Canada apologized to Mulroney as part of the settlement of his lawsuit and acknowledged that there was no basis to assert any wrongdoing on his part when the 1995 Letter of Request was sent – and that no evidence had emerged since, even though the RCMP had continued the investigation.

The judge could not have been unaware of the significance of Greenspan's remarks. He was, uniquely in this case, in a position to know exactly whose name had been blacked out, information not normally passed on to the court. But he had some legal concerns, based on his duty to apply the law that protects confidential informants. That duty was not dependent on whether the Information said the person was reliable or whether a number was assigned. The duty did not depend either on when the privilege was claimed. That duty did not disappear simply because the privilege was belatedly claimed. Protecting the privilege was so important and necessary that, even if claimed late in the day, as apparently it had been here, the judge was required to protect the identity of the informer from detection. The duty depended solely on the status of the person, the judge said, "because you've made an agreement of confidentiality with the person." Once that happened, he pointed out, the agreement, for good or for ill, had to be honoured. That was the way the system worked. "I have," the judge continued, "no interest in being involved in a scandal. I just want to do the right thing."

"I know you do," Greenspan replied, adding, "All I want you to do is this. If there is a confidentiality agreement as between either of the two people that I'm talking about, because my interest is piqued by everything in the book that suggests that there's something going on ... if they've entered a confidential agreement, the political enemy of Mulroney – and Herb Gray knew about it – before the letter of request went and [he] didn't stop this investigation, this case couldn't get off the ground. It would be the worst abuse of power that you could imagine, the worst abuse of power. And that's why, in my respectful submission, if this is what it potentially may be ... and the police ... and the Crown want to forge ahead in the face of this, which I submit ... would be an unbelievable, unbelievable story ... that would lead to an abuse of power of the worst kind imaginable, where ... it is possible that a reporter, the political enemy of Brian Mulroney, co-opted a national police force, and they've entered into some confidentiality agreement with that writer, or writers, in my respectful submission, that is an element that could be considered by you in quashing this search warrant ... This is serious business."

Just get them to tell us it's not her, Greenspan demanded. The police cannot and should not be permitted to go around making confidentiality agreements with the likes of Cameron. This, he argued, would "be about as serious as it can get. So just tell me it is not so." Greenspan continued. "I'm trying to be a responsible officer of the Court, and I look at what's in front of me and I see this. And this isn't just a question of saying that this may be a matter of some interest. This is, in my respectful submission, a matter of huge interest ... But at the end of the day, somebody has got to say, 'This isn't going to wash.' This isn't going to get by a judge of the Superior Court of Ontario, either on a motion to quash or a trial. This is an abuse of power of the worst kind. Why close your eyes and put your head down and try to say, 'We're going to try to justify this'?"

So, Greenspan suggested, as he concluded his submissions, the judge should defer the matter of rescinding the publication ban and opening up the proceedings. "Explore this further. Decide whether there has been a monumental abuse of process. If there has been, put an end to it." That, Greenspan argued, was the right thing to do.

The judge had some questions, but what he really wanted to do was to make sure he understood. Are you suggesting, he asked, again summarizing what he had just heard, that either the person is not a confidential informant, given the unusual way in which the privilege was asserted, or, if the person was a confidential informant, then that claim should be considered in light of the factual context that you have laid out, one in which the propriety of conferring the status on the individual you identified is put into issue? The answer was both, Greenspan answered, and he had something to add. The first thing you should do, he suggested to Justice Then, is not give us the name, but consider it in terms of the exercise of your judicial discretion. "And once you've made that judicial discretion, give us the name."

Crown attorney Bernstein got the last word. He slammed Greenspan once more for reading books. The judge knew it was hearsay, he claimed: "It's grand hearsay, even if it's a best-selling hearsay." There is, he pointed out, no best-seller exemption to the hearsay rule. Hearsay is evidence that does not originate from the witness but is the mere repetition, by him or her, of something he or she has heard or, in this case, something Greenspan had read. Hearsay evidence is usually rejected because it is often unreliable. Certainly, it is not the best evidence of what happened. Accordingly, if Greenspan was asking that the court "on the basis of those books and nothing else ... should tell those present the name of the confidential informant, then," he concluded, "I object."

For all intents and purposes, that is where the matter sat. Until the *Globe and Mail* got involved in September 2003 and wrote to the judge, asking what in the world was going on.

7 The Icing on the Cake

Word about these unusual proceedings began to leak before the *Globe and Mail* took matters into its own hands. In early April 2002 Crown attorney Michael Bernstein wrote to all the lawyers in the case: "I would like to advise you that on March 25, 2002, a clerk in the Crown Law Office ... received an inquiry from Ms. Tracy Tyler asking who the Crown handling the Eurocopter file was. Ms. Tyler also mentioned that it was a matter before Justice Then and had been heard a few weeks ago ... I understand Ms. Tyler is a reporter with *The Toronto Star*. We did not answer Ms. Tyler's questions. Does anybody know how Ms. Tyler learned of this information and why she is making this inquiry?"

Tyler was undoubtedly tipped, but had, as several of the lawyers pointed out, a good explanation. Even though the trial was secret, information about it could be found on the list of cases at the commissionaire's desk in the lobby. *R. v. Eurocopter Canada Ltd.* was also posted on the courtroom door. After April 2001 the heightened security surrounding the case notably diminished, though the public and the press were forbidden to attend. Tyler tried to find out what was going on but made no headway. "I went to the criminal trial office ... They claimed they didn't even know what I was talking about ... I also went to the Court of Appeal, just in case it had somehow ended up there." Nothing. "It was like," she later recalled, "talking about air."[1] No one seemed to know anything. With no other leads, Tyler moved on to other stories.

In June 2002 Shannon Kari, an argumentative journalist for Southam, wrote a short article about the case, noting that Eurocopter was the "subject of a mysterious criminal proceeding." Kari tracked down the different lawyers, all of whom refused to cooperate. Even the talkative Karlheinz Schreiber refused to go on the record. "Oh my God, no," Schreiber said when asked for a comment.

"Everybody goes to jail."[2] Until the *Globe and Mail* began poking around, the secret proceedings stayed completely off radar.

In Canada, the police are independent of the politicians. They decide who to investigate, how to investigate, and when to stop investigating. But there are a number of checks on their power. One of them is that they are ultimately accountable to the legislative branch. Federally, the solicitor general answers for the RCMP in the House of Commons. The solicitor general must be kept informed about matters that might possibly be raised in Parliament, though the minister must never interfere in a proper police investigation. Solicitors general are kept informed through briefings and briefing notes, which tell them what they need to know to answer questions in Parliament.

An RCMP briefing note first told Solicitor General Herb Gray about Stevie Cameron, her allegations of political corruption, and her direct involvement in this case in early 1995:

> Ms. Stevie CAMERON has stated that she has new information concerning political corruption which will be released in her paperback version in future. A German magazine called *Der Spiegel* has reported that $46 million in commissions were paid to a company controlled by Karl Heinz SCHREIBER, a Canadian businessman, and implied that payments were made to former Prime Minister MULRONEY. An evaluation of the information available with the media is being conducted to determine if a criminal investigation is warranted.

The briefing note continued: "On 95.01.25, Ms. CAMERON was interviewed and stated that the *Fifth Estate* had advised her that they had new information which she could include in her new book after their program aired. She did not know the new information at the time of the interview." Presumably, this was the meeting with the Mounties that Cameron was referring to when she addressed the University of Saskatchewan students the next month. The briefing note went on to state: "On 95.03.18, the German news media *Der Spiegel* advised the Canadian media that they were publishing an article on the Airbus contract in which they claimed a Liechtenstein shell company called International Aircraft Leasing Ltd. (IAL) received $46 million for their marketing assistance. They link Karl Heinz SCHREIBER to the deal and state that the late Bavarian Prime Minister, Franz Josef STRAUSS, and Rt. Hon. Brian MULRONEY were

friends of SCHREIBER. This information has been published in several Canadian newspapers on 95.03.19 and a copy of the German
article was given to us by Stevie CAMERON and is currently being
translated into English from German." At the very least, Cameron,
if this briefing note is accurate, began passing materials to the RCMP
on January 25, 1995.

The briefing note detailed further investigative initiatives being
considered by the RCMP, notably sending investigators to Germany
to interview *Der Spiegel* reporters. After these steps, an evaluation
would be made to determine whether sufficient evidence existed to
warrant a criminal investigation. The briefing note concluded: "This
matter was reviewed by the RCMP in 1989 and there was insufficient
evidence at that time to warrant a criminal investigation. The new
information which the media is currently publishing will be evaluat-
ed by the RCMP to determine whether or not sufficient information
now exists to warrant a criminal investigation."

There matters stood until after the *Fifth Estate* went to air at
the end of March 1995, broadcasting a program called "Sealed in
Silence." The result of a five-month-long investigation by the award-
winning series, it was clearly indicated at the outset that there was
no evidence that anybody with decision-making power had been
paid off for anything. There was evidence, however, that Airbus
Industrie had made payments to Karlheinz Schreiber in connection
with Air Canada's purchase of airplanes. Frank Moores was also
involved. Moores's close association with the former prime minister
was described. The show spawned another briefing note to the solicitor general. The RCMP, apparently, was still making efforts to contact journalists with information. If those efforts bore fruit, the RCMP
would decide its next step.

Yet another briefing note, the third, followed shortly thereafter.
"The source of the information and documents upon which the media
have based their reports has provided material to the prosecutor's
office in Augsburg, Germany. His allegations are believed to involve
tax evasion on the part of SCHREIBER in Germany." Although no
name was given, it was clearly Giorgio Pelossi, Schreiber's former
accountant, that the briefing note was referring to. Interestingly,
though, Stevie Cameron is also on record as travelling to Augsburg,
where she helpfully provided local prosecutorial authorities with
some of the documents she had collected.

Within a few weeks, another briefing note, this one dated July 5,
1995, was sent to the solicitor general. Cameron and her "new information" were referred to. The note made it clear that Mulroney was

suspected of receiving Airbus payments. It also reported that it had been "determined that there is sufficient evidence to warrant a criminal investigation." The briefing note concluded by describing the next steps: "The RCMP will be gathering the information on the contracts involved in order to support a request for the assistance of the Swiss authorities in divulging the contents of the Swiss bank accounts used to make the payments. Exact dollar amounts and the ultimate recipient of the secret commissions will not be known until the funds have been traced through the accounts. This process is expected to take up to six months if the holders of the Swiss accounts contest their disclosure in the Swiss courts."

The final briefing note in the series is dated August 24, 1995. Again Cameron was quoted as saying that she had new information concerning political corruption that would be released shortly in the paperback version of her best-selling book *On the Take*. Mulroney was under investigation for receiving payments from Schreiber for Airbus, MBB, and the aborted Bearhead project. In fact, the solicitor general was told that the *Fifth Estate* was at work on a second program on the topic and apparently had a document "which links Mulroney to the Swiss account." Finally, Gray was informed that the Letter of Request to the Swiss had been approved by the Department of Justice, was undergoing translation, and was being pre-approved by the examining magistrate in Bern, Switzerland, before formal submission. And, indeed, in September 1995, the Justice Department did send the Letter of Request to Swiss authorities calling Mulroney, Schreiber, and Moores criminals, accusing them of defrauding the Canadian people of many millions of dollars, and seeking details about their Swiss bank accounts (which, in Mulroney's case, did not exist).

A solicitor general in receipt of these increasingly alarming briefing notes asserting outright criminal conduct by a recent prime minister might have called the commissioner of the RCMP in for a chat. While making it clear that, as minister, he or she had no wish to interfere with the ongoing criminal investigation, he or she might have asked the commissioner what steps had been taken to ensure that the investigation was a proper one. After all, the briefing notes indicated that the investigation had been initiated because of some European media reports and had been given a boost by Giorgio Pelossi, a man the RCMP had to know had a grudge against Schreiber, and Stevie Cameron, a journalist with a recognized hatred of Mulroney. If the RCMP was relying on any other sources of information, it was keeping that quiet.

A lawyer and longtime member of Parliament, Herb Gray is as able and as experienced as they come. He is especially adept in answering difficult questions with long speeches that say nothing. But, as solicitor general, Gray had a special duty to ensure that the RCMP was properly supervised. This was an investigation that called for a deft touch. Yet Gray decided to keep his hands off. It would not have been appropriate, he later told reporters, to interfere with a police investigation. He is right about that, but his answer is just an artful way to sidestep the real issue: a police investigation was launched at least in part on information provided by Cameron. Years later, even though he knew about only one of the briefing notes, Greenspan had gone some distance in establishing that Cameron provided information to the police and then became a police informer in order to protect herself from discovery, to protect her name – a conclusion consistent with, if not wholly confirmed by, the series of RCMP briefing notes.

It is accepted wisdom that, in a free and democratic society, a journalist must be completely and totally independent of powerful interests, including the police. Journalism exists to serve the public and its right to know. It has other goals too, but that is the most important one.

Investigative reporters play a particularly significant role. They have to find out and report the stories that powerful interests would rather keep quiet. They have to be resourceful, careful, and brave. Theirs is not an easy task. As every investigative reporter knows, sometimes, to get information you crave, you have to trade information. Often, to obtain information, you must demonstrate knowledge. A delicate, appropriate, and mutually beneficial balance can be achieved. Frequently, the relationship between journalists and the world is adversarial. Sometimes the relationship is downright manipulative: excessive solicitude and interest aimed at lulling the source into believing that agendas and interests are shared. Ultimately it matters little what role a reporter plays, provided that independence is maintained.

What a reporter can never do is cross the line and compromise this independence. Without independence, there cannot be trust; and without public trust, the press cannot do its job. But how much cooperation is permissible?

Reporters depend on the police for information, but any reporter who relies on police press releases and the comments of official spokespersons is sure to miss the whole story. Good investigative reporters will have cultivated a wide range of contacts at all levels of police command, from the beat officer to the chief, if possible, and will succeed in doing so having established a reputation for integrity, fairness, and objectivity. Information is exchanged, and legitimate expectations are vindicated. The police favour trusted journalists with tips and advance warning of breaking events. Cooperation has its advantages. Everyone benefits.

The reverse is often true. A journalist publishes a story, and the police get leads. Journalists must work with the police. There is a certain symbiosis to the relationship. Sometimes, in the interest of assisting a criminal investigation, reporters will agree to withhold their reports for a time. Sometimes it means acceding to a request that certain information be publicly disclosed. Scepticism is required in either case, but both are often correctly considered legitimate requests. Underlying the consideration is the recognition that journalists and police have fundamentally different jobs: journalists must report, while the police are obliged to enforce the law. It is a fine line between permissible cooperation and impermissible cooptation.

The media, for example, never voluntarily hands over photographs and videos of events, unless they have been published or broadcast. If they did, their ability to function would inevitably become compromised. If the police want to seize videotapes or any other records, they have to persuade a judge to grant them a warrant or issue a subpoena, authorizing them to do so. Requiring a court order is a legal pretence, perhaps, but it is not just about form triumphing over substance. Real journalists are not, and cannot be seen to be, an arm of the police. As satisfying as it might be to assist the police by providing information so that criminals can be apprehended, that is not, and cannot be, the role of a reporter in a free and democratic society. The only possible exception is the need to speak out to prevent an imminent and serious crime.

A good citizen has certain obligations. Assisting the police when possible is one of them. A good reporter has many obligations, but working with the police to apprehend criminals is not among them, unless there are reasonable grounds to believe that a serious crime is about to be committed. Reporters are in the news business, not the police business. When reporters become part of the investigation, even if motivated by a genuine belief that their actions are in the public good, they lose their objectivity, impartiality and, perhaps most important of all, the ability to be fair.

In recent years, there have been frequent examples of journalists who have been exposed as working for police and intelligence agencies in right-wing regimes in South America, for the secret police in the former Eastern Bloc, and for the police in apartheid-era South Africa. Closer to home, there have been some publicized cases of journalists who assisted Western intelligence agencies during the Cold War. Whatever the reason or objective, no matter how high-minded, there can be no forgiveness. Every violation trespasses on the reporter's most basic responsibility: to maintain the public trust.

Reporters sit in daily judgment of the day's events. Fortunately, just as for the lawyers and judges who perform a similar job, there are rules to guide them. The CBC has issued guidelines to its reporters.[3] While governing only those who work at the CBC, they establish a benchmark applicable to the entire working press. The overriding obligation of CBC reporters, according to these guidelines, is to provide consistent, high-quality information that all citizens may rely on. To achieve this objective, three key principles have been identified: accuracy, integrity, and fairness. Accuracy means that the information conforms with reality and is in no way misleading or false. Integrity means that the information is truthful, not distorted to justify a conclusion. And fairness means that the information reports or reflects equitably on the relevant facts and significant points of view; it requires that persons, institutions, issues, and events are dealt with fairly. CBC journalists must also be credible: "Credibility is dependent not only on qualities such as accuracy and fairness in reporting and presentation, but also upon avoidance by both the organization and its journalists of associations or contacts which could reasonably give rise to perceptions of partiality. Any situation which could cause reasonable apprehension that a journalist or the organization is biased ... must be avoided."

Investigative journalism is singled out for attention in the CBC manual. It is "a particularly sensitive type of journalism, which can have a powerful effect upon the public mind and, consequently, upon the livelihood and well-being of individuals and the viability of public institutions and private enterprises. It therefore calls for heightened skills and the maintenance of strict standards of accuracy."

The Canadian Association of Journalists counsels its members to be wary of police requests for assistance, identifying many potential pitfalls: "If we are seen to be part of the judicial process, it damages our credibility as critics of the system and may limit our access to sources."[4] But no formal code of ethics is really required: just be fair, act with integrity, and avoid conflicts of interest.

The discussions reported in the briefing notes from the RCMP to the solicitor general were not the only times that Cameron had been too cozy with the authorities. She frequently boasted about her police connections to her colleagues.⁵ She clearly had a conflict of interest. Implicating Mulroney vindicated her life's work.

There was a police informer – that is certain. Inspector Mathews had sworn an affidavit to that effect. The most sacrosanct of all privileges known at law had to be protected in the Eurocopter case. Informer status was conferred on someone who provided the RCMP with information in 1995, perhaps even earlier. In November 1993 the RCMP, acting on a tip from the new minister of justice, Allan Rock, interviewed two journalists about alleged Mulroney wrongdoing. One of these journalists, Inspector Marc Beaupré of the Mounties later reported to the justice minister, "agreed to provide us with supporting documentations should [he or she] find something factual."⁶ By 1995 informer status was confirmed on someone: this fact was established by the redacted Information to Obtain and a number of the affidavits filed in support – affidavits by a senior officer in the RCMP, Inspector Mathews, sworn under oath. Eddie Greenspan took up two days of the court's time attempting to prove that the person in question was Stevie Cameron: the RCMP prepared briefing notes for the solicitor general, and Cameron figured prominently in those briefing notes; she bragged about her relationship with the RCMP; and she travelled to Germany to share documents with prosecutorial authorities. Greenspan's argument was persuasive – but it got even better when the Crown provided some additional details in a new affidavit from Inspector Mathews. This information was the icing on the cake.

The new affidavit had been sworn in April 2001, but it was not provided to the parties in the Eurocopter case until the end of February 2003. It had a number of objectives, but its prime purpose was to persuade Justice Then that, even though more of the information could be disclosed, parts of it had to remain blacked out to protect the identity of a confidential informant.

> Disclosure would compromise the identity of a confidential informant [name blacked out] who is named ... within the Information to Obtain. The confidential informant status of this individual was unknown to me at the time of writing the Information to Obtain, and was not recorded in file material which I reviewed then, and which I have again reviewed in preparation for this Affidavit. I first learned of the possibility of this on March 1, 2001 from Jim Shaw, a counsel for the

Edmonton Regional Office, Department of Justice (DOJ), representing the Attorney General of Canada, who asked me whether or not I understood the relationship to exist. I did not. On March 23, 2001 I learned of an intention to assert a confidential informant privilege in this regard, from Ingrid Hutton, also a counsel for DOJ at Edmonton, who advised me that she learned of the existence of this confidential informant relationship earlier in March, 2001, in conversation with S/Sgt Fiegenwald (now retired), the original investigator of this file, who said that the confidential informant privilege existed in respect of this individual. Hutton also told me that she subsequently confirmed the fact of the confidential informant status with the informant directly on March 20, 2001, who claimed the privilege at this time, and who also advised Hutton that Supt. Carl Gallant of the RCMP (now retired) was also present at the time. *Hutton advised me that the informant will not consent to the Crown's waiver of privilege, unless it was for the prosecution of Brian Mulroney.*[7]

This latest affidavit was somewhat confusing, and it is far from clear that it is even legally correct. Inspector Mathews, the lead investigator in the Eurocopter case, was indicating that he did not know, when he first swore the Information to Obtain that persuaded Justice Fontana in December 1999 to authorize a search, that there was a police informer. In the normal course, where there is a police informer, the Information makes that clear and the identity of the person is not revealed, even to the judge. Moreover, the whole point of being a police informer is the security and peace of mind that comes with knowing you will never ever be called to account for the information you have handed over. This case, however, presented a police informer with a twist: he or she was apparently willing to waive the privilege for one purpose: bringing Brian Mulroney to justice. It was questionable whether it was a proper application of the police informer privilege.

What was especially interesting is how Inspector Mathews came to learn that there was a police informer, so late in the game. In February 2001, the affidavit indicates, Greenspan examined two witnesses as part of Schreiber's $35 million lawsuit against the RCMP and the Government of Canada. One witness was Kimberly Prost, the Department of Justice lawyer who headed the International Assistance Group and helped the RCMP and other police forces prepare letters of request – including the 1995 Letter of Request to

Switzerland. The other witness was Staff Sergeant Fraser Fiegenwald (retired). There is a rule, called the implied undertaking rule, that the questions asked and the answers given in discovery – that pre-trial process in which one side gets to ask the other side questions about the pending case – cannot be disclosed or relied upon or used in any other proceeding but the case at hand. Until Schreiber actually begins the trial of his lawsuit against the Canadian government and the RCMP, as opposed to the pre-trial skirmishes, the transcripts of this examination, because of this rule, cannot be made public. However, it is clear, reading between the lines of Inspector Mathews's affidavit, that Fiegenwald was asked questions about his relationship with Cameron. Those questions, in turn, led to Ingrid Hutton, a senior Department of Justice lawyer in the Edmonton office, contacting Cameron and asking her about her relationship with the RCMP. Hutton then reported to Mathews that Cameron confirmed her informer status and claimed informer privilege. In fact, there was even more to it than that. Cameron also told Hutton, who told Mathews, that she would consent to waive her informer status for only one reason: to testify against Brian Mulroney. She also indicated that "disclosure would be disastrous to [her] career right now, and implied considerable monetary damages could result."[8]

When Mulroney heard about the new affidavit, he was flabbergasted. He felt a huge weight lift from his shoulders as the implications of the revelation began to sink in. His number one enemy was working with the RCMP! He tried to go to sleep at his usual bedtime, but could not and, around one in the morning, he got up, his mind racing. "It's delicious," he later observed to me. "It was just so astonishing to see it finally there in writing. All I can tell you is that every god-damn thing is a lie. They all knew that she was a police informer ... Basically what happened is that she coopted the national police force. There is no evidence except her own hatred ... She thought she was so clever and she thought I would not fight back. It has been going on since the settlement. I spent millions fighting against this thing ... As best as I can figure, the RCMP will try to keep this secret for quite a long time. It is clear that everything they have said is a lie. It is a corruption of the Privy Council and the independence of the police all done to destroy the former prime minister."

"I think she is now cowering," he continued, " – that she is fearful of what is going to happen to her when the public finds out that she has been on the police payroll and that she is a liar and a hypocrite ... She had to sell her soul. And because it is the RCMP, they put it all in writing. She knows what is going to happen to her."

It was really very simple. While there was no evidence that Stevie Cameron was paid for her services, the evidence of her continuing hostility to Mulroney was overwhelming. The RCMP, having no, or little, information of its own, was quick to confer informer status on Cameron to obtain information from her. Inspector Mathews may have learned about her status only late in the game – a rather astonishing state of affairs, it must be said, given his rank and his years of full-time work on the file. While she had clearly arranged for informer status to be conferred to protect her from any awkward questions about her activities, she was, in a strange way to her credit, prepared to testify and reveal her relationship if it would help send Mulroney to jail. That was her central preoccupation and longtime goal. Eddie Greenspan had figured it all out. Usually, reporters get information from the police, although the reverse can occur, and trading does, on occasion, take place. In this instance, Canada's best-known journalist, perhaps mistakenly believing she was acting in the public interest and for the public good, wanted to help out. Perhaps there were other motivations at work. Whatever the explanation, most journalists believe they should be the ones asking the questions, not answering them. The inhibitions do not work the other way around, and the police have no principled objection to good sources who want to snuggle up.

8 Brian and Me

Martin Brian Mulroney, eighteenth prime minister of Canada (1984–93), retired from office the most hated politician in Canada – possibly the most hated prime minister in Canadian history. Paradoxically, Mulroney had come to power on a wave of resentment against the long-lived, thoroughly decayed government of Pierre Trudeau and his hapless short-term replacement, John Turner. Mulroney ran an almost flawless campaign and won the largest number of seats in Canadian history in 1984 by promising to be different. His government *was* different. Almost from the beginning of his first term in office, there appeared to be a revolving door of ministers and MPs in trouble with the law. Mulroney stood loyally by: "Ya dance with the lady who brung ya," he always said, blurring the lines between personal friendship and public business.

There were other serious problems as well, and not just with the ragtag band of parliamentarians who came to power on Mulroney's coattails. Canadians did not believe that Mulroney kept his word. He said that social programs were a "sacred trust," but his government tried to de-index old-age pensions. He promised to make appointments based on merit, not political stripe, then demonstrated that the Tories, just like the Grits, knew how to divvy up the spoils.

A 1987 Angus Reid poll indicated that 78 per cent of Canadians thought that the Mulroneys lived like a "wealthy elite." Ridiculed and hounded by the press for his presidential style, Gucci shoes, and exquisitely tailored suits, Mulroney appeared to many as imperious, self-important, and fundamentally out of touch. How should the Mulroneys live? the pollster asked. Like the middle class or upper middle class, Canadians answered. The Mulroneys lived better – conspicuously better. Whatever impact their lifestyle might have had on the prime minister's personal popularity, however, it did not interfere with electoral success. Despite the public's uneasiness with Mulroney's party and image, and with the Free Trade Agreement, the Progressive Conservatives won a second majority in the 1988 general election.

The Canadian economy was strong; the Quebec separatists were weak. There was no political alternative worthy of consideration. Most important of all, the Conservatives won another term because Mulroney had a very good plan: free trade with the United States. In this context, it mattered little how he lived or what Canadians thought of him. Although close and bitterly fought, the election was all about choosing a different direction from the one Canadians had travelled for the previous one hundred years.

Mulroney continued to be hammered by the public-opinion polls in his second term. The numbers got worse and worse, and they got even more personal. When a 1989 Gallup poll asked Canadians about the most important quality in a prime minister, "honesty" and "trustworthiness" were by far the top choices. Mulroney consistently scored poorly on a trust index, and the popularity of the Tories dropped to historic lows.

He was, in part, his own worst enemy. He used ninety-cent words, his critics claimed, to inflate his ten-cent ideas. He appeared pompous, his sincerity rehearsed. His smiling subservient attitude towards the Americans made it appear that he wanted to be just like them. He boasted of his humble roots, and would not let people forget them. There was the blarney, delivered in his deep baritone voice, radiating self-righteousness. It all seemed so cynical and calculating. And, while some of the friends he kept were honourable, others were toadies and hangers-on, picked up along the way.

Canadians were dissatisfied with their government and with the man who led it. The failure of his constitutional initiatives, the introduction of the unpopular Goods and Services Tax, his famous "roll the dice" comment, which sounded as though he was gambling with the future of the country by cynically timing a final first ministers' conference just before the expiry of the time limit for the passage of the Meech Lake accord – all these measures were lightning rods for discontent, and Mulroney was at the centre of the storm. It was more than just unpopular taxes and policies, constitutional initiatives gone awry, and an economy that tanked out – Trudeau had often been in the same boat. There was something about Mulroney that particularly rankled. Only one in five Canadians, according to a 1990 Gallup poll, believed that the prime minister cared about the average citizen – the same low number that considered him to be honest and trustworthy. When Stevie Cameron published her book with a picture of a smiling, tuxedo-clad Mulroney on the cover, beside the words "On the Take," the image, and the claim, resonated.

By 1993, with the polls promising political disaster, Mulroney proclaimed his mission accomplished and stepped down. But, just like Trudeau, he then embarked on a lavish around-the-world tour, collecting kudos from the world leaders he had come to know. Usually when political leaders retire, the people become sentimental, magnanimous, even forgiving. Not with Mulroney. A *Globe and Mail* poll conducted in June of that year revealed that few Canadians believed history would judge his administration well. Mulroney was convinced he would be vindicated by history, and these initial results cannot have been encouraging. His economic policies were courageous and largely correct (and endorsed by succeeding governments), but credit for these and many other important accomplishments was elusive. Almost ten years after he stepped down from office, an EKOS poll conducted for the *Toronto Star*, the CBC, and *La Presse* in May 2002 indicated that Canadians believed that Mulroney's government set the standard for unethical behaviour while in office. Mulroney's friends always described a different type of man from the one Canadians got to know: even if his ego was larger than the Canadian Shield and his vanity truly unsurpassed, they said, he was extraordinarily generous, with a heart as big as all outdoors. These reports were routinely, and quite wrongly, dismissed as sycophantic tub-thumping.

Canadians were never given the opportunity to hand Mulroney the electoral defeat many thought he had earned. Instead, all they got was an ill-prepared, underqualified, self-absorbed, and entirely unsuitable successor, Kim Campbell, on whom to exercise revenge. It was brutal and swift retribution, burying her and the Progressive Conservatives forever. Canadians were ready, anxious almost, to believe the worst about Mulroney.

And that is probably why it was so important to Mulroney that his commercial relationship with Karlheinz Schreiber not see the light of day. After he left office, Mulroney returned to the practice of law and established an independent international consultancy. There was nothing wrong with any of that. Accepting a retainer from Schreiber was problematic, however. An important part of Schreiber's business in 1993 and 1994 was Canadian government business, and Mulroney had recently led the government. Making matters worse were the circumstances in which the retainer was paid. Ordinary Canadians would not begin to understand the payment of $300,000 in cash – payments made in hotels and for services that have never been adequately explained.

The size of the payment paled in comparison to the many millions the RCMP wrongly asserted in its 1995 Letter of Request to Switzerland that Mulroney had taken in payoffs for Airbus, MBB, and Bearhead, but it was still a lot of money. The distinction between the amounts was likely to be lost on the public if information about the retainer leaked. Mulroney's critics would have a field day. Where there is smoke there is fire, popular wisdom has it. This controversy would challenge even an old professional media manipulator like Mulroney. The best solution was to ensure that the story stay buried. The *National Post* had killed it early in 2001. Now, in the fall of 2003, with the Eurocopter secret trial about to become public knowledge, could the *Globe and Mail* be persuaded to do so too?

In the weeks, and then the days, leading up to the unsealing order and the end of the publication ban in the Eurocopter case, Brian Mulroney made telephone call after telephone call to me. The *Globe and Mail* had asked me to write a series on the case. Mulroney heard about this request, and he also knew that I knew about the money from Schreiber. Sometimes there were several calls a day, and hardly a day went by without at least one discussion. They began on a confident note. The government, he pointed out, had cleared him of misconduct. But that was not quite right. Dated April 22, 2003, the announcement was completely straightforward: "After an exhaustive investigation in Canada and abroad, the RCMP has concluded its investigation into allegations of wrongdoing involving MBB Helicopters, Thyssen and Airbus. In October 2002, a charge of Fraud was brought against Eurocopter Canada Ltd. (formerly MCL – Messerschmitt Canada Limited), and two German citizens, Kurt Pfleiderer and Heinz Pluckthun. The RCMP has now concluded that the remaining allegations cannot be substantiated and that no charges will be laid, beyond the charge of Fraud already before the courts. A preliminary inquiry in the Eurocopter Fraud charge is scheduled to begin September 8, 2003 at Ottawa. Today's announcement fulfills a commitment made by former Commissioner Phil Murray to announce the results of the Airbus investigation once the RCMP concluded its investigation."

Mulroney was informed first that the investigation was over. The RCMP came to see him and hand-delivered the letter from Commissioner Giuliano Zaccardelli. Would the RCMP have called off the investigation if it knew about the commercial relationship between Mulroney and Schreiber? According to Yves Fortier, the distinguished former Canadian ambassador to the United Nations and a law partner of Mulroney's, the RCMP had "full knowledge" of the commercial relationship between Mulroney and Schreiber before it called off the investigation. This assertion, in a June 15, 2004, letter to me and the publisher threatening legal action over this book, may be correct. Not so, says Inspector Mathews, who when informed of the claim responded, "I would dispute that assertion."[1] Another very senior retired RCMP officer told me, however, but not for attribution, that the Mounties did know about the transaction, but they decided the payment did not prove anything. It was also pointed out to me by that same source that other former politicians have gone on Schreiber's payroll. But what is especially puzzling is that the RCMP even had a chance to learn more. On two occasions, Schreiber made offers to tell them what he knew in return for favourable treatment. It was not exactly clear what Schreiber would have to say – it was "bigger than Watergate," he confided to me – but the quid for the quo was obviously turning down the German government's extradition request. The Mounties were not interested. Undoubtedly, Schreiber has more "get out of jail free" cards than any Monopoly game. If and when he is ordered extradited, and if all appeals have expired, he will likely produce one. It should be interesting to find out then what, if anything, he has to say.

Of course, Mulroney knew nothing about Schreiber's entreaties to the RCMP. The end of the investigation was another matter, however, and the former prime minister embraced the April letter as confirmation of innocence. Over the phone, Mulroney reasoned to me that if the RCMP did not care about his commercial relationship with Schreiber, why should anyone else? Why should I, in particular, the author of a supportive book about him and the Airbus affair, be concerned? I disagreed, and Mulroney tried another tack.

There was the promise of a huge scoop. Contrary to everything Jean Chrétien had said, there was, Mulroney advised me, reason to believe that officials in both the Privy Council Office and the Prime Minister's Office were well aware of the RCMP investigation and may even have reviewed the letter to Switzerland – the one that flat out called him a criminal – before it was sent. If this was true, it would be a huge scandal, demonstrating government interference with the police at the highest levels. Mulroney possessed an affidavit to that effect, he claimed, and would let me see it when the time was right. Mulroney eventually revealed what he knew. He must have realized, when the *Globe* called his bluff and refused to trade, that he might as well pass on a tip that served his interests. There was some disturbing evidence, but not enough to go to press.

Then there was the Mila angle. "There is something that I want to talk to you about," Mulroney said in another phone call. "Mila raised this question with me, and I decided to raise it with you. It has to do with that other matter you know about. I want you to know that it is not going anywhere. It has been thoroughly investigated. The income has been declared and I am as clean as a whistle. This thing involving Schreiber, someone told that to the RCMP and they investigated that and they concluded that it was all clean as a whistle. That was the final thing they were investigating prior to giving me the apology letter in April ... As I told you, and as my lawyers told the RCMP, I am innocent."[2]

More bait followed: "The money came to 'Britan.' This money was not for me. I know who Britan was. Now, there is a big story for you."[3] Many numbered Swiss accounts received Schreiber funds: "Britan" was one of them. Another famous numbered account was code-named "Devon." That account, it was wrongly asserted for a long time, held Mulroney's proceeds of crime. Schreiber had set up that account, according to Giorgio Pelossi, for Brian Mulroney. Pelossi even made a note to himself about it, writing the initials "B.M." on a business card. Mulroney had once lived on Devon Street in Montreal, informed observers knowingly pointed out. The only problem was that the account never belonged to him. It belonged, one story went, to Frank Moores's wife, Beth, explaining Pelossi's mistake in believing that "B.M." meant Brian Mulroney. Frank Moores was not confused about the ownership of the account, however. It was his, he told the *Financial Post* on December 16, 1995. He opened it to hold the proceeds of European business deals, which did not materialize. Why Devon? Because his parents came from Devon, England, and he had a relative named Devon. Whatever the explanation, the account was opened with a $500 deposit and, when it was finally closed in 1990, it held only $271.40 – the original amount having been diminished by bank charges. Moores had the records to prove it.

The Britan account was another matter. Britan, the same observers suggested, undoubtedly meant Brian, since Schreiber liked to assign code names that resembled the name of the beneficiary. Maybe Mulroney was going to tell me who Britan was – an interesting piece of information. And revealing that information would certainly be consistent with his obligation, as a citizen and former prime minister, in furthering the police investigation.

Bank records unearthed by Harvey Cashore for the *Fifth Estate*, and eventually published in *The Last Amigo*, indicate that, on July 26, 1993, following his visit to Harrington Lake to see Mulroney just after he stepped down as prime minister, Schreiber moved some of

his money around, including $500,000 CDN to a new Swiss bank
account he code-named Britan.⁴ Someone withdrew $100,000 the
next day. Schreiber's first payment to Mulroney, for $100,000,
followed not long afterwards. On November 3, 1993, another
$100,000 was withdrawn from the Britan account. Fifty thousand
more was taken out on July 21, 1994, and another $50,000 came out
on November 21, 1994.⁵ All the withdrawals were in cash.

In the spring of 1995 German tax police raided Schreiber's Bavarian estate and seized his 1994 diary, among other documents. Entries
in that diary indicate that, in the fall of 1994, *Der Spiegel* began calling Schreiber regularly – and that is when questions first began to be
asked in earnest in Europe about Airbus payoffs. In November 1994
Schreiber began, according to the diary, making plans for a trip
to New York and a meeting with Brian Mulroney, Elmer MacKay,
and others at the Pierre Hotel. As noted above, on November 21,
$50,000 CDN was withdrawn from the Britan account. On Decem-
ber 4, Schreiber travelled to New York, and he appears to have met
up with Elmer MacKay in the next day or two and, according to his
daytimer, with "Brian" soon after that. It would be extremely interesting to know who, exactly, was at the meeting and what was discussed. *Der Spiegel* is a serious news magazine. It was on to something, as subsequent events amply established.

Mulroney repeatedly denied being Britan, but he continued to
insist that he knew who Britan was and would, one day, tell me. This
account is the only one German authorities have not yet tied to a particular individual. It is impossible to say for certain who Britan is.
However, it is clear that the withdrawals and the total amount of
payments add up to $300,000, the amount that Schreiber says he
paid to Mulroney.

There is no reason to believe that Mulroney knew anything
about the source of Schreiber's cash. Moreover, Schreiber might
have had his own reasons for establishing the Britan account. Quite
possibly he was, legitimately under German law at the time, allo-
cating grease money or, perhaps, as German authorities later suspected, creating a ruse, keeping the money for himself and evading
taxation. There is a third possibility: that Mulroney agreed to go to
work for Schreiber, performed services, and was paid. That is what
Mulroney and his circle say happened. There is a fourth possibility
as well: that Schreiber just wanted to give Mulroney a gift. As historian Michael Bliss wrote, "If special commissions were paid in the
Airbus deal … it is quite possible that the recipients, whoever they
were, might have intended someday to give some of the money to
Mulroney. By the same token, Mulroney would remain entirely

innocent of any wrongdoing ... His only guilt might be by association."[6] Unfortunately, Mulroney never told me who Britan actually
was.[7] He had more pressing matters to discuss.

"The thing I want to get back to is that I do not want your story
to reflect badly on me," he insisted. "I don't want a sidebar that Stevie
Cameron can pounce on and say, 'See, I told you so,' when we have
her finally going down the tubes ... I don't want anything in there
that gives Stevie Cameron a pound of flesh to start chewing on. So
please think about what I said. I told Mila that I would be surprised
that Bill gives anything to Stevie Cameron to chew on ... the principal reason I want this as clean as a whistle is, following your series
of articles, let's say it starts out the week of November 5, 2003, I wait
a week and then I write a letter to the new prime minister, Paul Martin, asking for a new investigation and a royal commission into this
cabal and conspiracy. I plan to tell Martin that this is the only thing
that will clarify it all ... By the way, Paul Martin views this thing as
a huge scandal and it wouldn't offend him if his predecessor was
caught up in this."[8]

Then there was the children angle: "Now I want to clarify something with you that is important for me. I have told you that I lay
awake about what would be in the paper during this whole Airbus
thing and how that would affect my wife and kids. Then on April 22
we got the letter from the RCMP that there was no evidence for any
prosecution. Now I get the impression that you plan to say something about matters unrelated to the secret trial."

That was correct. Mulroney asked the question straight out, but
I did not give him the answer he was looking for. "It's part of the
story," I told him, feeling sick and uncomfortable as I did so. He did
not agree. "It's not part of the story at all. It is a different story. Don't
forget that I have already told you this, that I have never done anything wrong or been involved with anyone for any improper purpose. Everything has been fully legal and proper. Don't forget that it
has been fully examined by the RCMP ... So if you write about this it
will be a big red herring that will please Stevie Cameron and distress
myself because it is a false accusation, because there is nothing there,
you can be certain of that. The RCMP, before they signed off on April
22, had examined everything and had satisfied themselves about this.
I don't want to do anything to feed Stevie Cameron. With all this
stuff coming out, she would seize on this, as would her allies."[9]

But what about the fact that Schreiber paid you $300,000 in
cash? I asked. And what about the fact that when you were examined under oath, you never indicated a commercial relationship with
the German businessman?

"All that is false ... the transcript is fine," Mulroney retorted. "Regarding the money, I can tell you that there would be enough inaccuracy in what was just said to maintain a lawsuit. I will tell you what I have told you before – everything I have done is completely honest and above board. Before, during and after my political life."[10]

Then there was the warning: "If I have to defend myself again, I will. If I have to go through the courts again, I will. I don't need this ... It was like the Gestapo. You know, it just about killed me fighting alone against the government and the complete lack of any kindness from Rock or Chrétien. There wasn't a senior public servant who said to Chrétien, 'Look, you may have your partisan reasons for going against Mulroney, but we have worked with him for 10 years as prime minister and he was completely honest and fair minded.' It cost me hundreds of thousands of dollars to serve as prime minister. No public servant said we can't be party to this. This is what I found so terrible. No one said a word – they let me suffer while they listened to Stevie Cameron denigrate me. She had been saying that I was a criminal. In any event, if that is your intention, let me know. All I can do is tell you that you can be god-damned certain that before they signed the letter in April telling me everything was okay, they had to look at everything, including all commercial transactions. They investigated everything ... They were aware of any transactions I did after I left office ... I can give you a personal guarantee that everything I did with anyone was looked at by the RCMP. And also everything in the transcript is completely accurate."[11]

As our conversations often did, this one drifted on. What he liked to talk most about was the "squalid conduct and stunning hypocrisy" of Jean Chrétien and his Liberals. This time, the next issue up for discussion was who would lead the Conservatives to power. The answer was – Mulroney. He explained that he had recently seen a Quebec poll that gave the Liberals up to sixty seats. This was before the "adscam" sponsorship scandal that drove down Liberal numbers in Ontario and Quebec and across the rest of the country. But the poll also asked about voting patterns if Mulroney was the leader of a united Conservative Party. Assuming that to be the case, the poll indicated there would be forty Tory seats. "The first time I ran," Mulroney continued, "I took fifty-eight, then the second time I ran I took sixty-nine seats. So I would have a strong base just to start."

What did Mila think about the prospect? I asked. "She won't even let me talk about it. But if I thought it was necessary ... In April [2004] they will hold a leadership convention. If I decided to run next April I would win the leadership. I would have a handicap on Paul Martin, but I could defeat him easily in the debates. I would be prime minister by July 1. This is achievable. I would only do it if it became clear that the Conservatives had put themselves in a position where they could never win again."[12]

Later I told several people I knew about this conversation. The universal reaction was that Mulroney was nuts. I wasn't so sure. I was certain that, as prime minister, Mulroney would be an even more formidable opponent. "I don't exclude the possibility of running myself," Mulroney said. "At my age, having been there, I could do it – and the answer is yes. It would surprise you, as I walk down the streets in Toronto, how people mob me and how happy they are to see me."[13]

There was also the Jewish angle. I am Jewish. "Dear Mr. Kaplan," the October 17, 2003, note from Mulroney's longtime assistant began, "The Right Honourable Brian Mulroney asked me to send to you the attached articles for your information." And duly attached were two articles, both of which had appeared in the *Canadian Jewish News*. The first, titled "The best prime minister – for the Jews,"[14] by Morton Weinfeld, reported on a recent speech Mulroney had given in Montreal. It was essentially a repeat of his more widely publicized speech, given at the University of Toronto the previous February, condemning anti-Semitism and coming out forcefully in support of Israel. According to Weinfeld, "no Canadian prime minister ... has ever given such a thoughtful, informed and personal speech ... Mulroney demonstrated both an intellectual understanding of, and visceral empathy with Jews and Israel. His phrase 'Israel is the new Jew' underscored the potential linkage between anti-Zionism and anti-Semitism." Almost one thousand people gathered to toast the former prime minister at the Queen Elizabeth Hotel. John Crosbie was master of ceremonies. The dining room was beautifully decorated, all in black and featuring towering vases of calla lilies. Prominent Jews were in abundance. And, Weinfeld reported, the audience was "deeply moved." The speech, Weinfeld concluded, was "a signal event in Canadian Jewish history." The other attached article gave more details of an event referred to as the "Negev Dinner." Mulroney, whose speech "won round after round of applause," had been named the Jewish National Fund's "man of the year." I guess that was supposed to mean something to me, but it did not. It just left me feeling embarrassed.

Then there was the outright threat: "Do not feed Stevie Cameron. And I should tell you this, be prepared for a son of a bitch of a reaction from me. I will deal with it immediately. If you want my cooperation and friendship, then you cannot be a friend and an opponent at the same time ... You have gotta learn to let your enemies put out the crap ... We shouldn't be putting it out about each other ... I will be your friend or enemy but not both."[15] I was never Mulroney's friend. After *Presumed Guilty* was published, Mulroney kept in touch. He called me. If I heard something interesting, I would call him. Every once in a while, when he was in Toronto, he would invite me over to his hotel for a visit, usually late at night after official business was over. I liked him. He is very engaging, very funny, very insightful, full of good stories. I enjoyed his company. I found it very interesting listening to him. But I was never his friend. And I was very disturbed when I found out about the Schreiber money. However, having Mulroney as my enemy was not a priority. I am well aware that he has a lot of friends, truly powerful friends. I had seen first-hand how he went after his enemies in 1995. The Government of Canada, at least, had some resources. There was no way I could afford to be at the receiving end of a Mulroney lawsuit – and he knew it.

On September 25, 2003, *Globe and Mail* lawyer Patrick Flaherty wrote Justice Then seeking access to the Eurocopter court file. Flaherty, a leading litigator at the Torys law firm, with special expertise in defamation lawsuits and in challenging publication bans, requested an opportunity to appear before the judge to make submissions on the *Globe*'s right to attend the secret trial and to obtain copies of all the records that had been produced. "While we appreciate this request is somewhat unusual," Flaherty wrote, "we have been unable to obtain any additional information about the proceeding or order through normal channels of public access." Soon enough, Justice Then reconvened the case, but for the first time, in open court. On Friday, October 31, 2003, acceding to the *Globe*'s request, and with the support of the lawyers from the CBC, Schreiber, and the Crown, Justice Then agreed to release just about the entire record and to set aside the publication ban. All the parties were given one week to appeal that order, failing which everything – everything, that is, except for the name of the secret informer – would become public. All interested media outlets were entitled to immediate access to the materials, provided that nothing was published before the time for appeal had run out. I was one of the persons designated by the *Globe and Mail* to have a look. We began working around the clock. Publication was less than a week away – no appeals were anticipated – and even though I was generally familiar with the story, there was a lot of material to digest.

Patrick Flaherty – the *Globe and Mail* lawyer succeeded in persuading Justice Then that secrecy could no longer be justified.

Globe and Mail editor-in-chief Ed Greenspon assigned editor Jerry Johnson to make sense out of my prose. A journalist and an author, Greenspon was determined to shed light on the secret trial, and he was prepared to commit the *Globe*'s power and prestige in order to so. As far as I could tell, Greenspon cares about only two things in the world: telling the truth and the *Globe and Mail*. Johnson, a *Globe* editor for more than twenty-five years, was a University of Western Ontario graduate with both an Honours BA and an MA in journalism. It was amazing working with Johnson, the editor of "Focus," the *Globe*'s Saturday feature section. He could take a paragraph and reduce it to a much better-sounding sentence. We spent hours in his windowless room going over everything. He started calling me "Scoop," which was a bit amusing. When we were not working together, we were sitting with *Globe* libel lawyer Brian MacLeod Rogers, reviewing the text line by line as Rogers demanded justification for some of the possibly contentious claims. People looked at me as I wandered around the newsroom, wondering who I was and why I was spending so much time in Greenspon's office.

Telephone calls from Mulroney to me, and to Greenspon, escalated. Greenspon advised Mulroney that I would be telling the whole story. Let's meet, Mulroney suggested to me on Monday, November

3, 2003, and, he added, "I would be grateful if you brought what you wrote." But there was a little more about Jews. "I defended the Jews and got abused for that. That is the right thing to do, I know you got abuse about me, but it is because of Stevie Cameron. She put so much poison into the system. Israel is the new Jew. As far as she is concerned, I am the new Jew."[16]

Finally, there was our conversation early Sunday morning, November 9, 2003. I was completely worn out by the process of getting the series ready for publication, while working at my day job, and worn down by his effort to stop the publication of the last in the series of three articles in the *Globe and Mail*. The purpose of this conversation was, for him, to address my concerns with his misleading testimony at the examination on discovery. At some point in our conversation, not long after we began, Mulroney told me it was not an interview. This was the first time, in all the years I've known him and in countless conversations, many lasting hours, that he had ever said that. I should have said no, that it was an interview and that if it continued I could and would feel free to quote what he said. We reviewed the transcript. I directed him to the problems. It was an emotional conversation and, at the time, the stakes truly seemed enormous. We both believed, quite wrongly as it turned out, that Canadians would notice – and care. He talked about honour. I pointed out that he was not the only person with honour. I had sat in his house and he had told me that he barely knew Schreiber – and that was not true. He responded: "I regret any inconvenience that I may have caused."

I could not believe my ears. I had trusted Brian Mulroney. He had looked me in the eye. He had told me the same story he told the Canadian people – the same misleading story that he had but a "peripheral" relationship with Karlheinz Schreiber. He regretted the inconvenience? I had worked like a dog getting my book done, working early mornings, nights, and weekends, taking weeks off work criss-crossing the country to promote my book, all the time defending him while attacking the misconduct of the government and the RCMP. Raising my voice for the first time ever in a discussion with him, I told him it was not good enough. He then said, "I'm sorry." Although he called my house later that night, I did not answer the telephone. I have not spoken to Brian Mulroney since.

9 Confirmation

The series was published the moment it was lawful to do so. On Friday, November 7, 2003, part one, "Secret trial revealed," gave an account of the proceedings from the beginning. I spent the day at the *Globe and Mail* working on the Saturday story. The *Globe*'s libel lawyer, Brian MacLeod Rogers, was there too. There were meetings in editor-in-chief Ed Greenspon's office. People came and went. Mulroney called. A *Globe* reporter was assigned to contact Stevie Cameron. Mid-afternoon, word came back that Cameron denied she was the police informer. "Horseshit," she told reporter Paul Waldie.

I am not sure what I was expecting. If I had been her, I would have told the truth. For some reason, I thought she would too. Then I began to worry. What if we were wrong and about to make a terrible mistake? What if it was someone else, not Stevie Cameron? What if, in reporting the assertions made in court, which the newspaper was lawfully entitled to do whether they were right or wrong, we were hurting an innocent person? This denial was extremely troubling. The evidence appeared overwhelming that Cameron was the police informer – but it was circumstantial evidence. The existence of the principal fact – that Cameron was a police informer – could at the time only be inferred or deduced from the circumstances. There was no smoking gun because most of the proof was still under seal.

Eddie Greenspan's reasoning was persuasive. Moreover, there were other documents, such as the RCMP briefing notes, that supported the conclusion that Cameron was working for the RCMP. There was similar fact evidence – she had turned over information to the authorities in Augsburg, Germany. Having cooperated with at least one other police force made it more likely that she was also cooperating with the RCMP. In addition, there was the telephone call from Cameron's lawyer, Peter M. Jacobsen, to Allan Rock's lawyer,

Harvey Strosberg, in which Jacobsen informed Strosberg that Fraser Fiegenwald had told Cameron about the 1995 Letter of Request being sent to Switzerland. That letter should have been kept confidential. The fact that it was leaked to a journalist was the reason the government gave, in 1997, for settling the Mulroney lawsuit at the cost to Canadian taxpayers of $2 million plus. Sharing the secret letter with a reporter was simply inconsistent with the government's defence of scrupulous good faith in the conduct of the investigation. These facts all tended to support, strongly, the suppositions made in court. After a spirited discussion on the matter, the *Globe* decided to proceed with part two.

The next day, Saturday, the lead story asked "Could this journalist be the secret informant?" There was a picture of Stevie Cameron on the front page. This revelation was published on the second day of the series because that was the proper chronological order. At no point was there any discussion, at least none that I was party to or heard about, considering running the story out of order so that the revelations about Mulroney could be published on a big circulation day. Maybe the *Globe and Mail* should have done that. Maybe that made the most news sense because the payments to Mulroney, and his efforts to keep them quiet, were what really mattered. It just was not the proper order. On Sunday afternoon, Mulroney called Greenspon. The *Globe* editor-in-chief told him that tomorrow would not be a very good day. On Monday, November 10, 2003, the final part in the series appeared, headlined in 100-point type "Schreiber hired Mulroney." There were large pictures of both Schreiber and Mulroney. The story detailed the cash payments and Mulroney's misleading testimony at examination on discovery.

Astonishingly, there was next to no public or media reaction. The *National Post* ran a piece about the secret trial. The *Toronto Star* almost completely ignored the story, as did the *Toronto Sun* and most of the national media. No one asked Mulroney what he did for the money or why he was paid in cash. No one asked him when he declared the income or remitted the GST. No one asked him why he was not more forthright with Canadians when he testified in discovery. And no one asked me anything, except for one radio call-in show in Saskatoon, which inquired whether I would be willing to appear as a guest.

Mulroney, more media-wise than most, had forecast some of the reaction. Speaking about the likely CBC response to the secret trial, he predicted: "In my view, they will play it in a muted manner. The big stuff will be missing."[1] He got that right. But he was wrong to

Jerry Johnson and
Edward Greenspon at
the *Globe and Mail* –
Greenspon was offended
by the idea of a secret trial.

worry about the impact of the story about Schreiber's $300,000 pay-
ment to him in cash. There wasn't one. It was as if no one noticed.

There was, however, some predictable abuse from the beautiful
people, the Annex crowd, Toronto's intelligentsia, the in-people in
Ottawa, the movers and shakers, all part of Cameron's large coterie
of friends. A dinner party guest in my home reamed me out for what
I had done and, at the end of the evening, apologized, telling me
"that no one should be treated that way in their own house." I had
been quite unfair, many claimed, to Stevie Cameron. How could I
write a story based on Greenspan's unsubstantiated tirade? It was
all a set-up, others suggested, running the Cameron story on Saturday – when the *Globe and Mail* sells the most papers – and deliberately "hiding" the Mulroney revelations until Monday, when
the paper sells the least. We had buried the lead, others claimed,
although it was not evident to me how we could have been clearer

that the story was about Schreiber's payments to Mulroney. The pictures of Schreiber and Mulroney were oversize and, like the headline, above the fold. Stevie Cameron criticized me, Greenspan, and, most of all, the *Globe and Mail* on the CBC Newsworld program *Inside Media*. What I had written was simply wrong and completely unfair, she claimed. No informant she.

Robert Fulford came to see me. He is the unofficial dean of Canadian journalists. One of the most respected public intellectuals in this country, Fulford has a well-deserved reputation as a responsible iconoclast, often persuasively challenging received wisdom. He was writing a story for *Toronto Life* magazine about the *Globe and Mail* series. He told me it was his theory that Martians took over the newspaper for three days – and they were not good Martians. I told him that the *Globe* deserved a huge amount of credit for opening up the secret trial and for telling the truth about Mulroney and Cameron. I never heard from him again and am still waiting to see the story.

Antonia Zerbisias, the *Toronto Star*'s media columnist, soon weighed in, one of the few journalists in Canada to say anything about the series. She acknowledged the *Globe*'s role in shedding light on the secret trial but failed to mention that her paper had found out about it long before the *Globe* and had done nothing to open up the proceedings. What concerned Zerbisias most was that a journalist had been criticized. Instead of evaluating the evidence reviewed in court, and reported in the *Globe and Mail*, Zerbisias simply dismissed it as "thinner than the paper the stories were printed on."[2] The headline said it all: "Paper turns on one of its own writers." In case that point was lost, Zerbisias repeated it in her column. Reporters apparently cannot, in Ms Zerbisias's view, be fairly called to account.

A variation of this theme was offered by a Halifax journalism professor writing for *rabble*, "Canada's leading on line source for progressive news and views." Stephen Kimber, the author of many books and self-described "accidental academic," asserted that we had buried the story about the Schreiber payments, turning our guns instead on journalist Stevie Cameron. According to the professor, my "accusation" against Cameron was based solely on "the courtroom theatrics" of Schreiber's lawyer Eddie Greenspan. Kaplan and the *Globe*, Kimber wrote, were "indecently eager to serve as judge and jury" of Cameron. Professor Kimber, as *Frank* magazine did some years ago after publication of my admittedly pro-Mulroney book *Presumed Guilty*, concluded by suggesting that I had put myself in a position to perform on Mulroney what in the old days used to be called an indecent act.[3] What was especially odd about it all is that the professor, in his book *Not Guilty: The Trial of Gerald Regan*, asked the question: "What role should a journalist play in a police investigation?" Kimber's answer: "None."[4] There was a common theme to it all: along with the *Globe*, I had smeared the reputation of a liked and respected journalist by building a story around an accusatory question – in the style of Joe McCarthy – instead of by reporting the facts.[5]

I have no idea whether Antonia Zerbisias, Robert Fulford, and Stephen Kimber bothered to work their way through the now publicly available court file. If they had, they would know that I was not the person who swore under oath that there was a police informer. It was the RCMP who invoked the confidential informer privilege and who then, as required by law, refused to identify that person. It was the RCMP and the Crown who blacked out the name of the confidential informer in the search warrant documents. It was the RCMP who reported that that person, that informer, had invoked the privilege but agreed to be identified, provided it was for the prosecution of Brian Mulroney. Lawyer Eddie Greenspan had a theory about who that person was, about the motivations of that person, and about some of the possible implications of conferring informer status on this individual – implications for his client and for the administration of criminal justice in Canada. Rightly or wrongly, Greenspan believed that the investigation was irreparably tainted. He expounded that theory in court, as was his duty. It was not frivolous, and it added up. The *Globe* reported what Greenspan said in the series I wrote.

The *Globe and Mail* also gave Stevie Cameron, as it should, the opportunity to set the record straight. Here is what she wrote.

MULRONEY WAS THE REAL STORY
By Stevie Cameron, *Globe and Mail*, Nov. 22, 2003

Recently, *The Globe and Mail* ran a sensational three-day story about a secret hearing, a journalist who allegedly turned secret police informant and a payment to a former prime minister. In the high-profile Saturday edition, with a three-column, front page picture with 100-point type, I was the person portrayed as the secret informant.

But they buried the lead.

In fact, the most important element in the three stories *The Globe* ran wasn't about me. It was the revelation made the following Monday that shortly after stepping down as prime minister in 1993, Brian Mulroney accepted $300,000 over 18 months from Karlheinz Schreiber, an infamous German-Canadian arms dealer. In cash. To help promote a fresh pasta business and develop international contacts, said a spokesman for Mr. Mulroney.

Now that was the real shocker. Mr. Schreiber is the self-proclaimed master of the art of dispensing schmiergelder or "grease-money" to win contracts for German companies.

Although Germany has been trying to extradite him from Canada since August, 1999, on fraud charges involving three government contracts in Canada and one in Saudi Arabia, it was Mr. Schreiber's 1991 secret political contribution of one million Deutsche marks (DM) to Germany's Christian Democrats that brought him international infamy. Delivered in a suitcase to the party's treasurer, and as usual in cash, the undeclared donation brought down Helmut Kohl, the former chancellor of Germany, in the worst political crisis in that country since the war. Known as the Spendenaffare or slush-fund scandal, it spawned two parliamentary inquiries.

Investigations showed it was Mr. Schreiber who organized the payment of secret commissions on a DM 446-million deal to sell Thyssen tanks to the Saudis in the 1991 gulf war. Half the money went for secret commissions to pay bribes and kickbacks.

None of this money was his own; it was provided by German munitions companies. Mr. Schreiber's job was to spread it where needed and by his own admission, his main beneficiaries were politicians. He took a percentage as his fee.

He also received about $20-million (Cdn.) from Airbus headquarters in Toulouse, France, to spread around on the Air Canada purchase of Airbus planes in the late 1980s and about $6-million to kick-start a Thyssen tank plant in Nova Scotia that was never built. In one of his piddliest deals in the mid-1980s, he received secret commissions of about $1.2-million to spread around for the sale of MBB helicopters to the Canadian Coast Guard. That company is now known as Eurocopter Canada Ltd.

After a lengthy police investigation, as we know now, a secret preliminary hearing into the Eurocopter case began in a Toronto court three years ago. This is the hearing *The Globe and Mail* breathlessly reported on in the first instalment of its series. I tried to find and get into the hearing and failed, and had no lawyer there. That has proved unfortunate for me as no one was there to protest against the volumes of diatribe delivered against me by Mr. Schreiber's lawyer, Eddie Greenspan, a series of allegations reprinted by *The Globe* in the second part of the series, under the byline of William Kaplan. (Ironically, a couple of years ago, when I was a regular *Globe* contributor, I tried to interest editors in the whole Eurocopter story. At that time, the story of the aging Sea King helicopters was big news and the Chrétien government was backing Eurocopter's bid to replace them. But *The Globe* wasn't interested then.)

A Toronto lawyer who helped Mr. Mulroney tell his side of the Airbus affair in a 1998 book, *Presumed Guilty*, Mr. Kaplan blamed me for creating many of Mr. Mulroney's problems. He stated that I had betrayed the RCMP officer who was the lead investigator, Staff Sergeant Fraser Fiegenwald. In a glowing, 2,500-word review of Mr. Kaplan's book, which he published in his then-*Financial Post* and in most of his Southam newspapers, Conrad Black pounced on me, saying I had "ratted" on a police source. When Staff Sergeant Fiegenwald wrote a public letter to say the allegation was nonsense and that he admired my work, none of the Black papers would print it. Only *The Globe and Mail*, to its credit, published a story about the Fiegenwald rebuttal.

Mr. Kaplan's 1998 book had one interesting section that is relevant here. It described, from Mr. Mulroney's lips, the spin campaign his team designed to limit the damage threatened by the looming RCMP Airbus investigation that would name the former prime minister as a target. Mr. Mulroney's team would leak the story to a friendly reporter. The strategy was masterful; they controlled the story for weeks and the Mounties were left on the defensive.

This time, Mr. Kaplan revealed that the former prime minister did indeed receive a cash payment of $300,000 from Mr. Schreiber. This was the significant revelation, though it only appeared in the last part of Mr. Kaplan's 16,000-word, three-piece story.

In its astonishing treatment of me, *The Globe* ignored the fact that I had originally broken the story of Mr. Schreiber's influence in Ottawa years ago, for *The Globe*; that I had been edited and guided by their best people, and that I had never been sued for anything in the books I have published on this whole matter. The paper's treatment is incredible to me.

Journalists across the country have been in touch and given me strength and comfort. They know how difficult investigative work is. They know that our job is to dig to get the truth. It was my privilege to work for a *Globe* where reporters usually go through a rigorous editing process to make sure standards of fairness and accuracy are met. Now the paper suggests I may be a confidential informant.

So let's look at that. Mr. Kaplan isn't just saying I betrayed a Mountie any longer; now, he uncritically repeats Eddie Greenspan's accusations that I betrayed journalistic standards by becoming a confidential police informant. He even quotes from a 2001 fax Mr. Greenspan sent to me on behalf of his client in which the lawyer demands I answer how much I was paid to be an informant and whether or not I had a contract with the RCMP. (I never replied.) This was nonsense and deliberately insulting. Yes, I try to get help from police on stories. That's my job. That's what we do. Police reporters, investigative reporters, political reporters all share and swap information all the time with cops, business people, politicians. But in this case, I never approached the RCMP.

Instead, I was called in 1995 by officers who told me they had not started a formal investigation but were simply nosing around to see whether or not an investigation into the sale of Airbus planes to Air Canada was warranted. Could they come and see me? I was intrigued. Sure, I said, thinking I might get a good story out of this. I have never hidden the fact that they interviewed me, nor have the half-dozen or so other reporters they went to see. I answered their questions truthfully. Was I the one who approached the police? No. Did I give any information? Yes – information that was on the public record. It was in my own stories and in the 1994 book I had just published, *On the Take*; it was also in other media outlets in Canada and Germany. I did not give them any names of my sources or any information that was confidential. Paid police informant? Never. A confidential informant? Are you kidding me? Did they promise to protect me? There was no promise; indeed, police assured me that my interview would come out at trial. I never asked to be a confidential informant and if I had been in court the day Eddie Greenspan started throwing my name around, I would have said, "Who, me?" Did Mr. Kaplan interview me before writing his attack against me? Of course not. The only chance I had to respond to these charges came the day before all those pages went to press. I denied them vehemently.

In 1999, CBC Producer Harvey Cashore and I began work on *The Last Amigo*, our book about Mr. Schreiber. Our research extended to Costa Rica, Gibraltar, Saudi Arabia, the United States and Europe, as we followed Mr. Schreiber's money trail through his personal diaries, banking records, witness statements to police and testimony before a parliamentary inquiry in Berlin. By 2001, we finally understood the whole story. Perhaps now, *The Globe* is beginning to learn the truth about this story, too.

Mr. Mulroney's admission that, after leaving office as prime minister in 1993, he received $300,000 in cash from Mr. Schreiber was the real story in their recent series. I was the sideshow.

This comment was extremely upsetting. I was not sure what to do. I agreed with one thing Stevie Cameron wrote in her self-defence: the payments to Mulroney were the big story. She was just a "sideshow." But I did not believe her explanation: Cameron fiddled with the dial but never faced the music. Moreover, even though the *Globe and Mail* repeatedly asked her to say straight out that she was not a police informer, the best she would come up with was the retort "Are you kidding me?" I think the *Globe* would have given me a right of reply to her response. I was sorely tempted. If someone called me a police informer, I would sue. However, litigation is expensive and uncertain, even when you have a good case, so perhaps Cameron was content to make her case in the court of public opinion, something she was particularly well situated to do. I soon concluded that I had to write this book. I was working on it during the morning of February 24, 2004, when I got an email tip.

> Bill,
> You never heard this from me.
> Parties to what used to be the secret lawsuit have received notification that the RCMP has made application to the judge to have the name of the secret informant released. Why they would do this I cannot imagine, but apparently they have done so.

I called Justice Then's secretary. Yes, it was true. There was an application to reveal the name of the confidential informant. I had recently heard from a friend of a friend of Stevie Cameron – this is a small country – that she was telling people that the RCMP had cleared her of being a confidential informant and would be making a public statement to this effect shortly. Had I blown it? I wondered. Was I a party to harming an innocent person? I began to call around, letting Ed Greenspon at the *Globe and Mail* know first. Greenspon assigned justice reporter Kirk Makin to follow up on the lead. I continued to phone around. Different theories were advanced, but discussion soon focused on the two most likely scenarios. If it was Cameron, she was going to say it was all a big mistake. Perhaps the RCMP would acknowledge error as well. In that case I would be toast, not because part two of the series was inaccurate but because of the media onslaught that was sure to unfairly follow as friends of Stevie Cameron – who are legion – moved in for the kill. But I would be in even worse trouble, and more fairly, if she was not the confidential informer. What if it was someone else? What if someone else, the true police informer, had now decided to waive the privilege? Doing so would clear Cameron. The conspiracy theories advanced about the *Globe's* timing and the ordering of the stories would appear vindicated. I would look like a stooge and an idiot, Mulroney's pet. The whole thing would be a huge embarrassment. Even worse, I would be largely responsible for an injustice to Cameron, one that would be difficult, if not impossible, to set right.

Around 5:30 P.M. Kirk Makin called. "Bill, you are never going to believe this." He asked if I was sitting down, and then he told me. Cameron had admitted that she was the person identified by the RCMP as the secret informer. As predicted, her explanation was that it was all a big mistake. The RCMP, she told Makin, had made her a secret informer without her knowledge: "The fact is that I didn't know very much at the time. You think you're off the record – but when somebody decides for whatever reason to put you down as confidential informant, you don't even know about it."[6] Cameron went on to explain that the RCMP, on its own initiative, applied the confidential informant designation to her after she passed on some "pathetic scraps of information" to them when they came to see her in 1995. Cameron, however, was unable to explain away the March 2001 affidavit from Inspector Mathews, which indicated that the informant had been contacted by Justice Department lawyer Ingrid Hutton, had confirmed her status, and had refused to waive the privilege unless it was for the purposes of participating in the prosecution of Brian Mulroney. She claimed that her meetings with the Mounties were off the record and that she was not a coded informant. She did say, straight out, for the first time, "I am not, and never was, a police informant."[7] The *Globe and Mail* asked for my comment. I said I was glad that Cameron "has come forward telling the truth, sort of." I had no idea at the time that she was still lying.

There were more lies on Friday, February 27, 2004, when Cameron appeared on the CBC radio show *The Current*. It was all a horrible mix-up, Cameron told host Jane Hawtin. How did this happen? Hawtin asked. Well, Cameron explained, after the *Globe and Mail* series it "looked like ... I was indeed the person being named."[8] That was not what Cameron wrote in her *Globe* rebuttal, however. In any event, Cameron continued, it was all very confusing, so she hired Clayton Ruby. A lawyer since 1969 and a prominent bencher, one of the governors of the Law Society of Upper Canada, Ruby had an impressive curriculum vitae, having served as counsel in many important criminal law, constitutional law, human rights, aboriginal, and environmental cases. Like his client, Ruby was a lawyer with name recognition. He investigated, Cameron explained to Hawtin, and the RCMP person in charge of the case, Inspector Mathews, Cameron claimed, confirmed to Ruby that she was not a police informer. Someone, Cameron did not say who, unilaterally gave her the confidential informant designation. When Cameron learned what had happened, she continued, she had a choice: Let it blow over or tell the truth. She decided to tell the truth. Hawtin was a little sceptical.

"Right ... I mean, were you an informant or not?" "No!" Cameron replied. Cameron then asked her interviewer a question: "What do you think a confidential informant is?" Hawtin replied that she thought it was someone who gives information to the police on the condition that his or her identity not be revealed. Apparently not. According to Cameron, "every investigative reporter in the country does that." "That" was giving confidential information to the police on condition that the identity of the informer be kept secret. Cameron then rattled the sabre: "I'm getting calls now from investigative reporters who tell me that their major investigative pieces are being killed now by editors because ... They now realize the police will identify them in a trial." It was really quite astonishing, both the revelation of supposedly routine journalistic behaviour and the assertion that others engaged in this misconduct and were now having their investigations shut down. Hawtin, unfortunately, did not follow up on this lead. Cameron told her what had happened in 1995, however.

"It was back in '95. I had a new book out called *On the Take*. And they asked me about Airbus, what did I know. And I gave them documents and news clippings that were in the public record that I had either published in my book or were out ... *Der Spiegel* did a major story in Germany, *The Fifth Estate* did a major story on the CBC. What we all had were news clippings, company records, stuff like that, and material that was in the public record, in the public domain, and that's what I gave the RCMP ... And in fact, the Superintendent today in charge of the case said to me the other day that it

Clayton Ruby – one of the
high-profile lawyers advising
Stevie Cameron

is a fraction, you know, an infinitesimal part of the case that they
built against Mr. Schreiber." The RCMP, Cameron explained, came
to her house and sat in the kitchen. "It was very informal," Cameron
claimed at first, adding, moments later in the broadcast, that it was
"a formal interview, which I found very intimidating." Did you ask
the RCMP to keep your identity secret at this meeting?" Hawtin
asked. "The meeting was off the record … and I assumed it would
stay that way," Cameron replied. What were the implications of all
this for journalists? Well, Cameron explained, "I changed the way
I did business a long time ago because of this … I saw Eddie Greenspan going after me years ago, saying I was a confidential informant." That was odd: How could Cameron have possibly known
what Greenspan was saying about her in the secret trial? Her *Globe
and Mail* rebuttal indicates that the revelations of Greenspan's
"tirade" came as a bit of a shock. Perhaps she was referring to earlier correspondence from Greenspan when he asked her to confirm
her informer status.

In any event, although far from fully briefed about the underlying background, even Hawtin – who explained to me later that she
looked Cameron in the eye after the show and had the strong feeling
she was, overall, telling the truth – had difficulty with some of the

inconsistencies in Cameron's account.[9] Cameron told the CBC she had only recently learned that the RCMP considered her their informer, but, later in the show, she claimed that, because of the terrible RCMP mix-up, she stopped talking to the police a long time ago to ensure she was not further victimized by their silly mistakes. She also claimed that she was never coded: "Normally, a confidential informant has a code. So if it's "A" Division in Ottawa, you're A1234." Cameron never addressed the fact, probably because Hawtin did not know to ask her, that senior Department of Justice lawyer Ingrid Hutton called her in March 2001 and, in that call, confirmed her status as a confidential informer with her. There was a debate going on in the RCMP, Cameron explained, about whether she was really a confidential informer. In fact, the real definition of a confidential informer, she continued, was a big mystery to most people, including her. The interview concluded with Hawtin asking what next: "Nothing's going to happen. I mean, I just have to carry on. I've learned some bitter lessons, and this is ... But I learned those things some time ago. I think the only way to deal with this is to just hope that by laying out the truth and laying out the facts, that it ... this can perhaps help other journalists. I don't know. I mean, I'm happy to talk about it ... So this is why the irony of being called a confidential informant ... It's so astonishing to me." Following this interview, anyone with any knowledge about the background to the case was left with more questions than answers. Eddie Greenspan, Paul Schabas, and Kenneth Prehogan – the three lawyers on the file representing Karlheinz Schreiber, Eurocopter, and Brian Mulroney – arranged for transcripts.

Then it was time to go to court. Justice Then called a special hearing beginning at 9:00 a.m. on March 3, 2004. Stevie Cameron was not there, but her husband, David, a well-regarded University of Toronto professor who had won the 2002 Governor General's Award for Canadian Studies for his outstanding contribution to scholarship, was in attendance, and she was represented by lawyer Clayton Ruby. When the proceedings began, the Crown announced that it wished to unseal all the remaining documents. Ruby stood up and asked for standing on behalf of his client, Stevie Cameron. Eddie Greenspan objected.

The judge ran the proceedings in his usual polite, friendly, roundabout way. Ruby, it soon transpired, along with Cameron, had received advance copies of the documents the Crown wished to divulge. Ruby urged the judge to keep those documents under wraps. What Ms Cameron wanted, he explained, was for her name to be revealed, and the background information kept under seal until she was in a position to reply properly.

That was a big clue that, whatever else the Crown wished to disclose, it would not be of assistance to Cameron. The other lawyers disagreed. "Disclose it all now" was the common thrust. It was extraordinary that Cameron, who was not a party to the proceeding and who had not even been given standing before the court, had received the RCMP documents in advance. It was hard for Eurocopter lawyer Paul Schabas to keep his indignation in check. After giving everyone their say and, as is his habit, summarizing what each lawyer had said, Justice Then unsealed the rest of the documents in the Eurocopter case. Ruby then passed out a curious document he had prepared in which Cameron continued to assert that it was all a big mistake and that the RCMP documents would prove it. In fact, the arguments Ruby advanced on Cameron's behalf were correctly described in court by Greenspan as "preposterous, ludicrous, even laughable": the weight of the evidence was overwhelming.[10] Greenspan's theory had been vindicated in spades. Just about all the dots could now be connected.

According to the RCMP, Cameron first began to provide information to them in 1988. More documents were handed over by her the following year. "The attached package was received from ... Globe and Mail reporter Stevie Cameron," according to an October 10, 1989, RCMP Continuation Report. The package was various documents relating to Airbus, Frank Moores, and Karlheinz Schreiber, and to allegations of improper behaviour on their part. At the same time as Cameron was openly cooperating with the Mounties, she was under investigation by them in connection with two anonymous letters the RCMP had received.[11] "Consideration should be given to document examination of both anonymous letters, along with a control sample of Cameron's published work, to determine whether they were of the same writer; whether more than one writer produced the second anonymous letter; and whether Cameron was a contributor to either letter."[12] In 1990 Cameron continued her cooperation with investigators and passed over more materials.[13]

On January 25, 1995, Cameron met with Staff Sergeant Fraser Fiegenwald, the lead RCMP investigator in the Airbus file, along with his boss, Superintendent Carl Gallant, at Mountie headquarters in Ottawa. The meeting was initiated by Gallant, after media reports of her allegations of corruption in the Mulroney government, broadcast earlier in the month in the radio program *On the Hill*, hosted by Jason Moscowitz, were brought to his attention by the commissioner of the RCMP, Philip Murray. Would Cameron like to come in and talk to the RCMP? She accepted the invitation. The Mounties could barely wait, as their investigation had no legs. "At least for the moment," RCMP internal records dated January 19, 1995, indicate, "there is not enough evidence in Airbus file." With Cameron's imminent interview, the investigation was about to be given a significant boost.

Even before Cameron got to Ottawa, according to notes found in the RCMP papers, she began spilling the beans. The meeting on January 25, 1995, was more thorough. Inspector Gallant began the meeting by asking Cameron whether she had any proof to back up her on-the-air assertions that kickbacks had been paid in Airbus. "Mrs. Cameron did not divulge any information as a journalist; however, [she] stated she did have certain confidential information to pass along and would have to reflect on her position before discussing this any further. Mrs. Cameron eventually called back and agreed to meet investigators to discuss this information further."[14] After this interview, Inspector Gallant drafted a briefing note for the solicitor general, the first in the series, about corruption in the Airbus acquisition and about the information coming to the RCMP courtesy of Cameron. "Ms. Cameron," the briefing note sent up the chain of command reported, "offered her complete cooperation."

Anxious to develop this promising new source, Fiegenwald, entrusted with the task, followed up with a number of telephone discussions. In March 1995 the two discussed confidentiality. On March 20, 1995, for example, Cameron passed on a just-published *Der Spiegel* article claiming that $46 million had been paid by Airbus in commissions to IAL, Schreiber's company. Cameron told the RCMP on that day that "she will share with us any information she receives that suggest criminal activity on the part of former or present government officials."[15] On May 1, 1995, Fiegenwald must have felt he had hit gold. "A call was received this morning from Stevie Cameron indicating that she was in possession of all the documents that the 5th Estate and *Der Spiegel* had used to research their articles. She is willing to provide us with copies of these documents."[16] Cameron was the only source, the RCMP observed in another document, noting that "Harvey Cashore and Jock Ferguson have decided to not share the same information with us."[17] Fiegenwald and Gallant travelled to Toronto and, on May 4, met with Cameron at her house. She handed over various materials, including those materials that other journalists had shared with her and had declined to pass on to the RCMP.

Cameron told Fiegenwald and Gallant at this meeting that she was concerned about her cooperation with the police not becoming known and insisted that her identity be kept confidential as a precondition to cooperation. About ten days later, Cameron agreed to send to Ottawa copies of her "research diskettes."[18] Some time later, whether legally correct or not, given that Cameron at some point agreed to waive her privilege to participate in the prosecution of Brian Mulroney (a position notionally inconsistent with informer status), she was designated a confidential informant. The second and third briefing notes to the solicitor general soon followed. As the RCMP investigation progressed throughout the summer and fall of 1995, Cameron continued her informing activities. On November 8, 1995, for instance, she told the RCMP that she "had come up with a new lead concerning offshore accounts of Frank Moores."[19]

Normally, Cameron would have immediately been assigned a code number. Fiegenwald decided not to create a source file and number for two reasons: he did not want junior officers on the investigation to know that Cameron was his informer; and he concluded, because the file was "a secret one," with access limited to the most senior officers within the RCMP, that there was "no need for further protection." That decision was revisited several years later when Cameron was coded. "In retrospect," Superintendent Gallant reflected in 1997, "Mrs. Cameron had at that stage become an informant and should have been coded as such."[20] Henceforth, she was referred to in RCMP documents as A2948. "A" is the headquarters division of the RCMP, and the code indicates that she was handled out of Ottawa.[21] It was exactly as Cameron had explained it to CBC interviewer Jane Hawtin. It seemed she was speaking from first-hand knowledge and experience.

Cameron was extremely concerned, Fiegenwald later reported, that no one ever find out that she had become a police informer: "disclosure would be devastating to 2948's professional life and ... 2948's information had to be kept in a confidential manner."[22] Cameron explained to Superintendent Gallant that "being identified as a source would most definitely terminate her career as a reporter."[23] These concerns increased when the RCMP wanted to call her to give evidence in the disciplinary proceedings launched against Fraser Fiegenwald. Once Fiegenwald admitted to his superiors that he had leaked information about the 1995 Letter of Request to Cameron, the RCMP wanted her to testify about the improper disclosure. A meeting was arranged in Toronto, attended by Cameron, her longtime lawyer Peter M. Jacobsen, and Chief Superintendent Pierre Lange. Cameron was told that her testimony was required. She was informed that her evidence would remain confidential, but it was pointed out to her that an application had been made to the court to open up Fiegenwald's disciplinary proceedings and, as it turned out, that application was successful. Cameron would have to testify in public. After listening carefully, Cameron announced that she no longer wished to cooperate with the RCMP. She then made the following statement recorded by the RCMP:

> She originally agreed to provide the RCMP with her personal findings as a reporter under the agreement such cooperation would remain confidential. (It was pointed out this had been qualified with the exception that her cooperation might be revealed in the case of a prosecution against Mr. Mulroney. She made no response to this statement.) Following the civil suit by Mr. Mulroney, inference was drawn by some reporters that she had been a source of the RCMP. Her appearance as a witness in the internal process would confirm this inference and would damage her reputation as a reporter ... As a source she has no confidence in our ability to protect her identity should she testify in this case ... Her identification as a witness in the internal process would likely result in a mention as a source of the RCMP. For all of the above, Mrs. Cameron states that her participation in such an internal process is not possible. She emphasizes that the damage to her reputation as a journalist would be so serious as to prevent her from being gainfully employed in the future. In her opinion, it is contrary to the guarantees we had offered her during our initial contact.[24]

The RCMP was in a dilemma. It needed Cameron's evidence to make the disciplinary charges against Fiegenwald stick. But there were some larger issues that also had to be addressed. "I have no doubt," Chief Superintendent Lange wrote in his memorandum to his superiors, "that very serious civil repercussions would follow." What Lange was referring to was the inevitable lawsuit should Cameron be outed by the RCMP, given the Mounties' promise of confidentiality to her. More important, however, "it would seriously damage our reputation and future ability at recruiting confidential sources of information. I believe it would be extremely embarrassing on a very long term basis, for the RCMP to be the cause of it's own damage in that field. I have no doubt in my mind after interviewing the noted persons, that the RCMP made promises to Mrs. Cameron to the effect that her identity as a source of information would be protected in any proceedings other than criminal proceedings against Mr. Mulroney. I also have no doubt that Staff Sergeant Fiegenwald regarded Mrs. Cameron as a confidential source of information and that he is supported by management of the time in his belief."[25] In all the circumstances, the RCMP decided against making Cameron testify; they settled privately with Fiegenwald instead.

Cameron's respite was only temporary. In fact, although she had indicated in 1997 that she no longer wished to cooperate with the Mounties, RCMP and other documents indicate that she provided information to investigators as late as 2000.[26] In any event, she was contacted by the RCMP in December 2002. As a result of a Supreme Court of Canada ruling in a case called *Stinchcombe*,[27] the police, once charges are laid, are required to divulge just about everything to the accused. Criminal charges were forthcoming against Eurocopter and, when they came, that would require disclosure. Inspector Allan Mathews, now in charge of the case – Fraser Fiegenwald having been drummed out of the force – travelled to Toronto to meet with Cameron and her lawyer, Peter Jacobsen. The disclosure obligation was daunting because the police file contained 686 references to Cameron in more than fifty documents, many of which were multi-paged (but this included routine references to Cameron as a journalist). Mathews, Cameron, and, for some of the time, Jacobsen spent hours together, trying to separate what she had supplied to the RCMP as their confidential informant from her journalistic output, which the Mounties also intended to rely upon. The former, if traced back to her, would expose her status, so it had to be concealed. But the latter, being in the public domain, would have to be disclosed. There was no doubt in Mathews's mind that "Cameron understood the purpose of the meeting."[28] So too, Mathews believed, did her lawyer.

Inspector Mathews also took advantage of this December 2002 meeting to advise Cameron that her name was mentioned in the Eurocopter search warrant but had been redacted, blacked out, to protect her identity as a confidential informant. Any doubt about Cameron's confidential informant status was confirmed in further correspondence between the RCMP and Peter Jacobsen in March and April 2003. Mathews wanted to make some changes to the redactions in documents that they had agreed upon in their meeting the previous December. Jacobsen was not pleased. On May 8, 2003, on Cameron's behalf, he wrote to Crown attorney Michael Bernstein,

Peter Jacobsen – he insisted that the RCMP honour its confidentiality commitment to his client Stevie Cameron.

who would ultimately be the person making decisions on what materials were disclosed to Eurocopter, indicating: "Our client is very concerned that if the documents are released in their present form it will indicate that our client was a source, and that it would not be difficult for someone to conclude that our client was the confidential source with respect to whom privilege is being claimed by the Crown for certain documents. Accordingly, our client insists that the promise of the RCMP be honoured and that our client's reputation not be put at risk."[29]

Jacobsen also insisted that when his client Cameron became a confidential informer, the RCMP agreed that the privilege would extend to documents handed over before the establishment of the relationship. This was important because the RCMP file contained information she had provided to the force in 1988 and 1989. In simple terms, Cameron was claiming the informer privilege for everything she had given to the RCMP up to seven years before she became a confidential informer. Jacobsen's long letter is replete with references to when "the confidential informant relationship was formed," "when our client was designated as a confidential informant," "the relationship to be protected," and "the substantial risk of prejudice that our client would suffer."[30] Disclosure would lead to suffering. As Cameron told Inspector Carl Gallant in May 1995, her "identification as a source would be fatal to her career."[31]

Michael Bernstein replied to Jacobsen on June 25, 2003. If one reads between the lines, the seasoned prosecutor was more than a bit peeved. He pointed out that it was the Crown who decided what to disclose, and that the obligation on prosecutors to disclose was one of their highest duties. What Bernstein was getting at was the importance of ensuring that the criminally accused get complete disclosure of the evidence amassed by the authorities against them. Crown attorneys like Bernstein understand that their first obligation is to justice; securing convictions comes later. That means making sure that the rules are followed. A confidential informant like Cameron was, to be sure, entitled to privilege, but there were limits. She was entitled to claim the privilege for information handed over only after the confidential informant relationship was established. Cameron was not, therefore, entitled to claim the privilege back to 1988, when she began cooperating with the Mounties. Indeed, Bernstein was dubious about the claim to informer status, although he recognized that it had been extended. What was puzzling to the Crown attorney was the justification advanced: "In my years of experience, I have never come across an informer whose sole concern about being revealed was reputational ... In addition, I understand that your client was prepared to waive the privilege if Brian Mulroney were charged."[32] The point Bernstein was making was that, if Cameron was prepared to waive her privilege for this purpose, then she possibly would not technically qualify as a police informer. The reputational justification for extending the privilege, he also indicated, was suspect. Bernstein suggested that Cameron give careful consideration to her position.

Cameron might very well have been doing just that after the *Globe and Mail* went to court in the fall of 2003 to open up the Eurocopter proceedings and then published my account of Eddie Greenspan's in-court submissions: the "diatribe," as Cameron later described it. However, when Cameron went public after the series went to press, Mathews, now a superintendent, one of the highest ranks in the force, was more than a little disturbed. "On November 18, 2003," he swore in a lengthy affidavit presented to Justice Then, and later to all the parties and the public, "I watched a CBC Newsworld television broadcast called '*Inside Media*'. I made notes of this show as I watched. Ms. Cameron was a guest on the show. During the course of answering questions of the host Ms. Cameron denied having been a police informant in this matter."[33] She then, of course, followed up with her piece in the *Globe and Mail*. Mathews was even more alarmed by some of Cameron's published claims, especially the following statement:

I did not give them any names of my sources or any information that was confidential. Paid police informant? Never. A confidential informant? Are you kidding me? Did they promise to protect me? There was no promise; indeed, police assured me

Paterson, MacDougall
BARRISTERS, SOLICITORS

NO?

Box 100, Suite 2100
1 Queen Street East
Toronto, Ontario
M5C 2W5

T: (416) 366-9607
F: (416) 366-3743
Website: pmlaw.com

PETER M. JACOBSEN
Direct Tel: (416) 643-3319
E-Mail: pmjacobsen@pmlaw.com

May 8, 2003

DELIVERED

CONFIDENTIAL
SOLICITOR & CLIENT PRIVILEGE

Mr. Michael Bernstein
Ministry of the Attorney General of Ontario
Crown Law Office – Criminal
720 Bay Street, 10ᵗʰ Floor
Toronto, Ontario
M5G 2K1

This is Exhibit ___G___ referred to in the affidavit of Supt. A(Mathews sworn before me this 26th day of February A.D. 2004.

A Commissioner, Etc.

Dear Sir:

We are writing to you with respect to three letters and enclosures that we have received from Superintendent A.K. Mathews dated March 21, April 3, and April 7, 2003.

At the time the confidential informant agreement was made, our client understood that it would cover all documents that had been provided to the RCMP. At no time was our client advised that this agreement was somehow limited in time or scope. We are confident that if you speak to those who made the undertaking to our client, you will find that they placed no limitation on the promise of confidentiality.

Our client is very concerned that if the documents are released in their present form it will indicate that our client was a source, and that it would not be difficult for someone to conclude that our client was the confidential source with respect to whom privilege is being claimed by the Crown for certain documents. Accordingly, our client insists that the promise of the RCMP be honoured and that our client's reputation not be put at risk.

We will now deal with each package of documents as they were provided to us separately.

March 21, 2003

It is our understanding that each of these documents was shown to our client in December 2002 and that at that time an assurance was given that the agreed upon redactions were understood to be necessary and would be honoured in order to protect the identity of our client. At the time, Superintendent Mathews and Staff Sergeant Alexander were both well aware of the approximately date on which the confidential informant agreement was made, nevertheless, it was clearly understood by

Cameron's lawyer, Peter Jacobsen, was not confused about her status as a confidential informant.

all that the redactions proposed in these documents (some of which were created prior to the establishment of the relationship to be protected) were to be included. Further, this is consistent with my client's understanding of the nature of the agreement that was made that gave rise to the confidential informant relationship.

My client would not have entered into or co-operated with the RCMP further had the agreement not contemplated documents made prior to the establishment of the relationship to be protected.

April 3, 2003

Clearly the document enclosed under the letter of April 3, 2003 relates to information that was provided after the confidential informant relationship was formed. The information that was originally to be redacted identifies our client as providing information to the RCMP and co-operating with the RCMP on certain matters relating to the Airbus investigation. We understand that the Crown is proposing a much more limited redaction, however, this does not meet the concern of identifying our client as a confidential informant. It is hard for us to understand the logic behind the more limited redaction proposed by the Crown, when it leaves a clear indication that our client was providing information to the RCMP at a time when our client was designated as a confidential informant.

April 7, 2003

The materials sent with the April 7, 2003 letter also clearly fall within the time period after which the confidential informant relationship was formed. There is no question that the handwriting on these documents would tend to identify our client and, accordingly, it is our position that the disclosure of this material would be in direct contravention of the agreement that gave rise to the establishment of the relationship to be protected.

Conclusion

Our client co-operated with the RCMP in good faith and entered into an agreement, which our client understood to refer to all documents provided to the RCMP, regardless of whether the documents were created or provided before the establishment of the relationship to be protected.

Furthermore, at a meeting in late December 2002 with Superintendent Mathews and Staff Sergeant Alexander, our client took a very reasonable position with respect to the redactions that were proposed. I believe that both Superintendent Mathews and Staff Sergeant Alexander will confirm this.

It came as a shock to our client to understand that the redactions that our client understood were agreed upon were in jeopardy. It would appear that the documents in question are of very limited relevance and that the redactions discussed in December 2002 would not make any material difference to the defence or the prosecution. This must be weighed against the substantial risk of prejudice that our client would suffer if the Crown resiles from the redactions discussed in December 2002.

We request that you contact us prior to making any disclosure of these documents, and we look forward to hearing from you in the near future.

Yours sincerely,

PETER M. JACOBSEN

PMJ:cc

that my interview would come out at trial. I never asked to be a confidential informant and had I been in court the day Eddie Greenspan started throwing my name around, I would have said, 'Who, me?' … The only chance I had to respond to these charges came the day before all those pages went to press. I denied them vehemently.

In light of these remarks, Mathews decided he had to contact Cameron to "determine if she was in fact waiving confidential informant privilege, or was denying it ever existed, or if in fact her references to not being a 'paid' informant were intended to divert examination of a relationship with the police which she still intended to conceal under confidential informant privilege."[34]

Before Mathews could contact Cameron, her new lawyer, Clayton Ruby, was on the telephone on December 5, 2003, to the Crown attorney's office. He also left the superintendent a message over the holiday season that Cameron was reviewing her options. As part of that process, she called Mathews twice, on January 12 and 16, 2004. She offered various explanations about what had taken place – explanations that Mathews did not accept as consistent with the facts about the relationship and with his own observations and experience of it. "Ms. Cameron may find the designation of 'confidential informant' distasteful, but in my interactions with her she clearly wanted to benefit from the operational effect of the assertion of confidential informant privilege, namely that her identity and the fact of her cooperation with the police would be kept confidential from all."[35] Mathews told her that if she attempted to revoke her confidential status or deny it, he had an obligation to inform the court and would do so forthwith. He suggested that she consult a lawyer, and he laid out her only options: waive the privilege or hang tough and hold on to the privilege. Cameron told Mathews that "Clay" was advising her to hang tough. That was good advice, and she should have taken it. The whole thing would eventually have blown over, with most people believing her stories. Mathews continued, "she indicated that Mr. Ruby had told her that one of the advantages of Confidential Informer status was that she could deny it." However, she decided not to listen to her lawyer. That left Mathews with no choice but to inform his superiors, and in due course the Crown served its notice of motion of its intention to reveal Cameron's identity.[36] So began the extraordinary court proceedings on March 4, 2004, and the presentation of irrefutable evidence that Cameron was both a police informer and a liar.

Conclusion
The Difficulty in Getting to the Truth

It can be extremely difficult to get to the truth. When I wrote *Presumed Guilty* I thought I had the story right. To be sure, just about everything in that book is factually correct – there are a couple of mistakes, including one whopper – but the story itself is wrong because a key piece of information is missing: that Karlheinz Schreiber hired and paid Brian Mulroney $300,000 and that the payments were in cash and handed over in hotels. That single piece of information changes everything. No evidence has ever come forward, none whatsoever, that Mulroney had any improper involvement with Airbus, MBB, or Bearhead. What the evidence does demonstrate, however, is that Mulroney went to great lengths to conceal his commercial relationship with Schreiber: he misled the Canadian people, when his overriding obligation both as a citizen and as our former prime minister was to tell the whole truth, every single unvarnished detail, whether the government lawyers asked him about it or not. Instead, Mulroney turned the examination on discovery into political theatre and violated the public's trust. In all probability Mulroney's acolytes, who also blasted the government for its perfidy in the Airbus investigation, were, like me, unaware of the Mulroney-Schreiber commercial relationship. Mulroney's unrelenting campaign to persuade me not to publish the story about the money for one reason only – to protect his reputation – was brutal, heavy-handed, and extremely wearing.

No satisfactory explanation about the money and the commercial relationship has ever been given. Instead, all we have are mushy conflicting accounts from Mulroney and his circle. The payment was to assist Schreiber with his pasta business. It was for international introductions. It was legally privileged. It was to help out with Bearhead. The fact is that we are still far from fully informed about why the money was paid or, put another way, what exactly Mulroney did to earn it. What we do know is that, a short while after leaving office, the former prime minister took payments in cash from someone he had recently dealt with in an official capacity. There is no reason to believe that the money was a reward for official services rendered. But what exactly was it for? And how was it papered? Are there invoices, for example? If I were Brian Mulroney, the first thing I would do is give a full public explanation about the commercial relationship. It is odd, at best, that he has not done so. Call me old-fashioned, but I want former prime ministers to provide moral and ethical leadership. I want former prime ministers to withdraw from partisan politics. They should stay above the fray but enter public discourse with passion and purpose, from time to time, when the nation needs their experience, guidance, and leadership. And I want former prime ministers, if questions are raised about their conduct and behaviour before, during, or after they held office, to answer those questions by providing every single last detail, leaving it to others to decide what is relevant. Power and privacy have an inverse relationship in a democracy: the more of the former, the less of the latter. Put another way, being prime minister of Canada is the biggest trust of all, and the obligations that go with it last forever.

Mulroney did many good and important things as prime minister. History will judge him well for those accomplishments. But there was also this terrible bad judgment, not necessarily in accepting Schreiber's cash – that was, to all appearances, lawful – but in not being forthright about the circumstances of the retainer with the Canadian people.

This important story about cash payments should have been told years ago. But the *National Post*, for reasons it has never bothered to explain, suppressed it. If no one cared about the former prime minister, that would be one thing. That clearly is not the view at the *Post*. At the same time, knowing what it knew about Mulroney, that paper puffed, and continues to puff, him at every available opportunity. This too is a violation of legitimate public expectations that editorial policy will be separated from the news. Of course, the *Post* is not the only Canadian newspaper that behaves badly in this way, mixing news with editorial.

Newspapers play a vital role in our society. The insightful Alexis de Tocqueville wrote in his classic *Democracy in America*: "I am far from denying that newspapers in democratic countries lead citizens to do very ill-considered things in common; but without newspapers there would be hardly any common action at all."[1] Newspapers are strong. Individuals are weak. Newspapers, and other media, therefore counterbalance the power of the elite, the insiders who manage the workings of political parties and the government. We depend on the press and we rely on it to tell us the truth, even if the truth is at variance with the wishes of the editorial board. The *National Post* let us down.

And what about Stevie Cameron? Not only did she become a police informer, itself completely unacceptable and objectionable conduct for a journalist in a democracy, but, when called to account, she lied about her informing role and tried to explain it all away, apparently against her lawyer Clayton Ruby's good advice, as a terrible mistake. Whether she is found to meet the legal definition of an informer is a different question for someone else's book, as I do not intend to return to this particular subject again. What is absolutely incontrovertible, based on her actions and those of her other lawyer, Peter Jacobsen, is that she insisted on confidential informant status, fully appreciating the consequences to her career if her misconduct became known. That did not stop her from using her friends to defend her, telling them, as she told the Canadian people, that she was the victim, and then enlisting them in an unrelenting public relations campaign on her behalf. Even when the full story was about to come out, she still could not bring herself to tell the whole truth.

The *Globe and Mail* broke the story. The CBC had been in the courtroom for years and had fought hard, behind closed doors, to have the proceedings opened up. But it was not until the *Globe* took the unusual step of writing to the presiding judge at the end of September 2003 and asking what exactly was going on that the veil of secrecy began, slowly, to rise.

In the hearing on October 3, Justice Then turned to *Globe and Mail* lawyer Pat Flaherty: "Trying to make this process of justice work for everyone is a difficult task," the judge observed, adding, "I'm saying that much of the concern you have expressed is a concern the court has laboured with for some time." That was putting it mildly. Justice Then was exceptionally fair-minded but not very speedy. Were it not for editor-in-chief Ed Greenspon and the *Globe*, the fight over the unsealing would undoubtedly have dragged on much longer. The *Globe* forced the issue. "As you can see," Justice Then said to Flaherty, "your letter has, I think, had some results."[2] What the judge was referring to was the fact that the proceedings, thanks to the *Globe*, were secret no more.

It was interesting spending the better part of a week at the offices of Canada's national newspaper, the *Globe and Mail*. There was a seriousness and high-mindedness in all the discussions I participated in. What was the right thing to do? How best to do it was the question we repeatedly asked *Globe* libel lawyer Brian MacLeod Rogers.

Rogers, a fifth-generation lawyer, onetime newspaper reporter, and co-author of *Journalists and the Law: How to Get the Story Without Getting Sued or Put in Jail* (which was my objective), read and reread the articles. Do it this way, he would say, suggesting a better phrasing, or at least one less likely to attract a lawsuit. To his great credit, Ed Greenspon was absolutely determined to lift the veil of secrecy. "When I learned that a hearing had been conducted in the most extreme secrecy over such a prolonged period involving parties of obvious public interest," Greenspon later reflected, "not only was my journalistic curiosity piqued, I was offended as a citizen. I could not believe what was transpiring. And so the *Globe* decided, given our knowledge and the civic role a newspaper plays, that we had no choice but to intervene. Only afterward," Greenspon continued, "did I gain a fuller picture of what was at play. But the spark of our interest was lit by the principles, not by the story itself."

Opening up the Eurocopter proceedings cost the newspaper a small fortune. Greenspon was willing to take the flak for publishing a story that was as unpopular within the journalistic community as Stevie Cameron was popular. Even though the *Globe and Mail* did not bury the story about Mulroney and the money "in a subterranean crypt," to use Greenspon's own words, he too faced attack but defended the sequencing of the story and the way in which it was presented. Through it all, he demonstrated courage, integrity, and leadership. As a reward, he moved the story forward and received more than his fair share of abuse.

The Canadian Association of Journalists operates a Web site for its members. They log on and share their thoughts with each other. It was frightening to read what many of them had to say, at least where Stevie Cameron was concerned, in the aftermath of the publication of the series in the *Globe and Mail*. By and large, instead of conceding the possibility that a colleague had behaved improperly and engaging in a rational discussion, the members who contributed to the debate refused to contemplate the possibility that Cameron had done anything wrong. It may very well be that the majority of the 1,300 CAJ members, as in most organizations, stay silent. For those who spoke up, the villains were easy to identify: the *Globe and Mail*, Ed Greenspon, Eddie Greenspan, and I. How dare the *Globe* attack a journalist! How dare the *Globe* attack this particular journalist! How dare the *Globe* hire me! If some of the postings were to be believed, it was all a big set-up, a deliberate ploy intended to detract attention from the real story – that Mulroney took payment in cash. The obvious question the conspiracy theorists never both-

Brian MacLeod Rogers – the *Globe and Mail's* libel lawyer on the three-part series

ered to ask was why, if that was the goal, the *Globe* splashed the money payment on the front page. That fact was inconsistent with the stampede of the herd – to form a circle around Cameron, the evidence be damned. The police call it the "blue wall": the circling of the wagons to ensure that an officer in possible trouble is protected no matter what. This defensive stance is extremely corrosive to the system and the faith of the public in the independence of the press. Periodically, the vitriol on the Web site would be interrupted by the odd contrarian who would suggest that maybe there was something to it after all. But if the site is any indication of the state of journalism in Canada today, we are in serious trouble.

When Cameron finally acknowledged that she was the RCMP's confidential informant – although claiming, contrary to all the evidence – that it was a big mistake, the true believers rejected even that admission. Of course, few of the commentators on her behalf demonstrated any familiarity with the actual documentary evidence and the facts. Cameron relies on this ignorance and continues to try to explain away her misconduct with a series of vague, ambiguous, incoherent, and contradictory accounts, much of which many of her colleagues accept without comment or criticism, reporting them as gospel. "Never talk to the police," Stevie Cameron told a symposium on democracy and journalism at the University of King's College in Halifax in March 2004. "My encounter with the RCMP has been a disaster for me and I will never talk to the police again, and I think that would be good advice for you." It obviously serves her purpose to confuse working for the police, which she did and which was not part of her job, and dealing with the police, which is what journalists must continue to do.

In late April 2004, Cameron spoke on journalism and ethics at the Metropolitan Toronto Reference Library. "This is a perfect topic for me," Cameron began, "because I am so topical." The Friday night audience, mostly sympathetic senior citizens, appreciatively laughed as Cameron launched into her talk. Don't plagiarize, say no to "freebies," always be fair, avoid conflicts of interest, seek balance, don't be mean, snide, or vicious, resist favouritism, and protect your sources were among the pieces of advice she shared. Finally, Cameron got to Cameron. "Do you know," she asked, "the story about the RCMP ... that I gave the RCMP information?" There were scattered "no's" throughout the capacity crowd in the brightly lit atrium on the main floor. So much for the power of the *Globe and Mail*. "One of the rules of good journalism is that you don't become a confidential informant on any police force," Cameron said and then went on to explain what happened to her. "The police heard that I was looking into Airbus and called me to ask if they could talk to me about it ... I told them I would tell them what was in my book. I would only tell them what was already public ... I was one of a number of journalists that they talked to. In the spring I was formally interviewed again. Again, I only told them information that was already public ... I never had any idea that I was considered a confidential informant ... That's about all I can say about this, because otherwise Clay Ruby will march ... into this library and tear me apart."[3]

It is easy to speak before a friendly crowd. I know. When *Presumed Guilty* came out, I was invited to speak at the Albany Club, the National Club, and the University Club, three bastions of the Toronto establishment. It was as close to a "love-in" as I have ever experienced. But there is still an obligation to tell the truth, and Cameron's explanation of her relationship with the RCMP is at complete variance with the established facts.

"I will have a complete chronology of my relationship with the RCMP and this case up on my web site shortly," Cameron wrote as she joined the online CAJ debate in the early spring of 2004 (as of

July 2004 it has not appeared). "I welcome any questions from any-one ... I am not and never was a police informant ... I was never numbered, coded, paid or told I was a confidential informant."4 Unfortunately, the facts are to the contrary.5 The CAJ leadership finally entered the conversation on March 10, 2004, issuing a press release "denouncing" Cameron's actions in passing information to the RCMP in the Airbus investigation. "The issue is not whether Ms. Cameron, like many journalists, merely chatted with police officers about a certain case," said CAJ president Paul Schneidereit.

> The fact is that she fed information, whether she regarded it as worthless or not, to the RCMP in their investigation of former prime minister Brian Mulroney, the very man she severely criticized in her 1994 book, *On the Take*. Besides the obvious appearance of conflict of interest that arises here specifically, all journalists must always carefully guard against any perception that they are working for the police. To not do so weakens the credibility of all journalists.

As Schneidereit told me, "it became quite clear to us, given the position we have taken for years on the separation between journalists and the police, that we had to say something."6 To its great credit, the CAJ has recently circulated a draft code of ethics on investigative journalism for its members' comments. On relations with the police, the CAJ, institutionally, has a clear message: "Our first responsibili-ty is to the public. Journalists must not be seen to be agents of the police. When that happens we undermine our credibility and stifle the flow of future information from sensitive sources. Being seen to be affiliated with the police could even threaten our safety."7

Many journalists did not agree, and some of the journalism pro-fessors showed their true stuff. One assistant professor of journal-ism posted this contribution to the online discussion: "It seems to me that the CAJ should be there to help journalists who get into trouble, even when a journalist may have made questionable judg-ments in his or her pursuit of the truth. Helping doesn't necessarily mean exonerating or excusing, it just freaking means having a little compassion for a fellow professional." While the approach the CAJ employed left a lot to be desired in terms of natural justice and due process, it was not, as some of the other contributors to the online discussion described it, the "Salem witchhunt." Nor was it equiva-lent, as one contributor suggested, to mass-murderer Mao Zedong's cultural revolution.

Susan Riley, an excellent columnist and very good editorial writer, made this observation in the *Ottawa Citizen*: "It is supposed to be International Women's Day, yet everywhere prominent women are suffering losses. First Martha Stewart, then investigative journalist Stevie Cameron, accused of being a confidential informant."[8] Riley went on to explain, "Arguably, it is irrational to draw larger conclusions from the experiences of these disparate women," but she pointed out that Stewart, Cameron, Ottawa City Councillor Diane Deans (who lost a Liberal nomination battle), and Sheila Copps (who likewise failed to get the nod in Hamilton) were all women. "What is true is that many women are watching all of this with mixed feelings – and sadness and sympathy are a large part of the mix. Maybe it is irrational, or maybe intuitive, but the suspicion lingers that strong women are punished not only for their mistakes, but for being strong." In fact, Stewart will be punished for lying. Cameron also lied and seems to be doing a pretty good job in getting away with it. Deans lost because she was out-organized and out-smarted by a rival candidate graced with the prime ministerial blessing. Copps likewise lost because the prime minister made it clear he did not value her or her contribution to the party.

Some of the journalists who had spoken out publicly on Cameron's behalf in the fall of 2003 after the informer allegations were first raised, such as the *Toronto Star*'s Antonia Zerbisias, were initially silent after the final RCMP disclosures were made public. Her clever analytical skills were not immediately deployed when the only outcome would reflect badly on "one of our own." When Ms Zerbisias finally did comment, there was the ritual slagging of me and the *Globe and Mail*: "Why did the *Globe* rely on an outsider, author William Kaplan, no friend to Cameron, for so much of its reporting on this story?" Then she did what she could to spin the revelation Cameron's way: "The point is that the charges against Cameron – who has been celebrated for her work not only as a reporter but also as a church elder who feeds the homeless – have devastated her many fans while giving comfort to enemies of the Liberals and friends of the Brian Mulroney government ... Cameron, like Martha Stewart, made the mistake of appearing like too much of a good thing and, in an attempt to cover her tracks, ended up being buried in a dirt pile of her own making. But unlike Stewart, she broke no laws. Just many hearts."[9] It is hard to tell the truth in Canada when newspaper reporters and other journalists believe they are in a club and job number one is protecting the interests of club members. There were, however, some honourable exceptions.

As investigative reporter Michael Harris commented, "It now turns out, with full credit to *The Globe*, that there was another Stevie Cameron, the confidential informant of the RCMP known as A2948. It turns out that her denial of the fact was patently false ... It is fundamentally wrong for a journalist to work with the police while researching the same story for their own purposes. Stevie Cameron knew that. That's why she told officers in 1995, after sharing information with the RCMP since 1988, that to be outed as an RCMP informant would have disastrous consequences for her career. Cameron was wrong. What was disastrous for her career was not being outed. What was disastrous for the journalist Stevie wanted so much to be was working both ends against the middle; driving the very investigation she was herself carrying out and then lying about it. And so, Stevie Cameron ... now joins a long list of people who had a public trust and betrayed it."[10]

Globe and Mail columnist Margaret Wente got this right, as she usually does. "This is a tar baby of a story. Absolutely everyone connected to it comes out looking bad ... At the centre of it all two flawed protagonists, each utterly convinced of his or her own righteousness and the other's perfidy, locked in bitter combat for a decade. You can't help thinking that somehow they deserved each other."[11] There is something to that. It is hard to know which of the two behaved worse. Mulroney, who cares more about his place in history than he should, had his place ruined by Cameron's vitriol and overheated imagination. The title of her book, *On the Take*, and its claim of massive misconduct, is seared into the Canadian consciousness even though the book itself completely failed to deliver the goods. What should have been a public victory for Mulroney – acknowledgment that his longtime nemesis betrayed her profession and went to work for a police force so anxious to please their Liberal masters that it became complicit, in Wente's words, "in one of the most contemptible, absurd, politicized prosecutions of all time"[12] – was ruined, first, by his own actions and, second, by his failure to come forward and forthrightly take responsibility for what he had done.

Still, it must be admitted, the cash payments and Mulroney's misleading testimony at his examination on discovery have had very little public impact, when first revealed and since. In late April 2004, for example, the *Globe and Mail's Report on Business* magazine published a flattering 7,000-word profile of the former prime minister. According to journalist Konrad Yakabuski, RCMP commissioner Giuliano Zaccardelli had written Mulroney in April 2003 informing him "that he had been fully exonerated in the Airbus affair."[13] I would like to see that letter. How the commissioner of the RCMP can "exonerate" anyone is beyond me. In another letter, the commissioner did indicate that the investigation was over and "that the remaining allegations cannot be substantiated," which, of course, is not "exoneration."

Public office is a public trust, and the trust does not end with the term. Being a journalist is just as important. Our society depends on an independent free press – free from fear, free from favour, free from the police. Whether a politician or a pundit, or just a working reporter, the obligation is straightforward: tell the truth and nothing but the truth. If this sad saga tells us anything, it tells us that.

Perhaps we need new and better rules. "The greatest difficulties," John Tait, a former deputy minister of justice and dedicated public servant, wrote, "arise in that broad grey area that exists between behaviour that is clearly forbidden and behaviour that is clearly honest or ethical. Within this grey area, there is a wide continuum ranging from abuses or conflicts that are real, through those that are potential, to those that are apparent. One of the reasons why codes of conduct and appropriate ethical rules are important is precisely to address the difficulties created by this grey area: to reassure the public; and to protect public office holders themselves." The recent appointment of Bernard Shapiro as an independent ethics commissioner, responsible to Parliament and replacing an ethics counsellor serving at the obvious pleasure of the former prime minister, is an overdue but welcome step. While public service is a special calling, it comes, Tait observed, at a price: "The price is submitting to very high standards of professional conduct; accepting public scrutiny and accountability; learning to hold a public trust and to put public interests ahead of self."[14]

We need more openness and accountability in legal proceedings too. The Supreme Court of Canada has held that there is a strong presumption that any documents used to obtain judicial orders – for example, the background document used to persuade the judge to grant the search warrant in the Eurocopter case – should be public. That is part of the principle of open courts. Proceedings, including procedural steps taken by the police, should be done or made available in open court, both to protect freedom of the press and to ensure that the rights of accused persons are respected. The press needs to know what happens in court. It needs to know what prosecuting authorities are doing. It needs to protect democracy by letting the people know. And the accused needs to know in order to vindicate his or her rights. It all sounds very noble, and it is.

All documents used to obtain court orders should be made public. There must be a very high onus on the party who seeks a sealing order to justify it with clear, convincing, and absolutely compelling evidence. The section of the *Criminal Code*, the provision allowing warrants to be sealed, is a new provision. It was added to the *Code* in 1997, and it is part of an unfortunate pattern of the erosion of open court principles and an increase in secrecy of the judicial process. Like the power to order publication bans, to close the courts generally, to protect privacy in sexual offence cases, or to use initials to describe complainants in sexual assault cases, it is, at least in theory, an exceptional power.

The Ontario Court of Appeal has held in the *Toronto Star* case[15] that a justice or a judge should not seal a warrant or its supporting documents without applying the *Mentuck* test.[16] *Mentuck* was a case where the Crown wanted a publication ban to protect a "confidential sting" operation – a process that is commonly used to extract confessions. The way it works is that a suspect is lured into a fake criminal organization pretending to be the real-life Sopranos, or some "Mr. Big," with promises of riches. The target is not let in until he, and it is almost always a he, proves his worth. First he must show he has the guts to commit crimes by bragging about something serious he has done. Unbelievable as it may seem, this ruse has produced many confessions in major cases. The targets, in supposedly establishing their nerve, actually incriminate themselves by providing details directly to the police of their previous criminal misconduct. Many felons are not that smart.

The police were concerned in the *Mentuck* case that, if the public learned of this technique from the press, the sting process would stop working as the criminals cottoned on. The Supreme Court of Canada refused the request to ban publication of the sting. It developed a two-part test to be applied where publication bans are sought. The test is straightforward. The judge must first be satisfied that the ban or sealing order is necessary. The interest protected by secrecy must be shown to be not only important but impossible to accomplish without imposing the ban. In other words, the applicant has to convince the judge that there is no alternative. The judge must then decide whether conditions or editing can preserve the interest in the absence of complete secrecy and make the ban as narrow as possible. The second part of the test requires the judge to stand back and assess whether the costs of the ban or sealing order – the loss of public access to information about court processes or the denial to the accused of pertinent information relevant to his or her rights – are worth incurring, given the nature of the benefits to be achieved by secrecy.

As circumstances change, the need for secrecy can abate. It is still hard to understand why Eurocopter did not at least get some disclosure from the very beginning. Was withholding the entire lengthy Information and the hundreds of supporting documents really justified in a society of open courts and open court documents? There is an ongoing obligation on the party seeking to countermand the openness principle to justify secrecy. That is why, in the Eurocopter case, more and more documents and details were, belatedly, revealed as the case proceeded. Secrecy could no longer be justified – and it is questionable whether it was ever justified. Ironically, at the same time as the lawyers were arguing for and against continued secrecy in April 2001 and thereafter, just about every interesting fact about the case had already been broadcast by the *Fifth Estate*.

In this particular case there are other serious and troubling questions as well. Inspector Mathews insists, despite years on the file, that when he swore the Information to Obtain, he did not know that Stevie Cameron was a police informant. That is why her name appears in the list of witnesses. In February 2001, according to the inspector, he learned, because of the examination in discovery in Edmonton, that Cameron was a confidential informant and had invoked the privilege in discussion with Department of Justice lawyer Ingrid Hutton. When Mathews investigated, he found the overwhelming documentary record establishing her informer status. But he also learned that one former RCMP officer, Superintendent Carl Gallant, who was there when Cameron turned over the motherlode in May 1995, was uncertain about her true status. This uncertainty created a dilemma, and arguably it should have been brought immediately to the attention of the court.

What Inspector Mathews should have done (and he testified that he did) was tell the court that he was satisfied that Cameron was a police informer – looks like one, acts like one, says she's one. He had no shortage of evidence to offer in support, including, in due course, the correspondence from her legal counsel Peter Jacobsen, in which the lawyer repeatedly asserts police informer status on the part of the client. But because the discovery of her status was made late in the game, and because one RCMP officer, in any event, was apparently unaware of it, Mathews should also have told the court that there was one member of the force who should have known, but apparently did not, that she was cooperating with the Mounties. In those circumstances, Justice Then, in giving effect to the principle of open courts and open court documents, could have done so with open eyes on all the evidence. Informer privilege is arguably the most important privilege recognized at law, and only real informers should get it. Any issue about the technical status of an informer must be brought before the court for determination, and that means making *all* the evidence available. This failure to do so explains, perhaps, one of the reasons why the judge was so perturbed when Cameron came forward late in the game with the bogus explanation that, like Sergeant Schultz on *Hogan's Heroes*, she knew nothing, heard nothing, and did nothing (wrong). Telling the judge everything probably would not have made much of a difference, given the weight of the evidence about Cameron's police informer status and the promises of confidentiality that were repeatedly demanded, affirmed, and acknowledged, but the judge should have been immediately advised nevertheless. The assertion that he was not will be used by Schreiber and Eurocopter to cast doubt on the entire investigation, to divert attention from them. When Cameron came forward explaining it was just a terrible mistake, and then instructed her lawyer to try to prove it, the Crown had no choice but to ask Justice Then to reconvene the proceedings.

Eventually, the entire court file was opened up, including the name of the secret informant. But the case, even though it is not yet over, presents a cautionary tale. The Supreme Court of Canada has given extensive protection to freedom of the press. It has set high standards against publication bans and the closing of courtroom doors. When a sealing case eventually comes before it, the court will likely continue to insist on open documents, in the same way it has trumpeted open courts. But few cases end up in the Supreme Court. Police officers do not necessarily share the same sensitivity to an open judicial system. Nor do some of the line officers, such as justices of the peace and even some of the criminal court judges who administer the system day in and day out. Sealing orders are often granted on the basis of affidavits that contain no particulars other than general statements repeating the grounds set out in the *Criminal Code*.

Making matters worse, Parliament has, in recent years, become enamoured with secrecy. Legislation to ban the publication of the identity of some accused persons and almost all complainants in sexual offence cases, closing courtroom doors and going *in camera*, was all inspired by the sexual assault revolution that has swept criminal procedure in the past two decades. This trend, rightly or wrongly, has desensitized parliamentarians and some judges to the importance of the open court principle. Now, post–September 11, secrecy is the legislative buzzword. Changes to the *Canada Evidence Act* permit information to be suppressed in secret hearings before the Federal Court. There is a new power to conduct closed-door investigative hearings of those suspected to have evidence relevant to terrorist activities. This authority surely is contrary to the most basic principles of open courts and an open society.

Nowhere has the current challenge to the open court principle been more striking than in the Juliet O'Neill case. On January 21, 2004, O'Neill, an *Ottawa Citizen* reporter, awoke to eight RCMP officers with a search warrant who were demanding entry into her home. They stayed the better part of a day, going through every nook, cranny, and drawer in her house, before seizing boxes of documents, diaries, and contact numbers, and copying her entire hard drive. Simultaneously, they invaded the downtown Ottawa office of the *Citizen* and helped themselves to more boxes of documents. The RCMP claimed to be investigating violations of the *Security of Information Act*, the old *Official Secrets Act*, because someone apparently inside the security apparatus of the government had leaked information to O'Neill. Ironically, the leaked information did not expose Canadians to danger, but was meant to help rescue the embattled reputation of the RCMP by suggesting that Maher Arar really was a terrorist and not the innocent victim of overzealous police work that the press had been painting – a claim that precipitated the appointment of yet another royal commission.

As we know, in the ordinary course, after a search occurs where information is seized, the search warrants and all information used to obtain them are treated as public information. Yet O'Neill could not get access to anything. All the court record, the search warrants, and the affidavits had been sealed by a justice of the peace. Even the applications for the sealing orders were sealed. O'Neill found herself in the same conundrum as Eurocopter – the *Charter of Rights and Freedoms* gave her the right to challenge the constitutional validity of the search, but the sealing orders deprived her of the information she needed to effectively make that challenge. Like the Eurocopter lawyers, O'Neill's lawyers have spent days in court, and each time they reattend they force the government to turn over more and more information – information that has proved, as it turns out, to have been sealed needlessly. This exercise has cost the *Citizen* more than $100,000, and it will cost tens of thousands of dollars more before it is complete. An ordinary citizen would not be able to vindicate his or her rights in this way. These rights have been violated by an over-broad conception of secrecy on the part of government agents, one that has contributed to a culture of secrecy, contrary to the most basic principles of democracy – the principles of open courts and an open society. This culture, and many of the rules it has engendered, must be changed.

Many unanswered questions remain. Was the RCMP's case so impoverished, and its ability to obtain evidence so limited, that it had to ask Cameron for help? Actually, no. All the police had to do was go directly to the source: Giorgio Pelossi. In fact, if they had been just a little patient, Pelossi would almost certainly have come to them. He was making it his business to pass on incriminating documents about Schreiber and his friends to anyone who indicated any interest. Cameron just gave them a big head start, unnecessarily corrupting herself and the process. What the RCMP documents disclose is that A2948 fed information to her controller at the RCMP. The Mounties then used that information to continue their investigation, which had otherwise come up completely dry. They, in turn, then leaked information back to A2948 – Stevie Cameron – who published it without indicating that she was the main RCMP investigatory source. Garbage in, garbage out. As Andrew Phillips of the Victoria *Times Colonist* recently observed, "That is no way to run a police force – and it's no way to conduct journalism."[17] (Interestingly, Phillips was Cameron's boss at *Maclean's* at the time when some of her Airbus articles were first published.)

The revelation of Cameron's informer role, however, fills in many blanks, including why Cameron was always so well informed about Mulroney's lawyers' comings and goings at RCMP headquarters in the weeks leading up to the publication of the existence of the 1995 Letter of Request.[18] At least Cameron got something out of the relationship – but she did terrible damage to her profession in the process. "A journalist who serves as confidential informant is ... dangerous to the craft," William Thorsell, the former editor-in-chief of the *Globe,* wrote about Stevie Cameron. "They strike at the core of the presumed autonomy of all journalists in the perpetual crash of public events ... They poison the well, and endanger the mission."[19] Cameron sees things somewhat differently: "Thorsell hitched his wagon to the Mulroney star and I've ruined his idol. He's very stubborn and can't admit when he's wrong. He's highly susceptible to flattery. It's shameful that Bill just fell to his knees the way he did."[20]

This story is not just about a journalist who got too close to the police. It is about a journalist whose actions threatened the work of journalists everywhere by damaging the trust all journalists must enjoy with their confidential sources. This is a journalist who passed on information to the authorities that other journalists entrusted to her – to publish, not to inform. This is a story about a journalist who fed information to the police, which she then wrote about, enriching her professional reputation. While Cameron's decision to become a police informer might have been inspired by a sense of right and wrong and a desire to expose governmental corruption, her motives, at the very least, were mixed. As *Globe and Mail* columnist Lysiane Gagnon observed, Cameron was a "reporter who has tried for years to link Mr. Mulroney to criminal wrongdoings with a ruthlessness that has more to do with downright obsession than investigative journalism."[21] She got involved in a hopeless and irreconcilable conflict of interest.

In an editorial on February 26, 2004, the *Globe and Mail* asked why the RCMP pursued an investigation that had so few facts to back it up. "Why did the force continue when it had little more than dark innuendos from Ms. Cameron and other conspiracy theorists ... Just as important, if this was an investigation with a political motive, who directed the force to continue with its probe when it was apparent the case had no factual basis?" That is just not correct. There has always been a "factual basis" for the investigation and, notwithstanding the RCMP's April 2003 letter to Mulroney, there still is.

Pelossi's documents established the existence of secret commission schemes in Airbus, MBB, and Bearhead. The evidence is incontrovertible that millions and millions of dollars were deployed through middleman Schreiber and that some of that money ended up in Canada. There is no doubt, none whatsoever, that Airbus Industrie paid millions in bribes and commissions all over the world to sell its planes. There is no doubt that Airbus Industrie entered into an agreement with Schreiber's company, IAL, giving IAL a whopping commission for every Airbus sold in Canada. According to a German indictment, more than US $22 million came Schreiber's way between September 1988 and October 1993 as a result of the Air Canada acquisition.[22] It has been clearly established that the agreement between Airbus and IAL provided for its cancellation in the event of a major change in the Canadian government. The last Airbus from the 1988 purchase was to have been delivered by the end of September 1993, close to the date when the last commission was paid. The timing of the final commission payment and the change of government was undoubtedly a coincidence. Nevertheless, it has been convincingly established that through IAL Schreiber received millions of dollars in Airbus funds. Clearly, there was a "factual basis" for the RCMP investigation.

As soon as Mulroney found out about the 1995 Letter of Request that called him a criminal and asserted, without any evidence whatsoever, that he had profited from the Air Canada purchase, he retained Roger Tassé and sent him to Ottawa to see the commissioner of the RCMP. Mulroney offered to come to Ottawa to answer any of the Mounties' questions. He offered to bring all his financial records and income tax returns. He offered everything, but was told that the force was just beginning its investigation. If the offer had been accepted, the investigation could have significantly advanced. The RCMP presumably would have learned about the Mulroney-Schreiber business relationship.

But the offer was turned down. It is not clear why, but one is often left wondering whether Dudley Doright is a cartoon or a documentary. Tassé was certainly not told that much of the relevant information that had been collected to that point came courtesy of Cameron. He did not know then, nor did the *Globe and Mail* know on February 26, 2004, when it wrote its editorial – the RCMP's disclosure of A2948's informant file came later – that the commissioner of the RCMP at the time, Philip Murray, had signalled to the investigators his personal interest in continuing the investigation. Why was that? Moreover, this indication of interest from the very top of the force is at variance with what Murray said when Tassé came calling. It also completely contradicts the statement of defence filed by the RCMP in the Mulroney lawsuit, where the claim was made that the commissioner was not involved in the investigation or in the forwarding of the Letter of Request. Murray testified before a parliamentary committee that there had been no political interference in the Airbus investigation from anyone in the Liberal government. Maybe. But was he involved or not? Certainly, the relationship between the RCMP and the Prime Minister's Office while Jean Chrétien was prime minister would benefit from further exploration.[24]

With hindsight, the RCMP's defence to the lawsuit also merits some new attention.[24] For years there had been rumours of payoffs in the Airbus sale to Air Canada. No formal investigation was begun, the RCMP indicated in its pleadings, because the force believed that it "could not begin an investigation based simply on rumours in the media." The situation changed in 1995, the RCMP continued, when "vast information" about the secret commissions arrived at RCMP headquarters. A "serious and meticulous investigation" was launched, culminating in the sending of the 1995 Letter of Request. It is now clear that Cameron passed on much more than some "pathetic scraps" of readily available information. The "Grey Book," introduced into evidence before Justice Then in June 2004, is filled with private banking and other corporate records. Inspector Mathews testified that the RCMP could not have readily obtained these important documents "without a great deal of legal intervention." They certainly were not in the public domain. Moreover, Cameron's name is mentioned hundreds of times in the RCMP file, and she spent several days, together with her lawyer, helping the RCMP redact more than fifty documents. Clearly the investigation was relaunched solely on her say-so and initially based on the materials she provided. It seems that not too much information went the other way, although one important detail certainly did: that Mulroney was named in the 1995 Letter of Request.

What are especially revealing are the steps Cameron took to avoid detection, beginning with the betrayal of her control in the RCMP, Fraser Fiegenwald. Cameron had her lawyer, Peter Jacobsen, call Harvey Strosberg, Allan Rock's lawyer, with the news that Staff Sergeant Fraser Fiegenwald had advised Cameron that Mulroney was named in the 1995 Letter of Request. Ironically, Cameron, who had been stalking the Mulroney family for years, was at least partially responsible for scuttling the government's defence of scrupulous good faith in the drafting and sending of the letter. That leak led to the settlement of the lawsuit, on favourable terms, for the man Cameron had spent years trying to expose. What would be interesting to know is whether Jacobsen also told Strosberg that Cameron was informing for the RCMP. Cameron had been subpoenaed by Mulroney to testify in the lawsuit and, if knowledge of her informer status had become known outside the RCMP, the government would have had even more incentive to settle with Mulroney before his lawyers called her to the stand and put her informer status in issue. No matter what anyone thought of the former prime minister, the Canadian people would not countenance a police investigation based on information supplied by a journalist with a known vendetta.

Cameron knew that Mulroney's legal team intended to pose that question. After receiving her subpoena requiring her to travel to Montreal and testify, Cameron told reporters that it would be a "big fat zero for them." Behind the scenes, as we know, she had Quebec City lawyer Michel Jolin contact Jacques Jeansonne, one of Mulroney's counsel, who replied that Cameron would be extensively questioned on her RCMP relationship. Jeansonne, because of some pre-trial procedures leading up to the lawsuit, was already convinced that Cameron was a police informer. Cameron did an end run on the whole thing: she got Jacobsen to call Strosberg with the news about the Fiegenwald leak. At least, that is all we know so far. In comparing Mulroney and Cameron, it is hard to tell which one is more crafty. Reluctantly, one must admire their ability to think ahead.

In April 2003 the RCMP finally folded its tent and announced that the Airbus investigation was over. Why? Quite possibly it was fatigue and a realization that it would never be able to build a case. A new political caravan was pulling into town. There was no longer any need to please Jean Chrétien. There was no reason to believe that his successor had any interest in getting Mulroney. What was odd about the announcement was that Schreiber, twice, offered through intermediaries to cooperate – in return, presumably, for the Canadian government's turning down the German extradition request. The Mounties were not interested. It is somewhat puzzling. If Schreiber was prepared to sing, why not, at the very least, let him audition? Alternatively, the RCMP may have concluded that there was no evidence of wrongdoing in Airbus and Bearhead. "I was part of the decision-making process," Inspector Allan Mathews told me, "and there was a rationale." What was it? "No comment."[25] Likewise, the commissioner refuses to elaborate on any aspect of the case.[26]

What were the Mounties possibly thinking? Unsolved murder investigations are not ended – no unsolved criminal investigations are. They become cold files, not dead files – except this one. At the end of the day only Eurocopter and two MBB officials in Germany were ever charged with anything. The Germans, Kurt Pfleiderer and Heinz Pluckthun, declined the Canadian invitation to attend the preliminary inquiry, which began in September 2003. An Interpol arrest warrant for the duo was issued, but as long as they remain in Germany, the chances of their being brought to face any charges in Canada are nil. The preliminary inquiry, under way before Justice Paul Bélanger in Ottawa, is not expected to be concluded until some time in 2005.

The Crown has an excellent chance of persuading Justice Bélanger that there is enough evidence to commit the company to trial. Not that there is a lot of evidence, but the legal test for committal is extremely low: Is there a scintilla of evidence? If there is, the judge has to remit the case for trial. How the company could be party to a conspiracy that took place, without its knowledge, between its parent company, MBB, and IAL is, conceptually, hard to understand. At worst, there was a breach of contract. The Canadian people got the helicopters for the negotiated price. Surely the Crown might be expected to deploy its resources more fruitfully in cases where there is a greater chance of success. Schreiber has been subpoenaed to give evidence. On his behalf, lawyer Eddie Greenspan consented, provided the Crown agreed to ask him only about the helicopter deal. Crown counsel Michael Bernstein said no – everything was fair game. That has sent Greenspan to the courts, where he is trying to quash the subpoena. He might succeed in persuading a judge that it violates his client's constitutional rights to require him to give evidence in Canada, when that evidence might be used against him overseas. Schreiber, obviously, is not anxious to answer questions under oath.

Karlheinz Schreiber is wanted in Germany to face tax evasion, bribery, and other charges. The extradition proceedings began on January 25, 2000. As expected, Schreiber lost round one on May 18, 2004, when Mr Justice David Watt committed him for extradition. But it is just the end of the beginning, as the fight to keep him in Canada will continue. The point must be made that Schreiber is a Canadian citizen, and his extradition raises important legal issues. Extradition agreements between countries require reciprocity. The Germans never extradite their nationals and they would refuse to extradite anyone to face allegations of income tax evasion. Why then should Canada extradite one of its citizens to Germany when the Germans would refuse an identical Canadian request?

The revelations about Cameron's role are already being used by Schreiber's attorney, Greenspan, and Eurocopter's lawyer, Schabas, to muddy the waters. Their position is entirely predictable. The proper administration of justice requires a stay of all proceedings, including the preliminary inquiry in Ottawa on the Eurocopter charges and the extradition request. There will be bells and whistles, lots of smoke, some good newspaper quotes, and much fun in different courtrooms. There will be appeals and motions. There will be learned legal submissions in the court and more colourful ones outside the court. Delay and divert – that's the approach. It is legal trench warfare for the rich; no one else has the resources to resist the power of the state. Hopefully, the important legal issues at stake in the extradition will be carefully considered apart from all the other commotion. But a stay? That will be ordered only if the abuse would undermine the fairness of the proceeding.

Even if the RCMP erred in not notifying the court in a timely and normative way that Cameron was a police informer, or even if she is found not to qualify technically for the designation – given her willingness to testify against Mulroney – despite her repeated claiming of the privilege and her insistence on confidentiality as she handed over materials, the consequences are not likely to be considered so shocking that they would undermine public confidence in the administration of justice and require that the legal proceedings be brought to an end. Surely, corrupting a willing journalist is insufficient to bring important legal proceedings to a halt. At the same time, there is no predicting what other evidence might emerge. Round one, in any event, did not go either Schreiber's or Eurocopter's way. On April 9, 2004, Ottawa Justice Gerald Morin denied Schreiber's request for an adjournment of the previously scheduled hearing considering whether he should be compelled to testify in the Eurocopter preliminary inquiry – the judge was not convinced by Schreiber's argument that the evidence he gave might be used against him in Germany, and so he should not be compelled in Canada. On that same day, in a different Ottawa courtroom, Justice Paul Bélanger rejected Eurocopter's request, also for an adjournment, pending the outcome of the ongoing Eurocopter proceedings in Toronto scheduled for the end of May 2004, when Inspector Mathews was called to testify about who, in the RCMP, knew what and when.[27]

This proceeding was extremely unusual. Initiated by Justice Then on his own motion, the purpose of the hearing was to determine whether the court had been misled by the RCMP assertion, made late in the day, that Stevie Cameron was a confidential informant. Justice Then was determined to discover the bona fides of that claim "in circumstances where Ms. Cameron has recently disavowed any status as a confidential informant." In a nutshell, he wanted to make sure that the belated RCMP claim was legitimate and that the integrity of the court process remained unsullied. Obviously, had she said nothing, had she followed lawyer Clayton Ruby's advice, none of the evidence about her police informer role would ever have come forward. There would have been clues – good ones – and well-founded suspicions, but no smoking gun. However, as a result of Justice Then's inquiry, even more materials and information documenting her informer activities would soon be filed in court.

Just before the proceedings began, Justice Then, on May 25, 2004, rejected applications by Mulroney and Schreiber that they be allowed to participate in the new phase of the proceeding. He turned down their requests, reasoning that they had nothing to add to the process. It was a strange decision, particularly in Schreiber's case, as his counsel, lawyer Eddie Greenspan, had made the most important contribution to date in uncovering the truth. When the case finally began, it was déjà vu all over again. As usual, the hearing went from one day to the next and, at the end of June 2004, no end is even in sight. Crown attorney Bernstein left no stone unturned, the lawyers fought about everything, molehills were transformed into mountains, and the judge judged. Inspector Mathews testified at length, one day after another, as the Crown led him through a detailed chronology of what he knew and when.

When Eurocopter lawyer Paul Schabas got his chance to ask questions, he tried to poke holes in the Crown's case in pursuit of his objective of getting the charges against Eurocopter thrown out. If he could establish RCMP wrongdoing, he would lay an evidentiary foundation for attacking the charges themselves. While he made some progress around the outer edges, it was clear to everyone sitting in the courtroom, including me, that Inspector Mathews was one honest cop, diligent, responsible, and forthright. There is no predicting legal outcomes, but, based on the evidence elicited in court, it is inconceivable that the judge will conclude anything other than that the RCMP and the Crown acted completely properly.

Fraser Fiegenwald, evidently, did not follow proper procedures when Cameron became a confidential informant – procedures relating to coding and oversight. But that did not mean that the status had not been requested and granted. The only other mistake that was possibly made was in not telling the judge that a retired Mountie, interviewed years after the events in question, was uncertain about her status. But given the weight of documentary evidence confirming her informing activities and the repeated assertion by her and her lawyer that she was a confidential informant entitled to protection against disclosure, not to mention Mathews's own experience of the relationship once he found out about it, this omission, if it could be called that, was inconsequential and certainly not reflective of a lack of good faith by anyone.

As Inspector Mathews testified in May and June 2004, he painted a very unattractive picture of Stevie Cameron. Mathews dismissed comments attributed to Cameron after the fact – that she was trying to protect journalists who had provided her with information – as inconsistent with the facts as he personally knew them. Cameron displayed interest in protecting one person only – Stevie Cameron – the inspector told the court. Moreover, Mathews testified that he was shocked when Cameron, turning on her own longtime lawyer, attempted to repudiate Peter Jacobsen, who had written to the Crown on her behalf claiming confidential informant status and demanding that it be respected. Indeed, in a letter filed with the court, Mathews observed, Cameron claimed that Jacobsen had written to the Crown asserting confidential informant status without her knowledge and approval. That, of course, was not true, as Clayton Ruby conceded in a follow-up letter to Inspector Mathews.

"Dear Superintendent Mathews," the March 2, 2004, letter from Ruby began, "I am writing to follow up ... [on an earlier letter from Cameron to Mathews in which Cameron stated] that she had never sought confidential informant status nor authorized anyone to seek it on her behalf." Ruby was writing now "to correct and clarify that ... statement." There was an arrangement to keep Cameron's identity and activities confidential: "Ms. Cameron's lawyer wrote to you to make these arrangements. Ms. Cameron authorized him to do so ..." One had the feeling of a desperate person grasping at straws instead of acknowledging a mistake, apologizing, and moving on.

Accepting responsibility was not, however, on this particular buffet, where denial continues to be the daily special. Ironically, Inspector Mathews also testified, by the time Eurocopter was finally charged, the evidence Cameron had supplied had become peripheral, to use an unfortunate word. However, while Cameron's involvement did not, ultimately, prove all that important, other than giving the stalled investigation new life in early 1995 when she handed over key documents the Mounties would otherwise have found difficult, if not impossible, to obtain, she had frequent contact with the RCMP over many years. One cannot help thinking, what a waste of a career.

Meanwhile, Cameron continues to deny that she was a confidential informant, telling the Medico-Legal Society of Toronto on June 2, 2004, for example, that the RCMP had made a big mistake and everything would be corrected soon when her lawyer got to start asking the questions. Unfortunately for Cameron, the "mistakes" remain uncorrected, even after her lawyer, Clayton Ruby, got his chance in court. For several hours on the last day of June 2004, he put question after question to Inspector Mathews in what turned out to be a completely futile attempt to get the long-serving RCMP officer to agree that since he was confused about Cameron's status, then it was understandable that she would be too. Unfortunately for Ruby, his cross-examination plan failed miserably. The inspector testified over and over again that no one was confused about anything: he knew that Cameron was a confidential informant, she knew it, claimed it, demanded it, threatened to sue when there was talk of waiving it, and her police informer status was confirmed by her lawyer, Peter Jacobsen, in writing. By the end of the day, the only interesting piece of information Ruby was able to extract was that when Cameron was belatedly coded, she was not informed about the code number the RCMP assigned. She did not need to be advised, Inspector Mathews testified, because by this time she had stopped passing on information to the police. Ruby was in a difficult situation, so was left with little to do but poke some jabs at his arch-rival, Eddie Greenspan, and then, in a final flourish, to suggest that Stevie Cameron was simply a good citizen doing her duty by helping the police. When Justice Then suggested that Ruby might like to call his client to give her side of the story, Ruby quickly declined the opportunity, even when Justice Then made it clear that he would be left with little choice than to believe the largely uncontradicted evidence about her informing activities.

Cameron was not in court to view the efforts made on her behalf, but her disinformation campaign continues, aided by the same large coterie of friends that denounced the *Globe and Mail* in the fall of 2003 for reporting on the earlier assertions made in court. Indeed, a Friends of Stevie Cameron committee was formed to help her pay legal bills of $117,000 – and rising. "Ms. Cameron," the blog spot asserts, "says she neither asked for nor consented to designation as a confidential informant:

> This is a highly damaging accusation. The ethical compromises and breaches implied by the confidential informant label could be fatal to any reporter's career, and with some justification. We report on the state – we are not the state.
>
> The accusations were prominently reported in the press and even earned her a swift condemnation from an association of her peers, the *Canadian Association of Journalists*. The publicity and accusations have wounded her deeply.
>
> The issues are complex, the accounts contradictory, the motivations for some participants seemingly Byzantine. This is not the place to adjudicate them.
>
> Ms. Cameron has denied any wrongdoing and fought back, at great cost to herself.
>
> Stevie's friends are people who don't know the whole story yet, but believe passionately that one of our colleagues who has served her country and her profession so well, should not face ruin as she tries to get her side of the story out.
>
> And so we gather to lend our support.

Friends of Stevie were then invited to a party to raise money for her, with tickets $100 each. But there was a little more disinformation:

Why is this happening?
Good question. More than ten years and two books after Stevie Cameron shone a bright light into some very dark doings in this

country's civilian and military aircraft procurement processes, she finds her career and reputation under attack from those she exposed. They are not suing her, because they'd lose, rather they're using the protection from libel offered by the court to attack her name, her reputation, her career. She has no choice but to use the courts to fight back. The Friends of Stevie Cameron are offering support to a fellow journalist in her time of need.

Given all the exhibits and sworn testimony, not to mention accurate newspaper accounts, the Bourque Newswatch might, I suppose, be forgiven for calling the fundraising affair a "moochathon." The *Star*'s Antonia Zerbisias immediately responded and, characteristically, again attacked me in print with an absurd, nonsensical, and defamatory column that displayed a profound ignorance of any of the underlying facts. This time I wrote to her and asked why, given well-established journalistic rules requiring fairness and balance, she never bothered to contact me and request my side of the story before attributing unflattering conduct, motives, and behaviour to me.

More important, however, is the effect of all the various proceedings, dating back to 1995, on our system of justice. As an internal RCMP history of Project Airbus observes, "With the onslaught of time and events, the criminal investigation was increasingly sidelined. Tremendous resources had been marshalled in opposition to the [Mulroney] civil suit, the internal [Fraser Fiegenwald] investigation, [and to ensure that] political masters and senior management were properly resourced. Such was not the case with the criminal investigation."

One thing is for sure: no evidence has ever emerged that Mulroney had anything to do with Air Canada's decision to buy Airbus planes, other than his government's approval of the recommendation from the Crown corporation. To be sure, there remain unanswered questions about the transaction. Airbus Industrie was paying bribes all over the world to secure markets for its product, and millions in commissions were paid as part of the Air Canada transaction – with much of that money earmarked, according to Schreiber's records, for Canadian payments. Why did the Crown corporation choose a supplier, instead of leaving that decision to the private sector shareholders who would soon be taking over? Boeing seemed to be the shoo-in. What happened there, especially in the run-up negotiations leading to the Free Trade Agreement? How did that American company lose its home-field advantage to European Airbus? And why? Perhaps it was very straightforward: Airbus had the better product.

While Mulroney ultimately declined to give his government's green light to the Bearhead project, his officials did sign a letter of intent with Thyssen just before the 1988 election. Thyssen money, in the millions, began to flow soon after. Where did that money go? Schreiber considered suing over the letter of intent and even got an opinion from a leading counsel that the German industrial giant had a good case. Schreiber wanted to proceed with the action, but Thyssen said no. Some losses are best just written off. The commissions in the helicopter deal were, in contrast to the other deals, chump change. So what was it all really about?

There are a number of interesting theories about the movement of Schreiber's money, to Mulroney and to others. One of them is that Mulroney needed money, so Schreiber gave him some. "I can tell you," Mulroney told me on June 4, 1998, "when I first started out, I needed … money quite badly." There were certainly indications at the time. In the summer of 1993 the Mulroneys were moving back home to Montreal. Between April and October, Boyd's Moving made many trips between Ottawa and Montreal with trailers filled with Mulroney stuff, as they transported their 24 Sussex lifestyle to Westmount. Initially they made a deal to sell sixty-five pieces of furniture, along with bedding, carpets, wallpaper, curtains, and assorted knickknacks, to the government for $150,000, but the media got wind of the arrangement and a public outcry erupted, forcing the Mulroneys to rescind their offer and return the government cheque.[28] Schreiber was aware of Mulroney's financial situation the day he went to visit him at Harrington Lake, and he was more than willing to help out.

Still pitching his Bearhead project, Schreiber believed the former prime minister would be an excellent ambassador for the company – at home and abroad – with its peacekeeping vehicles and other products. "I am aware that many of the companies that Brian Mulroney is involved with today have similar reasons for employing him," he told me. "After Mr. Mulroney left office he was looking for clients to generate income that, in my opinion, he badly needed in those days. When I look back, I have to say that I like Brian Mulroney. I liked him from the beginning … I was introduced to him at the request of Mr Strauss through Walter Wolf and Michel Cogger at the time that he was president of Iron Ore. From then on I was involved to support his political activities … Whatever comes, whatever shows up in the public as negative about me coming from Mr

Brian Mulroney, Karlheinz Schreiber, and Helmut Kohl – together
in happier days

Mulroney or his circle will not excite me because he has done something that I begged him to do, and that is to support the reunification of Germany. At the time, François Mitterrand and Margaret
Thatcher were not in favour. George Bush, James Baker, and Brian
Mulroney were the ones who supported the idea of reunification and
made it happen with the governments of Mikhail Gorbachev and
Helmut Kohl."

Canada and Mulroney played a part in German reunification,
although not, perhaps, as significant a role as Schreiber believes.
Former president George H. Bush recalls in *A World Transformed*
(co-written with Brent Scowcroft) various discussions with the Canadian prime minister on German reunification – an initiative that,
with certain reservations, Mulroney supported. When Soviet leader
Gorbachev agreed in late September 1989 to negotiate Bush's proposed Open Skies Treaty, Mulroney offered Ottawa as the first site
for talks. The Ottawa Conference took place February 12–24, 1990,
attended by all member nations of the Warsaw Pact and NATO.
Before the participants turned their attention to Open Skies, however, discussions were initially dominated by the German question. On
February 13, 1990, the foreign ministers of the Federal Republic of
Germany, the German Democratic Republic, the United States, the
Soviet Union, Great Britain, and France reached agreement on the
start of the "two-plus-four" talks, which culminated in reunification
later that year. When Mulroney was examined in Montreal as part

of his lawsuit against the RCMP and the federal government, he mentioned Schreiber's interest in German reunification.

"Whoever reads this," Schreiber continued, "should understand that I would have done a lot more for him if he had asked me ... The most important thing he ever did for me and for the German people and for the world was the final release of 17 million Germans who were in a Communist jail ... Even if he were to call me an asshole every day of the week, I do not know why he would do so. If he needs my help, I am there, based on what he did for Germany. If he needed $2 million at the time, I would have given it to him. I was appalled by his financial shape and I would do whatever I could to help him. And if he asked me tomorrow, I would do it again."[29]

That is not too likely. By all accounts Schreiber and Mulroney no longer speak to each other. Mulroney clearly regrets his dealings with Schreiber. To be sure, in the summer of 1993 he had no way of knowing that he was going to become a great success in the private sector. In the meantime there were bills to pay and an expensive lifestyle to maintain. Quite consistent with these circumstances, Mulroney agreed to go to work for Schreiber – and he did so. But the money that Schreiber paid and Mulroney received pales in comparison to the many millions of dollars that moved in and out of Schreiber's various Swiss bank accounts. It does not come even close to adding up to the millions in commissions identified in Schreiber's own records for distribution in Canada. The question remains: except for the $300,000 that we now know about, and the relatively modest MBB payments acknowledged by Frank Moores, where did the money go? Millions and millions were paid in commissions in Airbus, MBB, and Bearhead. Perhaps the different commission schemes served different purposes.

One possible explanation is that some of the commissions were part of an elaborate mechanism to redirect money to the Strauss family for its business losses in Alberta, losses incurred by Schreiber with investments that had gone bad. Another theory, one broadcast by the CBC's *Fifth Estate*, is that the offshore money that helped dump Joe Clark had to be repaid and that it was reimbursed through secret commissions. These commissions eventually made their way back to the German Christian Social Union and the Christian Democratic Union parties, which had helped to fund the initiative to get rid of Clark in the first place.[30] Schreiber did, after all, hand over a million German marks in a parking lot to a CDU official, igniting the major German political scandal of his generation. There could be no commissions without contracts, and there was one big and one small contract: Airbus planes and MBB helicopters. Another possibility is that the money was paid to purchase influence. Schreiber's German lawyer testified as much.

Giving evidence in the Schreiber extradition hearing in Toronto in December 2002, Olaf Leisner, who had earlier told the *Fifth Estate* pretty much the same thing, testified that, until 1999, paying bribes to secure export business was perfectly lawful in Germany, provided they were paid to "foreigners of influence" who could help secure contracts. Mr Justice Watt, who was presiding over the hearing, expressed surprise, asking the German lawyer to confirm that bribes were really legal in Germany. They were at the time, and all Schreiber ever did was comply with the law. Outside the court, Leisner told reporters that Canadians were among the influential foreigners who had received legal bribes between 1988 and 1993. When asked who exactly he had in mind, Leisner replied that he knew only "parts of their names." He insisted that Schreiber was only a conduit for Liechtenstein trustees who represented European companies in those transactions.[31] Obviously, it is in Schreiber's self-interest to have his German lawyer characterize the payments in this way.

Whatever happened, Mulroney takes no responsibility. "What I can tell you now is that I have had poor judgment from time to time as Prime Minister. Being introduced to Karlheinz Schreiber by Elmer MacKay and Fred Doucet is one of the biggest mistakes that I regret the most. I know Schreiber peripherally. If I had my druthers I would never have seen a guy like that. I was told that he was a prominent person from Alberta trying to sell a legitimate and lawful piece of equipment. If you accumulated all the sorrow over all my life, it does not compare to the agony and anguish that I have gone through since I met Schreiber ... I did say that I regretted meeting Karlheinz Schreiber and that is true. You had better believe it. I should never have been introduced to him because the people who introduced me to him didn't know him."[32] But what about the money? "Anyone who says anything about that will be in for one fuck of a fight."[33]

Maybe. It would certainly be interesting. Even more about this story would then come out, including what exactly Mulroney did do to earn the payment in cash. Who else attended the meetings when the money was exchanged? What was discussed? If the matter ever does end up in court, one thing is certain: no relevant questions will go unasked.

Afterword

NORMAN SPECTOR

Bill Kaplan set out in 1998 to write a book about a botched investigation into alleged criminal activity by Brian Mulroney. He ended up with a bestseller on his hands – *Presumed Guilty* – and having to write a second book to correct the first. As readers of *A Secret Trial* will appreciate, there's still no end to the questions about "Airbus" – itself convenient shorthand for two controversial procurement decisions and one that never got off the ground. Yet, in discovering the difficulty of ferreting out and telling the truth about this slice of history, Kaplan has uncovered how Canada works below the radar screen – at least as I've experienced during my career in government and the media. What emerges, however, is not what most of us learned in high school.

As I write these words in July 2004, I have yet to meet Kaplan, and I wouldn't recognize his voice if he phoned today. All our exchanges have been by email, beginning in 1997 when he interviewed me for *Presumed Guilty*. I was pleased when he sent me a complimentary copy of the book, but less pleased after reading his criticism of me. "What would you have done with the RCMP's request not to tell anyone about the investigation?" I asked. "I would have told my former boss," he replied, "out of loyalty."

That's where matters stood until Friday, November 6, 2003. Like hundreds of thousands of *Globe and Mail* readers, I was fascinated by Kaplan's front-page article about a secret trial involving Eurocopter. Having worked in Mulroney's office on Schreiber's "Bearhead" proposal to build light armoured vehicles in Cape Breton, I had a particular interest in the long exposé – and a nagging premonition about what was to come. A few days later, after finishing the series, I asked Kaplan whether he stood by his criticism, but probably should have resisted the temptation. Though he quickly conceded the point, he also asked for help with this book, *A Secret Trial* – for the sake of history, for the sake of the truth.

In the past, I'd resisted requests by several publishers to write my memoirs. In reviewing a collection of my Mideast columns published in 2003, Robert Fulford and Norman Webster asked for more of the autobiography contained in the introduction. Kaplan's request was timely, and it provided an interesting framework to explore media and government issues I'd been thinking about for many years. This afterword is my contribution to his book – and, more important, to history and the truth.

THE CONTEXT

Even after working for Brian Mulroney, I cannot say for certain why he wanted to be prime minister. He didn't seem to have strong ideological views, nor did he have any particular policy agenda. In the 1983 Tory leadership review, he campaigned against free trade and attacked Joe Clark for being weak on Quebec; the rest, as they say, is history. The Conservative government's fiscal agenda, which Michael Wilson pursued during his long tenure as finance minister under Mulroney, was waiting in the deputy minister of finance's drawer when the Tories arrived in Ottawa the next year.

Winning was important, ego and social status were no doubt involved. From a modest background himself, Mulroney and his family had very expensive tastes. He was broke when he left office, according to a former colleague. In the words of another who stayed in touch, he did the stupidest thing in his life by accepting cash payments from Karlheinz Schreiber. Kaplan concludes that it's never been clear "why the money was paid or, put another way, what exactly Mulroney did to earn it." However, he's troubled that though "no evidence has ever come forward, none whatsoever, that Mulroney had any improper involvement with Airbus, MBB, or Bearhead ... Mulroney went to great lengths to conceal his commercial relationship with Schreiber."

Kaplan's outrage comes through as the story of the payments unfolds. The challenge he faced in exposing the truth was compounded, however, by an unlikely source – the media. What Kaplan learned about journalists may surprise many Canadians, particularly those who came of age during the Watergate era. What he uncovered, however, may help these baby boomers understand why their children and grandchildren, in addition to turning away from party politics, are tuning out the mainstream media.

Better at dishing it out than receiving it, many reporters, in my experience, tend to be notoriously thin-skinned and loath to admit error. Ottawa-based journalists, who operate in a unique hothouse, are a special class. Relative to the Canadian population, the parliamentary press gallery harbours disproportionately fewer Conservative and more NDP voters. Unlike Foreign Service officers, these journalists are not rotated to other postings before "going native" in the town that lives well off public spending. More than a few are married to, or in longstanding relationships with, senior government officials, so they have a personal reason to be anxious about a change in government.

Stevie Cameron, married to a senior public servant who had done well in Pierre Trudeau's Ottawa, was no exception in the press gallery when the Conservatives arrived in the Liberal town in 1984. At various points in my career I'd worked closely and well with her husband, David. I visited their home for dinner when I lived in Toronto. After reading her phenomenally successful book *On the Take*, I was puzzled why she had not asked to interview me about my experience as chief of staff to Brian Mulroney.[1] We had, after all, talked in 1986, and she had written about my appointment as secretary to the Cabinet for federal-provincial relations.[2]

Kaplan, who is by no means naïve, seems surprised at the difficulty he encountered in criticizing her. Even after she was outed, many of Cameron's colleagues circled the wagons to protect her. Ironically, they helped bury an explosive story about the former prime minister she had been stalking for years. Fortunately, in *Globe and Mail* editor-in-chief Edward Greenspon, Kaplan found a man of integrity. Canadians, in turn, owe Kaplan a debt of gratitude for his persistence and honesty.

An increasing number of Canadians are exiting the political system. Only 60 per cent of registered voters turned out in 2004, compared to 64 per cent in the 2000 federal election, 67 per cent in 1997, and nearly 70 per cent in 1993. Nearly all the decline is explained by apathy in the eighteen-to-twenty-four age bracket. Some analysts and interest groups, including the Law Reform Commission of Canada, attribute the decline to "wasted votes" and advocate various forms of proportional representation or preferential balloting. The Russian system, which requires that an election be re-run with new candidates if the turnout falls below 50 per cent, would more effectively force politicians to address Canadians' "pox on you all" attitude.

Voters are cynical because they think their votes don't matter.

They don't see the relevance of party politics to the issues that affect their daily lives. They see politicians promising to do one thing to get elected, and doing the opposite once safely ensconced in power. And they suspect that many politicians are more interested in advancing their private interests than the public interest. Once, politics was about doing good, and it still is for many; increasingly, however, it is about doing well – an arena for the ambitious to pursue personal quests for wealth, status, or power.

With improvements in pay and pensions – and opportunities to travel to pleasanter climes during increasingly frequent parliamentary adjournments – being elected to Parliament is, for many, the best job available. Nomination battles have become fiercely contested mass membership sign-up campaigns, sometimes featuring third-party payers in ethnic communities. Appointment to Cabinet puts you at the top of the social heap: wealthy, influential people and huge corporations or their lobbyists offer tickets to hockey and baseball games, or family stays at fishing lodges and vacation condos. Important political couples are invited to the best parties.

Unless one is personally wealthy, however, these lofty positions are temporary, and the politician knows it. In most careers, second place is not a bad showing; in politics, by contrast, it means you're a loser and potentially a bum. No more fine wine and restaurants; no more good-looking young aides to carry your bags. As former BC premier Bill Bennett told me more than once when I was working for him, people who had clamoured for the attention of his father, Premier W.A.C. Bennett, during the twenty years he was in office would cross the street rather than look him in the eye after he lost the 1972 election. Not surprisingly, a politician will do just about anything to postpone defeat, which is inevitable unless death or voluntary retirement intervene.

Pierre Trudeau was the last of our prime ministers to enter politics with a well-defined agenda. With the passage of time, Canadians increasingly came to disapprove of many of his foreign and domestic policies, but few ever doubted his integrity. Although he allowed his ministers to engage in the seamier side of patronage and he accepted gifts from anonymous donors to build the swimming pool at 24 Sussex Drive, no one ever suspected that he cut corners for personal benefit. Wealthy, charismatic, and intellectually gifted, he had no concerns about his political afterlife.

For his successors, politics has been about power more than principle. With what burning agenda did Jean Chrétien come to office? And what, after all, was the decade-long dispute between Paul Martin and Chrétien about? The power of the Prime Minister's Office is enormous, and for many it's worth the huge expense of getting to the top. Paul Martin raised $12 million from anonymous donors, whose names were disclosed only after Jean Chrétien announced his resignation. Money never seemed to be an issue for Chrétien, either, in his campaign to destabilize John Turner's leadership.

Over the years, money has become more important in politics, just as it has in society generally. As political discourse stresses image and emotions over ideas, policy takes a back seat to advertising and marketing. Politicians hire professional pollsters and advertising experts to help define their adversaries in negative terms. Election campaigns are run by highly skilled volunteers who, the day after the vote, transmogrify into high-priced lobbyists or receive lucrative government contracts.

Politicians like to hobnob with the rich; aside from their other attractions, they are the best source of campaign funds. Limiting corporate and union contributions – as have Manitoba, Quebec, and more recently Ottawa – is an imperfect solution because big money will generally find a way around the rules. Politicians also seek out wealthy people because they've always got one eye on the day after an electoral defeat. A good job in the wings is a relief when, as is the case with many career politicians, they have no marketable skills. However, the relationship is symbiotic: the wealthy want government policy to favour them, and to protect them too: as a tiny minority unable to shelter under the language of human rights, they are vulnerable to various forms of expropriation by the masses, also known as voters.

The dominant figure at the intersection between power and money in Canada is Quebec entrepreneur Paul Desmarais, our finest practitioner of the art of herding politicians. As chairman of Power Corporation, a multi-billion dollar company that ranks eleventh in assets and twelfth in sales in Canada, Desmarais has every reason to invest in politicians, with party stripe being of secondary consideration. At the same time, his role is a source of strain in a political system premised on the equality of citizens.

Brian Mulroney had done work for him as a labour lawyer, but Desmarais's connections with Jean Chrétien were even closer: they shared grandchildren from the marriage of France Chrétien to André Desmarais. Power Corporation executive John Rae ran Chrétien's election campaigns and was one of his closest confidants. Yet Paul Martin, who forced Chrétien from office, is also well connected to Desmarais. Martin began his business career at Power Corp in the 1960s, working for Maurice Strong, the company's president. Desmarais gave Martin the presidency of its subsidiary, Canada

Steamship Lines, and Martin and a partner eventually bought the company. Martin became a very rich man.

Paul Desmarais has survived two decades of stormy political waters, going about the business of acquiring wealth and adding ex-politicians and their aides to his stable. No wonder that, to many of my neighbours in British Columbia, the power elite in Canada looks like one big happy family.[3]

MY LIFE WITH BRIAN

I met Brian Mulroney once before going to work for him – if seeing him at the 1983 Grey Cup game qualifies as a meeting. I'm quite sure we did not exchange words, and I was surprised, three years later, when Paul Tellier, the Clerk of the Privy Council, asked if I'd be interested in coming to Ottawa to help with a major constitutional initiative.

In the 1984 election, Mulroney had promised to secure Quebec's consent to the Constitution, "with honour and enthusiasm." Now, just before the 1986 Premiers' Conference and my arrival in Ottawa, he wrote to the provincial premiers requesting that they defer "a more extensive revision of the constitution." They agreed and I, along with Lowell Murray, government leader in the Senate and minister of state for federal-provincial relations, was assigned to the case.[4]

In March 1987, after several cross-country tours, we advised Mulroney that a constitutional agreement could be achieved. However, Murray left our final briefing with Mulroney shaking his head at the prime minister's obvious lack of preparation. He persuaded Mulroney to have me sit at his side during the first ministers' meeting at Meech Lake on April 30, 1987, which turned out to be a very long but exciting day.

Mulroney was brilliant as a negotiator, alternating between letting others talk and cajoling them towards an agreement. On each of the issues, I pulled from an accordion file alternative drafts that Murray and I had prepared with the assistance of my excellent staff. Mulroney occasionally asked for clarification before passing the text around the table. Always he made it clear that he would not be leaving without an agreement. Advisers were kept out of the room, though the premiers were able to consult them over dinner. To the great surprise of journalists who had been waiting sceptically all day, shortly before 10 P.M. he announced a unanimous agreement in principle.

A few days later, Mulroney sent me to Montreal with my colleague André Burelle – Trudeau's constitutional adviser and speech-writer during the 1980 Quebec referendum and subsequent constitutional discussions – to brief the former prime minister. We did not know how unpersuasive we had been until a few days later, when Trudeau published a scathing denunciation of the accord in both English and French.

As we worked with officials through May on the legal text of the Meech Lake agreement, I could sense the nervousness that Trudeau's intervention had caused in some provincial delegations. Mulroney invited the premiers to a meeting at the Langevin Building on June 2 to work out the remaining problems. After considerable pushing and pulling overnight, he ended with a unanimous agreement. To bring Ontario's David Peterson and Manitoba's Howard Pawley onside, however, he agreed to refer the accord to a parliamentary committee for public hearings. Changes would be accepted only if "egregious errors" were identified; still, New Brunswick premier Richard Hatfield, a veteran of past constitutional wars, sniffed the risk in the three-year ratification process and insisted that all governments commit to passing it "as soon as possible."

Mulroney remained engaged for about a month, until the first polling results arrived. I did not know it, but his entourage had been boasting about their man's historical accomplishment where Trudeau had failed. However, to their and Mulroney's chagrin, though the majority of Canadians supported the accord, the polls indicated that it was unlikely to sway their vote. Mulroney became less engaged and, with Peterson keeping his head down in the face of mounting opposition, Murray and I were left on our own to play defence.

Notwithstanding a doctorate in political science, I had much to learn, I discovered, about the depth of the cleavage between Canada's two solitudes, the power of the media, and the interaction between interest group and partisan politics. As I watched Chrétien use the accord to destabilize John Turner's leadership, and then to attack his rivals in the subsequent race, I also learned a great deal about the Liberal Party of Canada.

During the summer of public hearings, several journalists placed bets on when the government would accept amendments. Later, nervous premiers insisted they had three years to adopt the constitutional resolution, which was legally true, though unhelpful. In hindsight, I wonder whether Mulroney should have replaced Murray and me at this time. Both of us were acutely conscious of the fragile compromises that underlay it. I've always found it hard not to give a straight answer to a straight question, and did not gladly suffer interest-group leaders – many of whom posited impossible worst-case analyses – after the accord was signed. Murray, a dour Cape Bretoner with an MPA from Queen's, is literate, considerate, and unflappable; however, his considerable strengths do not include public communication. Though he chaired the Cabinet Committee on Communications, the government did not undertake any advertising program, as it did in previous and subsequent federal initiatives of this kind.[5]

Increasingly, Mulroney was preoccupied with the negotiations that ultimately culminated in the Canada-U.S. free trade agreement. On the evening of Saturday, October 3, a small group of us gathered on the second floor of the Langevin Building for the final sprint. Just after midnight he asked me to inform the premiers that an agreement had been initialled by our negotiators in Washington. Peterson in Ontario was not pleased, and Pawley responded in Manitoba by dragging his feet on ratifying the Meech Lake resolution in his legislature.

Later that month Mulroney sent me to Fredericton to brief the new Liberal premier, Frank McKenna. In his election campaign against Hatfield, McKenna had promised to change the Meech Lake accord. He had also expressed misgivings about free trade, which, by that time, was a higher priority than Meech Lake for Mulroney. It may have been a coincidence, but in December 1987, two days after their premier had come out in support of the free trade agreement, the Irving-owned Saint John shipyard received a $6 billion contract – without tender and over the objections of Quebec – to build an additional six frigates for the Canadian navy.

By then I enjoyed Mulroney's full confidence for having delivered provincial support for his government's two major initiatives – constitutional reform and free trade. In his entourage I was considered a "helpful" deputy – a category that included Ray Hession, the deputy minister of the Department of Supply and Services, which had procured twelve MBB helicopters for the Coast Guard. Colleagues who were less well positioned sometimes turned to me for assistance, including Undersecretary of State Jean Fournier, who arrived at my office one day in 1988 looking very anxious.

Senator Michel Cogger was pressuring Fournier to fund a computerized document translation system. After listening to his concerns about a system he thought was a dog, I handed him a draft speech Mulroney had reworked and suggested he feed it into the system. I promised Fournier I would show it to Mulroney if he ran into any further difficulty telling Cogger that the government was not interested in the GigaText system. He was able to turn Cogger off; however, to the eventual chagrin of Saskatchewan taxpayers, Cogger's sales pitch moved to the government of their small, have-not province.

Shortly after the 1988 election, the Supreme Court struck down a Quebec law on the language of commercial signs. The minister responsible, Claude Ryan – a former Quebec Liberal leader and editor-in-chief of *Le Devoir* – insisted on using section 33 of the *Charter of Rights and Freedoms*, the notwithstanding clause, to foreclose any challenge to the replacement legislation. Sensing the landmines, Mulroney hesitated to condemn and ended up temporizing. Essentially, notwithstanding their public spats, I always felt that Mulroney's views on bilingualism were similar to Trudeau's; with the reaction in English Canada intense and emotional, Mulroney eventually ignored the advice of his Quebec lieutenant, Lucien Bouchard, and criticized the Bourassa government. However, the controversy provided a perfect excuse for the newly elected Conservative premier of Manitoba, Gary Filmon, not to proceed with ratification of the constitutional amendment. Filmon headed a minority government, with Liberal leader Sharon Carstairs – a devotee of Pierre Trudeau and Jean Chrétien – holding the balance of power. Another Trudeau fundamentalist, Clyde Wells, had been elected premier of Newfoundland in the fall of 1989, and he withdrew the ratification resolution adopted by his Conservative predecessor.

With prospects for its success dimming, Mulroney re-engaged on Meech and told me that he was adding Paul Tellier and his chief of staff, Stanley Hartt, to the constitutional team. He also told me that he had been consulting with Paul Desmarais, and that Hartt was already meeting with two very close Chrétien confidants, Eric Maldoff and Eddie Goldenberg.

Murray and I were dispatched to help McKenna draft a "parallel accord" that would add elements to the Meech constitutional amendment without, we insisted to Quebec, modifying it – at least not too visibly. Eventually, Roger Tassé – Chrétien's deputy minister in the 1980–82 constitutional discussions – was brought in from the outside to help out.[6]

After a parliamentary committee chaired by Jean Charest completed its hearings on the parallel accord and proposed changes to Meech Lake, Mulroney invited the premiers to a meeting at the Museum of Civilization in Hull on June 3. McKenna agreed almost immediately to the "improved" accord, and attention turned to

Manitoba and Newfoundland. Miraculously, at this point near the end of the Liberal leadership campaign, Chrétien began to soften his opposition to Meech Lake. His people lobbied Carstairs, and New Democratic Party leader Ed Broadbent urged Gary Doer, who was then the leader of the third party and is now the Manitoba premier, to move simultaneously with the others to pass the accord in the legislature. However, after a full week of negotiations, Mulroney got only part way. Even after Peterson gave up six Senate seats, Clyde Wells would commit only to putting the amendments before his legislature, or to the people in a referendum, with no recommendation. Yet, in a move that puzzled me, Mulroney convened a formal signing ceremony late at night on Saturday, June 9, which ended in the early hours of Sunday morning.

On Monday, as a favour to *Globe and Mail* editor William Thorsell, Mulroney agreed to be interviewed by three of his reporters, including Susan Delacourt. Thorsell had deliberately assigned Delacourt – a fierce though professional Meech sceptic – to the file to counterbalance the *Globe*'s generally supportive editorial line. I still recall the surprised faces in Paul Tellier's boardroom when press secretary Gilbert Lavoie popped in to inform the prime minister's closest advisers of the interview that had just taken place. We were even more shocked the next day when we read Mulroney's boast in the *Globe* about having timed the conference to maximize pressure on the premiers. Mulroney protested vehemently and demanded a retraction, which was quickly drafted. However, with talk of resignations in the air, *Globe* Ottawa bureau chief Chris Waddell persuaded Thorsell not to run it. The "rolling the dice" interview was the final nail in Meech Lake's coffin.

Once the mourning for Meech was over, Stanley Hartt was free to return to the private sector, but first he had to find a successor as Mulroney's chief of staff. Despite my repeated demurrals, Hartt continued to inquire whether I'd accept the position if asked. In the late summer of 1990 Mulroney invited me for the first time to Harrington Lake, the prime minister's summer residence. As I drove past the cut-off to Meech Lake, it crossed my mind that the invitation might be his way of saying goodbye. Instead, he spent about half an hour outlining his determination to try again to reach a constitutional accord. His chief of staff would have to keep an eye on Joe Clark and the new team of officials who'd be responsible for the file. I felt some responsibility to manage the aftermath of the Meech failure; I suppose I was also flattered. Though I knew I would be jeopardizing my public service career by going to work in the PMO, I accepted his offer.

I was unhappy almost from the first day when, unannounced, Premier Grant Devine arrived to plead for federal monies to assist a dam project in Saskatchewan. Over the next months, it was very frustrating to watch Joe Clark make up what became the Charlottetown accord as he went along. The pressures were intense: Mulroney would telephone at all hours, and regularly after the lead item on the national news. Very soon, I brought Hugh Segal – who had also been on Mulroney's short list – into the office as deputy chief of staff. Paul Tellier asked incredulously if I knew what I was doing, and I assured him I did.

Before leaving, Stanley Hartt – a brilliant but disorganized man – had handed over forty-one "active" files. I farmed most of them out to the relevant departments, including one related to the Montreal Bronfman family. The second generation's wealth was sheltered by the so-called twenty-one-year rule governing family trusts. Its imminent expiration threatened their pocketbook and the third generation's inheritance; for several weeks I received increasingly frantic calls from a Bronfman senior executive. Eventually I told him I had handed the file to Finance and asked that he stop calling. Several months later, I pointed to the Bronfman file as an example of the mess I had found when I arrived in the PMO, and was determined to clean up. Mulroney replied that he'd never heard of the issue, and I wondered to myself whether Hartt may have been freelancing. Today I don't honestly know what to believe, just as I don't know what to think about so much of what I experienced working for Mulroney.

That's not to say I did not like him. According to Tellier, who had worked alongside him from the beginning, Mulroney had never once raised his voice in anger, no matter how stressful the situation. He's also a great family man: when one of the children came into the room, everything stopped, no matter how important the issue we were discussing. He's charming, particularly in small groups, and a great storyteller with a fantastic sense of timing. Beneath the cloying exterior Kaplan describes, he has a wicked sense of humour. Yet, in reading *A Secret Trial*, a powerful disquiet came over me. Closing my eyes, I could see and hear my former boss as he badgered Kaplan with one argument after the other not to publish the story of the cash payments. All his weaknesses, and some of his strengths, are on display in the narrative. After I got to know Mulroney better, I understood that he carried the insecurities of an outsider who had grown up as a working-class anglophone on Quebec's North Shore. More than once, for example, he warned me never to believe that Canadians were a generous and tolerant people.

Mila Mulroney, ensconced with her own staff in an office on the first floor of the Langevin Building, was a constant challenge. Believing it an honour to work for them, she constantly made it clear that the Mulroneys had done me the favour by hiring me. She had an expensive lifestyle, and Mulroney was not a rich man. Party funds were being drawn, and one of our staff was assigned to pore through personal expenses to determine if some might be reimbursed. Every month I cashed a cheque at a local bank and remitted the funds to Mila.

For the leader of an important G7 country, Mulroney spent what I thought was an inordinate amount of time doting on the wealthy. A trip to Paris coincided with the ceremony conferring the Légion d'Honneur on Paul Desmarais. The Varis, Helen and George – a Hungarian-born millionaire who ran Sefri Construction – popped up there and everywhere. During the Meech saga, Conrad Black received special attention when he turned negative after Premier Bourassa used the notwithstanding clause. Indeed, Black's long letter on Meech provoked a mini-crisis in our office. Though it would be several years before I met him, Mulroney asked me to draft what turned into a fourteen-page reply that he reworked, in his own hand, several times.

Other than dutifully signing correspondence, Mulroney, I soon learned, was a telephone addict – and that, perhaps, explained why he had not done his homework for the Meech Lake meeting. He loved to trade political gossip, and he regularly called wealthy and influential people. He never missed an opportunity to stroke caucus members celebrating a birthday or mourning a loved one. He was magnificent at this and, unlike the more popular Chrétien, never faced a caucus revolt.

I don't know for sure, but I guessed that the phone calls were one source of the notes about specific files that Mulroney referred to Paul Tellier at nearly every meeting. However, since Tellier had thrown Karlheinz Schreiber out of his office for alleging a public service conspiracy against him, Mulroney handed the Bearhead project file to me. He asked that I meet with senior federal officials and "ensure it was approved expeditiously." I smelled trouble, so I invited Robert Fowler, the deputy minister of national defence, to my office. Fowler had prospered under Trudeau and had had a "good transition" under Mulroney, but he was not on the "helpful" list. I listened carefully as he explained that the Bearhead proposal to manufacture light armoured vehicles (LAVs) would threaten the viability of GM's existing operation in Ontario.

At the urging of Nova Scotia regional minister Elmer MacKay, I agreed to meet Schreiber in my office and listened politely as he wove his picture of an elaborate conspiracy. I knew I would need witnesses, and I gathered all the players around a table, including Minister of National Defence Bill McKnight and MacKay – who had introduced Schreiber to Mulroney. After listening to a rambling discussion, I asked the participants to prepare jointly a cost-benefit analysis. Someone, perhaps Schreiber or MacKay, had told Mulroney that the project would not cost a dime. However, the agreed-upon analysis indicated that $100 million would have to be booked in the fiscal framework if it went ahead.

A few days later, seated beside Mulroney in the back of the armoured Cadillac limousine, he asked whether I had made any progress on Bearhead. We were en route to a speech in Quebec, but I had brought notes and informed him about the cost. He seemed surprised and declared immediately, "In that case, the project is dead." But it wasn't – at least not completely.

In 1998, long after I had resigned as Mulroney's chief of staff, I learned that the Bearhead project had not been buried that day in the limousine. The first inkling came in an email from Lowell Murray, whom I had asked about a newspaper report, which I found very bizarre, that former Liberal minister Marc Lalonde had posted bond for Schreiber. In the course of our exchange, I learned that Hugh Segal had dealt with the Bearhead project after I left the PMO.

Kaplan raises a number of questions Crown lawyers should have asked Mulroney during the discovery phase of his defamation suit in 1997. I've long wondered why they did not ask why a project that he said had been killed on my recommendation never, in fact, died.

AFTER LIFE WITH BRIAN

In early December 1991 I submitted my letter of resignation to Brian Mulroney, and someone close to him leaked the news almost immediately. Eventually, the prime minister turned his attention to what to do with me. Tellier raised the idea of sending me to Paris as ambassador, but Mulroney opted for Tel Aviv.[7]

Abroad, I had little contact with former colleagues. A few Cabinet ministers visited, but most wanted to discuss Mideast politics. From time to time I read about issues with which I was familiar. While abroad, for example, I learned that the government had tabled legislation just before the deadline to exempt family trusts from taxation until the last beneficiary had died. And later I read that two related trusts had moved $2 billion from Canada, without paying capital gains taxes, thanks to a secret advance ruling made late in 1991 by senior officials at Revenue Canada. I also made a mental note when Mulroney named Conrad Black and Charles Bronfman to the Queen's Privy Council, an appointment that will allow them to use the honorific "Honourable" for the rest of their lives.[8] This seemed strange: I knew Mulroney had been irked by his lack of control over the Order of Canada. However, I didn't understand why non-ministers would be appointed to a body that provides the sole constitutional underpinnings of Cabinet government.

After the 1993 election I continued to serve Jean Chrétien's government as ambassador to Israel and the Palestinian Authority. During this very productive period, Canada and Israel began negotiations that eventually led to a free trade agreement. And I was able, twice, to bring Israeli prime minister Yitzhak Rabin to Canada. It was with mixed emotions, therefore, that I took a telephone call late one night in January 1995 and was advised by Tellier's replacement as Clerk of the Privy Council, Jocelyne Bourgon, that I'd be coming home at the end of the normal three-year term, to be replaced by David Berger, a Liberal MP and thorn in Chrétien's side. Following instructions, I informed the Israeli foreign ministry and obtained the necessary *agrément*. However, after word of the patronage appointment leaked, the government denied all and Berger was appointed as an adviser in the PMO – a delay that meant I was allowed to stay on in the Mideast for six more months.

To my pleasant surprise, Bourgon confided in her phone call that the prime minister wanted me to remain in the public service. A few months later she called again to report that Chrétien wanted me to run the Atlantic Canada Opportunities Agency (ACOA). She explained that a senior deputy minister was needed to keep an eye on David Dingwall, whose proclivity for pork-barrelling – though much appreciated by Cape Bretoners – had attracted negative press. I had first met Dingwall in Israel and had shown him around the country. His major ministerial portfolio was Public Works, where he put in place an advertising-management process that would later be extended to deliver sponsorships in Quebec.

Though ACOA's head office was in Moncton, I was in Ottawa one day a week. A month after taking up my new job, Sergeant Fraser Fiegenwald of the RCMP came calling to ask for the agency's files related to the Bearhead project – particularly the agreement in principle signed on the eve of the 1988 election.[9] I mentioned in passing that I had served in Mulroney's PMO, which surprised him. He asked me about Airbus, and I told him the transaction had been concluded before my time. However, I also informed him that I had been involved with the project that was the subject of his visit. Fiegenwald and his boss, Inspector Yves Bouchard, later returned to take a sworn written statement. Before leaving, they asked that I not tell anyone.

I agonized for a couple of weeks before advising Jocelyne Bourgon – the person to whom all deputy ministers report (aside from their minister). I sensed she was surprised, and more than a tad perturbed, that the RCMP had not informed her about the investigation. I left with the impression she'd be on the phone immediately to rake Commissioner Philip Murray over the coals.

Back at ACOA, I was having difficulty stopping the agency's embarrassing proclivity to lend cash to companies that didn't need it, deserve it, or have the ability to use it profitably. Liberal MPs complained to Dingwall that ACOA was slowing down the approval of project loan applications and financing requests. One MP summoned me to her office and explained that she, not I, should decide who received government money because she had to get re-elected every four years.

In 1996 Chrétien shuffled his Cabinet, and industry minister John Manley was given responsibility for ACOA. We now had a secretary of state too – Laurence MacAulay, the regional minister for PEI. Dingwall moved to Health but maintained an active and unhealthy interest in Cape Breton. When the government announced the closing of the Devco coalmine and the elimination of 600 to 1,200 jobs, he demanded that MacAulay set aside $60 million to cushion the blow.

MacAulay would have preferred to use ACOA's budget to fund projects in PEI, but he understood that Dingwall was better connected to Chrétien, so he agreed. Although the Liberals could have flowed the dollars through ACOA's existing programs, Dingwall wanted to approve projects himself. Because most of the applications flooding in to his political staff contained no analysis and no rationale, he did not want normal program criteria to apply.

At first I tried to negotiate the least problematic proposals with him. However, Dingwall was insatiable, and the projects were of increasingly dubious merit. Eventually I suggested that he sign off on the projects. Not surprisingly, he was anxious that public servants take responsibility for "economic development" projects that included refurbishing the Sydney waterfront, a chair in tourism, a new student residence at the local college, and a variety of forestry projects that ACOA did not fund in any other province. I tried to protect my staff from political pressure, but Dingwall called on an ally in the PMO – Dominic LeBlanc, son of the former governor general and later a Liberal MP from New Brunswick. Privy Council Office officials, who are supposed to preserve the integrity of the public service, looked the other way when they were not adding to the pressure on my staff. Though I complained to Bourgon, she just smiled. Eventually, I was summoned by Jean Pelletier, Chrétien's chief of staff, and warned about my growing reputation for having an "uncooperative" attitude.

In contrast to the charmed existence I had led under Mulroney, now I had no friends at court. For a time Eddie Goldenberg, whom I had known at McGill, tried to help. John Manley and his staff initially ran interference with the PMO, but they moved on after divining that MacAulay and Dingwall had the full backing of the Boss. Faced with a choice of giving in to political pressure or resigning, I advised Bourgon that I would be leaving the public service. Though not in the way I had feared when I went to work for Mulroney, ultimately the change in government did, then, spell the end of my public service career.[10]

Seated beside Jocelyne Bourgon at the retirement dinner she hosted in my honour, I asked how RCMP commissioner Murray had reacted when she upbraided him for not mentioning the Bearhead investigation. Bourgon told me that he insisted he had no obligation to inform her, as Mulroney was no longer a minister. Later, when I publicly disclosed my first conversation with Bourgon, the RCMP denied she had ever contacted Murray about the issue.

While Bourgon never disputed the substance of that conversation, the Privy Council Office issued a written statement declaring that she had not concluded from our meeting that Mulroney was under criminal investigation. The deputy minister of justice, whom I had also informed, issued an almost identically phrased written statement. In political and bureaucratic circles these are known as non-denials, since no one can quarrel with the conclusions another person reaches.

In the best tradition of a lawyer arguing on behalf of a client, Bourgon's staff added that even if she had understood that Mulroney was under investigation, she would not have informed Chrétien. I would have, because it is always dangerous to withhold information from a prime minister. Had she informed Chrétien, there's no reason to believe he would have interfered politically. However, it would have been reasonable for him to issue a sharp admonition that officials and the police carry out the sensitive investigation with the utmost care.

After I resigned, the *Globe and Mail* editorialized: "The Liberals put respected public servant Norman Spector in charge. They billed him as the man who would henceforth disburse grants based on economic merit, not political connections. Then he started living up to the advance billing. The Atlantic Canada caucus was shocked; the MPs think that ACOA's funds should continue to be doled out on a 'political' basis. Mr. Spector is no longer with ACOA. Ah, that a politician's reach should never exceed his grasp, else what is being in government for?"[11]

REFLECTIONS

As I write these words and reflect on current events in the context of my career experience, I am reminded that the odour of corruption was not unique to Brian Mulroney's Ottawa.[12] This observation is not meant as an excuse; however, it does suggest that the problem is systemic, not personal, as any solution must be.

Kaplan reminds us of the offshore money that fuelled Mulroney's two leadership campaigns. These costly contests inevitably leave many people feeling they have IOUs. Hangers-on in "consulting," advertising, investment banking, and legal firms expect rewards. Like Mulroney, many of those who accompanied him to Ottawa in 1984 had memories of having been shut out of the best patronage opportunities up to that point in their careers. Yet Mulroney came to office promising to clean up Liberal patronage and corruption.

In 1993 Chrétien too came to power promising new ethical standards and an independent commissioner reporting to Parliament to enforce them. Yet it sometimes seemed that the biggest change under Chrétien was in the political coloration of the lobbyists, law firms, investment brokers, and advertising firms that did business with the government.[13] It was only after he left office that Canadians saw the full dimension of the rot. With a historically weak parliamentary opposition, one has to wonder where the media were during these years.[14]

The seeds of the sponsorship scandal that exploded after Paul Martin entered the Prime Minister's Office were planted in a strategy document concocted at the Pearson Building towards the end of the 1995 referendum campaign. Chrétien's advisers, in near panic, were open to ideas from any quarter, including the department responsible for Canada's foreign relations. More remarkably, a public servant (George Anderson, a close friend of Eddie Goldenberg) expounded on the need to defeat Bloc Québécois MPs – which, in the political landscape that existed after the 1993 election, amounted to electing Liberals.

Five years before he nearly lost the country in that referendum, Chrétien had predicted that the death of Meech Lake would be no big deal. It was like getting stuck in the snow: you could always try again to move forward. Yet he made no attempt to amend the Constitution during his years in office. And, rather than trying to win the hearts and minds of Quebecers through democratic dialogue, he chose to conduct a propaganda campaign. Like most of his boondoggles, the sponsorship program grew out of Chrétien's desire to escape the rules of prudent public administration. Resorting to tactics he had honed as the minister responsible for the Canadian Unity Information Office during the 1980 referendum, his government discovered a supreme national interest in funding car races and comedy festivals.

David Dingwall had ACOA for purposes of pork-barrelling. Backbenchers looked on enviously and, eventually, they too got a turn at the trough through the Transitional Jobs Fund of the Human Resources Development department, but that eventually led to another scandal and came to an end. Ultimately, unhappy backbenchers fuelled Paul Martin's internal party coup against Jean Chrétien. For the first time in Canadian history an elected prime minister was forced from office. Fundamentally, Martin's decade-long campaign was about who should govern, not about good government. Is it any wonder the public has grown increasingly cynical?

If a deputy minister in Ottawa is fortunate, he'll never have to manage dollars dear to a prime minister. Alternatively, she'll be working for a minister motivated solely by the public interest (yes, they do exist). My luck ran out when I went to work for Dingwall. Ran Quail, the deputy minister of public works, found that his luck ran out when Chrétien turned to his department to deliver sponsorships in Quebec. Just a few years previously, Dingwall had landed on his doorstep as his minister, with responsibility for government advertising. Quail and I used to commiserate over drinks about the boss we shared. A veteran of the Coast Guard, Quail is straight as an arrow and mild-mannered, and was therefore no match for Dingwall's heavy-handed tactics.

The rulebook says that a deputy minister should inform the clerk of the Privy Council when a minister applies pressure to break the rules. Quail later testified that he had not done so when problems first popped up with sponsorships, because Chrétien had signed the

Treasury Board submission and he assumed that the prime minister and the clerk wanted the program to be run that way. No doubt, he also knew from our conversations that the Privy Council Office would back Dingwall and would even help enforce the wishes of Jean Pelletier, Chrétien's chief of staff. In the end, Quail went along when Dingwall chose Chuck Guité to run advertising programs. He promoted Guité at the request of a subsequent minister, Alfonso Gagliano, and allowed the two to deal directly on sponsorships. Later, when it was time for Guité to go, Quail accepted the parachuting of Gagliano's chief of staff into the civil-service position.

When I left Ottawa for the Mideast in 1992, he and other deputy ministers were working on a public service revitalization project called Public Service 2000. One group was assigned by Paul Tellier to write a paper on values and ethics. When I returned in 1995, deputy ministers were hard at work on a similar exercise launched by Jocelyne Bourgon. While I was dodging Dingwall's efforts to pork-barrel with ACOA funds – and Bourgon was doing nothing to help me resist political pressure – another working group was writing another paper, at her behest, on public service values and ethics. Completed a few months after I resigned from the public service, this otherwise excellent paper is flawed by a fundamental contradiction. By assigning the highest ethical value to carrying out the wishes of the government, deputy ministers were proposing, in the most charitable interpretation, an amoral definition of the public service.[15]

The deputies' talk about ethics was just that, notwithstanding their recommendation to adopt a formal code and a mechanism to resolve disputes when an ethical public servant balks at something that is going on – one modelled on the system used in the United Kingdom. For, in the very next breath, the deputy ministers rejected their British counterparts' legal and political accountability to Parliament for the financial administration of their departments, arguing that it would undermine ministerial responsibility. As I watched the Public Accounts Committee hearings on the sponsorship program, I found it hard to see how the situation could get any worse. The instinct of ministers was to blame others when found out; and the instinct of officials was to find ways to be out of the loop when "just following orders" would be an inadequate defence. You could call it the banality of corruption.

Some politicians seek public office to change the world; others try to hang on to office by buying support with public funds. They can always find a Chuck Guité to deliver the goods, and they're quick to blame anyone but themselves if things go wrong. Aside from high living on expense accounts and the unfair stereotype that they are lazy layabouts, complicity in government boondoggles is the major cause of the deteriorating image of federal public servants.

The sponsorship program was not an aberration, nor was it the result of relaxed management controls, as the current clerk of the Privy Council suggests. The scandal was the inevitable outgrowth of longstanding malignancies in the system. I know one very courageous woman who refused to knuckle under to PMO and PCO pressure to approve dubious projects. Today, she is raising dogs and walking the beach in Nova Scotia. However, most bureaucrats have mortgages and kids, and, sometimes, the only option for the ethical ones is to hunker down and take notes. But where, pray tell, were two successive clerks of the Privy Council during the sponsorship years?

Properly structured, direct accountability of deputies to Parliament would enhance ministerial responsibility. On most decisions, a minister and his deputy are as one. When they are not, the minister should take the decision and be accountable to Parliament. Twenty-five years ago the Lambert Commission on Financial Management recommended something along these lines. Had the Lambert recommendation been adopted (a simple amendment to the *Financial Administration Act* would suffice), the deputy minister of public works would not have been able to look the other way and give Guité free reign to run the sponsorship program. Before setting it up to operate outside normal channels, Liberal ministers would have had to gauge whether they could persuade Canadians that funding comedy festivals was about the national interest, not their partisan interests. And ministers and prime ministers would have to think twice before giving instructions to have "regional development" projects or defence-related procurements approved "as soon as possible."

For most of his decade of one-party rule, Chrétien trumpeted that Canada was the best country in the world in which to live, according the UN's Human Development Index. He never once mentioned that, at the same time, our position was deteriorating markedly in Transparency International's "Corruption Perception Index." In 1995 we ranked fifth; by 2003 we had fallen to eleventh. According to the Berlin-based watchdog, construction companies vying for public works projects in developing nations are most likely to bribe government officials to win contracts. Businesses operating in the energy and defence industries – which would include Eurocopter, Thyssen, and Airbus Industrie – are also apt to engage in shady dealings. Who knows where we would have ranked had Transparency International examined Canada between 1984 and 1993.

While reading Kaplan's *A Secret Trial*, I thought back to Mulroney's first chief of staff, Fred Doucet, who, with Elmer MacKay, had introduced Schreiber to Mulroney. After leaving the PMO, Doucet went to work as a lobbyist and he still occasionally brought people to Mulroney's Parliament Hill office after Question Period. Perhaps he was on charity missions or working for private clients pro bono. I cannot say for sure, since we prepared no briefing material and were not present for the discussions. The appointments were not booked through our office and did not appear on our weekly schedule.

Kaplan concludes that there was a clear "factual basis" for the RCMP investigation of Airbus, MBB, and Bearhead. Yet he also raises questions about the force's competence and political independence. In 1995 Commissioner Philip Murray was personally interested in the investigation continuing. In 2003 the RCMP shut down the investigation without taking up Schreiber's two offers to tell all. As Kaplan notes, "Unsolved murder investigations are not ended. No unsolved criminal investigations are. They become cold files, not dead files. Except this one."

However, questions can and must also be asked about the RCMP's investigation into Jean Chrétien's role in securing a Business Development Bank loan for an insolvent hotel in his riding, adjacent to a golf course in which he still, technically, owned shares. Chrétien's lobbying to secure the loan likely contributed to Canada's slide in international rankings of corruption. For, in professing that he was not in a conflict of interest, Chrétien set a dangerous standard for ministers and backbenchers. Had not the prime minister – Shawinigan's number one constituent – repeatedly stressed that ministers are first of all MPs, and that it's the duty of MPs to represent constituents?

The Auberge Grand-Mère story took a serious turn when a document, ostensibly the BDC's, arrived at the *National Post*. This time editors had no interest in burying a potential scandal (though they eventually took Andrew McIntosh off the case).[16] However, they were unsure about the document, which showed that the Auberge owed $23,040 to Chrétien's holding company. If it was authentic, he would have been an indirect beneficiary of the loan for which he was lobbying – potentially, a criminal matter.

The PMO claimed the document was a forgery, and the BDC

obtained a court order permitting a search of the home and office of its fired president, François Beaudoin. For months the RCMP made no progress and, in December 2001, it announced that "the investigation was being wrapped up." As McIntosh reported, investigators were "unable to confirm" the document was a forgery, but also "unable to conclude" that it was not.[17] Subsequently, the RCMP raided Beaudoin's home and cottage looking for evidence; then, when the police went to court demanding that the *National Post* turn over its copy, it provided what it said was the original from BDC files. It turned out that someone had forged the hotel owner's signature on the *Post*'s copy.

For me, a non-lawyer, the most troubling aspect of Kaplan's two Airbus books is his description of the criminal justice system. In *Presumed Guilty*, he exposes Keystone Kops who bungle investigations, mid-ranking officials who don't consult with superiors on politically sensitive matters, and an RCMP commissioner who's proud not to know what his officers are up to. In *A Secret Trial*, Kaplan describes the tactics used by high-priced and highly skilled lawyers to get their clients off. Simply put, the police and the courts have not been, and perhaps cannot be, an effective instrument for rooting out political corruption.[18]

Convictions such as Senator Michel Cogger's on charges of influence peddling are rare. Even that prosecution had to go through multiple appeals, strung out over more than a decade. And it had to survive political pressure on the RCMP when, in 1990, the government asked René Marin, a retired judge, to look into Cogger's declaration in the Senate "that the RCMP was trying to destroy me, no more and no less." Cogger would call me periodically to ask about the timing of Marin's report. Sixteen months after being appointed, he rejected Cogger's allegation of entrapment. However, he found that the RCMP had been manipulated by an undercover agent who was hired despite a prohibition on his services, and he recommended better training and updated manuals for the force. Eventually, Cogger seized on his one glimmer of hope and argued on appeal that first-term MPs and senators too needed to be educated in the law. In the end, however, he was convicted and he eventually resigned from the Senate in September 2000. In May 2001, Cogger was given an absolute discharge by the Quebec Court of Appeal that, while not reversing his 1998 guilty verdict, had the effect of erasing his conviction. The court reasoned that he had already suffered enough and that, while ignorance of the law is no defence, Cogger had acted in good faith without knowing that his actions were prohibited by the *Criminal Code*.

The court also found that there was no evidence of corruption and that his fees were not excessive.

As Kaplan explains, investigations of prime ministers inevitably raise doubts about police independence. In future, when any politician is suspected of wrongdoing, Ottawa should follow British Columbia's practice of appointing a special outside prosecutor to decide whether charges should be laid.[19] Parliament should also have a veto over the appointment of the commissioner of the RCMP. In order to maintain both the perception and the reality of the police force's independence, the next commissioner should not have deputy minister status and should not be treated as part of the deputy ministers' community in Ottawa.

"Independent" is not a term anyone would ever have thought of applying to ethics counsellor Howard Wilson, who was responsible for ruling on conflicts of interest and compliance with the code on post-employment activities during the Chrétien decade. Repeatedly, he determined that the two-year "cooling-off" period for public office holders applied only to lobbying Ottawa or taking jobs from firms with which a former minister had "direct and significant" official dealings in his final year in office.

As prime minister, Jean Chrétien hosted a state visit in June 2003 for Kazakhstani dictator Nursultan Nazarbayev, who lobbied for the invitation after his country's "poor [and worsening] human-rights record" was noted by the U.S. State Department. After leaving office, Chrétien signed on with three major law firms; his first announced client was PetroKazakhstan, a Calgary-based oil company.

As prime minister, Chrétien was very busy on the China front, visiting six times, leading two Team Canada trade and investment missions, and meeting frequently with top leaders. He purposely chose to meet Prime Minister Wen Jiabao on his last day in office. Less than two months later, the former prime minister travelled unannounced to China with son-in-law André Desmarais and a team of Power Corporation executives. The company has interests in property development in Shanghai's Pudong district and in manufacturing railway cars in Qingdao. Like the PetroKazakhstan relationship, the trip to China raised eyebrows in the Canadian business community. The *Globe and Mail* learned about the visit, but Chrétien's law office and the Canadian Embassy in Beijing refused to give out any details. A *Globe and Mail* reporter eventually discovered that the visit was organized by CITIC, China's biggest and most powerful conglomerate, which has a vast range of interests on four continents in financial services, military exports, energy, real estate, and hotels.

A month later, Chrétien travelled to Niger to meet with President Mamadou Tandja on behalf of TG World Energy Corp., a small Calgary oil company. Chrétien became well known in Africa because of his involvement with the Commonwealth and la Francophonie, and is well respected among African leaders because of his promotion of Africa's economic needs, particularly at the 2002 Group of Eight summit in Kananaskis.

What's been novel in the odour of corruption permeating Ottawa during the past two decades is its bipartisanship – a rare spirit in this very political capital city. Take, for example, the "consultants" who live well off their access, or perceived access, to the powerful, and whose shared interests sometimes outweigh their partisan differences.

At Cabinet one day, Mulroney looked up from writing notes, his main activity during ministerial discussions, and asked me to check which company being discussed around the table was represented by his former press secretary, Bill Fox, who was working as a lobbyist. After the Conservatives lost power in 1993, Fox eventually sold his interest in the firm with which he was associated, Earnscliffe.[20] It transmogrified into a well-connected adjunct of Finance Minister Paul Martin, becoming his PMO-in-waiting and the core group that deposed Chrétien. When Earnscliffe's name came up during the sponsorship controversy, the government pointed to its contracts in the Conservative period as a certificate of probity.

What was also new was the public role played by lobbyists. The Tories' pollster, Alan Gregg, after selling Decima Research, reappeared a few years later in partnership with Chrétien's ex-director of communications Peter Donolo. After Auditor General Sheila Fraser released the first report on the sponsorship program in May 2002, Gregg – who was a regular on *The National's* "At Issues" panel – explained frankly to the CBC's Peter Mansbridge how the "system" works: "At the root you have a situation how political parties run their election advertising as they pull together a consortium of essential volunteers. They're either unpaid or if they're paid, they're paid significantly below market value. And at the end of a winning campaign ... there's kind of a nudge, nudge, wink, wink, you know, we owe you one."[21]

After Fraser's second audit in 2003, Gregg accused the auditor general of "behaving more like the leader of the Official Opposition than the accountant she is" and belittled the sums involved.[22] The tag line in his *Globe and Mail* opinion piece identified him as "chair of the Strategic Counsel, a polling and research firm." It did not mention the name of his partner or that the firm does business with the federal government.

Throughout his decade in power, Chrétien dodged the Red Book commitment to appoint an independent ethics commissioner reporting to Parliament. To his credit, Paul Martin – the author of the Red Book – moved on the promise immediately after taking office. However, the post-employment code needs strengthening: it should apply to office holders who have had any dealings with a prospective employer for four, not two, years after leaving government, and the regulations should cover lobbyists and government contractors who move in and out of the system.

Kaplan was surprised and disappointed that the *National Post* proved to be a lapdog for the powerful, and not a watchdog. However, anyone who knows about Brian Mulroney's relationship with Conrad Black would not have been. Still, to the *Post*'s credit, another of its reporters, Andrew McIntosh, uncovered Jean Chrétien's dubious dealings to secure the Business Development Bank loan.[23] For the longest time, it seemed to me that the CBC's chief political correspondent, Jason Moscovitz, minimized the significance of the story. Eventually, he crossed the street to a senior job at the Business Development Bank of Canada.

There's something Orwellian, even at the best of times, in the government's owning a major source of news and information; Ottawa's power to appoint the president and the board could easily bring on the worst of times.[24] In my experience, the public broadcaster is always conscious that the PMO has the final say on its budget and the appointment of its president. In the one-party Chrétien decade, the government cleverly provided one-time funding increases that were not added to the budgetary base. Peter Mansbridge did not follow up on Allan Gregg's surprising confession about how the advertising and polling game works.[25] Nearly two years would pass before the CBC's flagship news program, *The National*, took an in-depth look at the sponsorship program.

The CBC did, however, run a brief item on Schreiber's cash payment after the *Globe and Mail* published Kaplan's series. No *Sun* newspaper published details of the payment: that chain is owned by a company chaired by Mulroney. Nor did any of the seven Gesca

newspapers owned by Paul Desmarais find the revelations newswor-
thy. As prime minister, Mulroney could always count on the publisher of its foremost newspaper, *La Presse*, to find the right words at
the right time on the Constitution or free trade. This was not a partisan act: a few years later *La Presse* removed columnist Chantal
Hébert – a thorn in Chrétien's side.

As publisher of the *Jerusalem Post*, I learned that many readers
are like Chrétien: they prefer not to read discordant views at the
breakfast table and gravitate to niche media that confirm their prej-
udices. Yet, any Canadian who has the time to read more than one
daily newspaper or watch more than one TV news broadcast will
often find differing reports of the same event.[26] Competition and
diversity are our only safeguard against media bias.[27]

A Senate committee chaired by Joan Fraser, who was removed
as editor-in-chief of the *Montreal Gazette* by Conrad Black, is examining issues of media competition and diversity, particularly in the
private sector. Public broadcasting should not be left out of the
equation, given the CBC's huge presence and power in radio, television, the Internet, and cable news and information programming.
The corporation and large newspapers should appoint truly independent ombudsmen, as have the *New York Times* and the *Washington Post*; smaller newspapers should consider the industry-wide
model of the Canadian Broadcast Standards Council established by
private broadcasters.

As he prepared to leave office, Jean Chrétien pointed to national
unity as one of his two main achievements – and journalists, for the
most part, nodded in agreement. Anyone examining public opinion
polls in Quebec in the wake of the sponsorship scandal and the
results of the 2004 election, however, would have come to a less san-
guine conclusion.

After taking office, Paul Martin maintained he had not known
what was going on in the sponsorship program. However, nothing
costing a quarter of a billion dollars moves in Ottawa without the
Finance Department and other central agencies knowing; only Chrétien's pet project could have escaped scrutiny. Many Canadians suspected Martin had heard rumours in his home province and knew a
lot more than he was letting on – he could have found out the rest
and put a stop to it by asking a few questions, they reasoned, but he
chose not to because a different war against Chrétien had higher priority. Preparing for an imminent election call, Martin and his minis-

ters insisted they wanted to reform the way Ottawa did business.

Almost daily, Stephen Owen, the man who had Dingwall's job at Public Works, would rise in the House of Commons to assure Canadians that he would get to the bottom of the scandal. Yet his government never embraced the non-partisan process he devised in British Columbia when serious allegations are made about politicians. In Ottawa the Cabinet appointed the special counsel assigned to recover sponsorship monies. Cabinet named the RCMP commissioner responsible for most of the criminal investigation. (Quebec government prosecutors were also involved but their ultimate boss, Premier Jean Charest, has deep links to some of the firms being investigated.)[28] Liberals were in the majority on the public accounts committee looking into the sponsorship program. And the government appointed the head of the judicial inquiry set up to look into the scandal. Mr Justice John Gomery was named to the bench by the Trudeau government and, later, to head the Copyright Board by the Chrétien government.[29] His wife too owes her judicial appointment, and later her promotion to the appellate court, to the Chrétien regime. The two will benefit from special survivor pension provisions Chrétien legislated for a very few judicial couples.

In announcing Mr Justice Gomery's appointment, Paul Martin told the House of Commons: "I would suspect that this particular inquiry will be up and running faster than almost any others we have seen." Not before the election, it turned out. Before beginning his inquiry, Justice Gomery left on summer vacation after appointing two co-counsels. One, Bernard Roy, Mulroney's first principal secretary, recruited Tory candidates for the 1984 election alongside Marc Lefrançois, who was fired by Via Rail after Auditor General Sheila Fraser's report. The other, Neil Finkelstein, served as senior policy adviser to Ian Scott, the attorney general of Ontario in the Liberal government of David Peterson, and worked closely with Chrétien's constitutional team against the Meech Lake accord in the late 1980s. In Ottawa, the Martinites spun the appointments as proof of a bipartisan process. Out where I live on the west coast, the commission would not pass the smell test.

In his conclusion, William Kaplan wonders why Karlheinz Schreiber paid Brian Mulroney $300,000, or, as he puts it, what Mulroney did to earn the money. He also notes that this amount does not "come even close to adding up to the millions in commissions identified in Schreiber's own records for distribution in Canada." Even after writing two major books on the Airbus affair, then, Kaplan does not have the foggiest idea of what happened to more than US$22 million that was paid to Schreiber in commissions by Airbus between September 1988 and October 1993. Pelossi's documents also show that there were secret commission schemes in the MBB and Bearhead projects. As Kaplan writes, "The evidence is incontrovertible that millions and millions of dollars were deployed through middleman Schreiber and that some of that money ended up in Canada."

It's in the public interest that these questions be answered – not just to reduce public cynicism, though that too is important. We must learn the truth in order to assess whether we have adequate safeguards in place to prevent unethical behaviour. If the millions in sponsorship commissions merit a judicial inquiry, so do the Airbus commissions – and the mysteries surrounding the loan to the Auberge Grand-Mère, for that matter – ideally under a new chair and with new co-counsel.

Canadians watch, and wait, as governments repeatedly break election promises and, safely in power, blame each other for deteriorating services – including their number one priority, health. While provinces starve most programs to keep waiting lists from growing longer, Ottawa, awash with cash, is eager to step into additional provincial areas while neglecting its own. Restoration of a competitive political system at the federal level outside Quebec, as a result of the partial reunification of the conservative family, should help revive ministerial accountability. It should also prevent further erosion of Parliament's first duty – to control public spending. But there's no substitute for integrity in high office.

The instinct of ministers at both levels of government is to take credit for anything that goes right and to point fingers at the other or their officials when anything goes wrong. If the guilty are not punished by the courts, if no one can be held accountable for screw-ups or punished at the ballot box, citizens will ultimately question why they bother to vote. Unchecked, this growing public cynicism will provide fertile ground for simplistic solutions that do nothing to address the problem of corruption.

The root of the problem is that money always looks for power; regrettably, the powerful sometimes violate their public trust in the hope of becoming wealthy. The time for concrete action against political corruption, Ottawa's bipartisan problem, is now.

Notes

Many of the documents mentioned in the notes to this book are court records or materials ordered disclosed in the Eurocopter proceedings. None of these materials are generally available (although they can be accessed in the public court file). However, I will deposit all these documents, in due course, with my papers at the archives of the University of Toronto, together with the interview transcripts. Only one person did not agree to an interview: Stevie Cameron.

CHAPTER ONE

1 Schreiber interview, February 13, 2004.
2 Schreiber interview, May 11, 2004. RCMP records are subject to a retention period varying by type. Records confirming, or disproving, Schreiber's visit to Harrington Lake no longer exist.
3 Approximately $750,000 Canadian, depending on currency fluctuation.
4 Mulroney interview, October 12, 2003.
5 William Kaplan, *Presumed Guilty: Brian Mulroney, the Airbus Affair and the Government of Canada* (Toronto: McClelland & Stewart, 1998), 214.
6 *Globe and Mail*, January 8, 1997.
7 Mulroney interview, December 2, 1997.
8 CBC, *Fifth Estate*, transcript, March 2001. See Stevie Cameron and Harvey Cashore, *The Last Amigo: Karlheinz Schreiber and the Anatomy of a Scandal* (Toronto: Macfarlane Walter & Ross, 2001), 274.
9 See L. Ian MacDonald, *Mulroney: The Making of the Prime Minister* (Toronto: McClelland & Stewart, 1984), 138–43; John Sawatsky, *Mulroney: The Politics of Ambition* (Toronto: Macfarlane Walter & Ross, 1991), 432–57; Ron Graham, *One-Eyed Kings: Promise and Illusion in Canadian Politics* (Toronto: Collins Publishers, 1986); CBC, *Fifth Estate*, transcript, March 2001.
10 CBC, *Fifth Estate*, transcript, March 2001. See also Cameron and Cashore, *The Last Amigo*, 66.
11 CBC, *Fifth Estate*, "Choppers, Plots and Cold Hard Cash," March 14, 2001.
12 Schreiber interviews, February 13, March 31, 2004.
13 CBC, *Fifth Estate*, transcript, March 13, 2001.
14 Ibid.

CHAPTER TWO

1 Michael Bernstein to E.L. Greenspan, April 9, 2001.
2 *A-G N.S. v. MacIntyre*, 65 CCC (2d) 129 (SCC) at 142.
3 Ibid.
4 Ibid., 143.
5 Ibid., 144–5.
6 Ibid., 147.
7 Ibid.
8 Ibid., 148.
9 Ibid., 149.
10 Affidavit of Inspector Mathews, December 1999, 1.
11 Ibid., 3.
12 Paul Schabas to Justice Fontana, December 15, 1999.
13 Ibid.
14 Justice Fontana to Schabas, December 16, 1999.

CHAPTER THREE

1 *Eurocopter Canada Inc v. The Queen*, proceedings before Mr Justice Fontana, January 28, 2000, 4–5.
2 Ibid., 5.
3 *The Queen v Eurocopter Ltd.*, Respondent's Preliminary Factum, January 28, 2000, 3–4.
4 *Eurocopter Canada Ltd v. The Queen*, Ruling on Motion, February 14, 2000.
5 *The Queen v Eurocopter Ltd.*, March 23, 2000, transcript, 1.
6 Factum of the Respondent, March 17, 2000, 7.
7 March 23, 2000, transcript, 78–9.
8 Ibid., 79ff.
9 Affidavit in support of an application for an order for further detention of things seized, June 12, 2000, 4.
10 *The Queen v Eurocopter Canada Ltd.*, Reasons for Judgment, January 10, 2001, 7.
11 The application for judicial review on the basis of overseizure was abandoned by Eurocopter before Justice Then issued his reasons for decision.

CHAPTER FOUR

1 Information, 80.
2 Ibid., 86.
3 Ibid.
4 Ibid., 95.
5 Ibid., 118.
6 Ibid., 125.
7 Ibid., 126.
8 Ibid., 128.
9 National Speaker's Bureau, speaker profile, Stevie Cameron, www.nsb.com/speaker-bio.asp?name=Stevie+Cameron.
10 Garry Loeppky to Aly Alibhai, Media Lines, Airbus.
11 Information, 63.

12   RCMP Report to Crown Counsel, 2002-0230. Fiegenwald also indicated that he might not have.
13   Information, 34.
14   Ibid., 139.
15   Ibid., 42.

CHAPTER FIVE
1   *CBC v New Brunswick* (AG) (1996) 110 CCC (3d) 193 (SCC).
2   (1994) 94 CCC (3d) 289 (SCC).
3   *R v. Eurocopter Ltd.*, Intervenor's Factum for application to be heard, July 25, 2001.
4   *R. v. Eurocopter Ltd.*, Factum of the Applicant Eurocopter Canada Ltd. (Motions – July 25 & 26, 2001), 2.
5   Ibid., 3.
6   Ibid., 4.
7   Ibid.
8   Ibid.
9   Ibid., 13.
10   *R. v. Eurocopter Ltd.*, Reasons for Decision of Justice Then, October 4, 2001, 2.
11   Ibid.
12   Ibid.
13   Ibid., 4–5.
14   Ibid., 7–8.
15   According to Inspector Mathews, the court knew about the informer exemption in April 2001. Mathews interview, March 23, 2004.

CHAPTER SIX
1   112 CCC (3d) 385 (SCC).
2   Ibid., 390.
3   Ibid., 392.
4   Ibid., 392.
5   Ibid., 396.
6   *R v. Eurocopter*, Transcript, February 12, 2002. The following section is quoted from this transcript.
7   Preface to the paperback edition, *On the Take: Crime, Corruption and Greed in the Mulroney Years* (Toronto: Seal Books, 1995), xvi.
8   Peter Jacobsen to E.L. Greenspan, April 18, 2001.

CHAPTER SEVEN
1   Tracey Tyler to William Kaplan, March 22, 2004.
2   Shannon Kari, "Firm bidding to replace Sea Kings the subject of mysterious court case: Public excluded from trial involving Eurocopter Canada," *Ottawa Citizen*, June 5, 2002.
3   www.cbc.ca/english/codes/rtnda.htm.
4   www.eagle.ca/caj (approved at 2002 Annual General Meeting).
5   Canadian Association of Journalists (CAJ) List, Andrew Mitrovica contribution.
6   *Globe and Mail*, August 10, 1996.

7   Affidavit of Inspector Allan Mathews, April 24, 2001, *Eurocopter et al.*, Further Release of Redacted Materials, February 28, 2003. Emphasis added.
8   RCMP Continuation Report, March 23, 2001.

CHAPTER EIGHT
1   Mathews interview, March 23, 2004.
2   Mulroney interview, October 5, 2003.
3   Ibid.
4   Stevie Cameron and Harvey Cashore, *The Last Amigo: Karlheinz Schreiber and the Anatomy of a Scandal* (Toronto: Macfarlane Walter & Ross, 2001), 228.
5   Ibid., 232, 238, 247, 311.
6   Cited ibid., 230.
7   A number of people claim that "Britan" meant "Breton," that the account was a slush fund to support the Bearhead initiative in Cape Breton, and that funds were widely distributed.
8   Mulroney interview, October 5, 2003.
9   Ibid., October 12, 2003.
10 Ibid.
11 Ibid.
12 Ibid.
13 Ibid.
14 *Canadian Jewish News*, June 26, 2003.
15 Mulroney interview, October 24, 2003.
16 Mulroney interview, November 3, 2003.

CHAPTER NINE
1   Mulroney interview, October 5, 2003.
2   *Toronto Star*, November 13, 2003.
3   Stephen Kimber, rabble.ca, November 24, 2003.
4   Stephen Kimber, *Not Guilty: The Trial of Gerald Regan* (Toronto: Stoddart, 1999), 15.
5   Alan Bass, "Stevie Blunder," seemagazine.com, March 18, 2004.
6   *Globe and Mail*, February 25, 2004.
7   Ibid.
8   *The Current*, February 27, 2004, Bowdens Media Monitoring.
9   Jane Hawtin interview, March 1, 2004.
10 Written submissions on behalf of Karlheinz Schreiber, March 12, 2004.
11 Michael Bernstein to Peter Jacobsen, June 25, 2003.
12 RCMP Project Airbus, 95A-517, prepared by S/Sgt R.G. Muir, February 8, 1997.
13 Affidavit of Superintendent Mathews, February 26, 2004.
14 RCMP Memorandum, 1997-10-20, C/Supt Pierre Lange.
15 RCMP Continuation Report, March 20, 1995.
16 RCMP Transit Slip, May 1, 1995.
17 RCMP Continuation Report, May 1, 1995.
18 Ibid., May 15, 1995

19 RCMP Endorstext, run December 10, 2002, 1995, 11 08.
20 RCMP Memorandum, 1997-10-20, C/Supt Pierre Lange.
21 "Notes made following meeting with Ex S/Sgt F Fiegenwald and Insp. Mathews and S/Sgt. Alexander 01-12-21 at 'A' Division."
22 Ibid.
23 RCMP Memorandum, 1997-10-20, C/Supt Pierre Lange.
24 Ibid.
25 Ibid.
26 Affidavit of Superintendent Mathews, February 26, 2004. See also Michael Bernstein to Peter Jacobsen, June 25, 2003.
27 *R. v. Stinchcombe*, [1991] SCR 326.
28 Affidavit of Superintendent Mathews, February 26, 2004.
29 Peter M. Jacobsen to Michael Bernstein, May 8, 2003.
30 Ibid.
31 Affidavit of Superintendent Mathews, February 26, 2004.
32 Michael Bernstein to Peter Jacobsen, June 25, 2003.
33 Affidavit of Superintendent Mathews, February 26, 2004.
34 Ibid.
35 Ibid.
36 RCMP Continuation Report, Project A102, A2948, January 13, 2004.

CONCLUSION
1 Alexis de Tocqueville, *Democracy in America* (New York: Harper & Row, 1966), 491. See Moisei Ostrogorski, *Democracy and the Origin of Political Parties* (New York: Macmillan, 1902).
2 *Globe and Mail*, October 4, 2003.
3 Notes from Stevie Cameron address at Metropolitan Toronto Reference Library, April 23, 2004.
4 CAJ site, Cameron contribution.
5 Canadian Press, March 20, 2004.
6 Paul Schneidereit interview, March 11, 2004.
7 CAJ, Draft Statement of Principles and Guidelines for Investigative Journalism, March 2004.
8 Susan Riley, "Rebuke to Copps rebuke to many," *Ottawa Citizen*, March 8, 2004.
9 *Toronto Star*, March 9, 2004.
10 Michael Harris, "Making the News," *Ottawa Sun*, March 5, 2004.
11 Margaret Wente, *Globe and Mail*, November 11, 2003.
12 Margaret Wente, "Stevie told us a story," ibid., March 6, 2004.
13 Konrad Yakabuski, "The Prime of Brian Mulroney," *Report on Business Magazine*, May 2004, 38.
14 *A Strong Foundation: Report of the Task Force on Public Service Values and Ethics* (Ottawa: Canadian Centre for Management Development, 1996), John Tait, Chair, 63.
15 *Toronto Star Newspapers Ltd v. Ontario* (2003), 232 DLR (4th) 217 (Ont. CA).
16 *R v. Mentuck*, [2001] 3 SCR 442.

17 Andrew Philips, *Times Colonist*, March 6, 2004.

18 As George Bain observed in the summer of 1996, "It is reasonable to assume that some-one, perhaps a reporter with good connections … received a private briefing and both made personal use of the information and passed it on in outline to others to raise the story's news value and to strengthen its authenticity. Exclusive stories at times can be too exclusive. In this instance, the explanation of apparent incuriosity in the media may not be incuriosity at all. Rather, it may be that because of where their information came from and their commitments not to tell, the reporters simply cannot give it to us." *Maclean's*, July 29, 1996.

19 *Globe and Mail*, March 29, 2004.

20 Jazz Miller, "The Cook, the Spy, the Prof and the Scribbler," *www.ryersonca/rrj/content/print/backissues/jazz.html*.

21 William Kaplan, *Presumed Guilty: Brian Mulroney, the Airbus Affair and the Government of Canada* (Toronto: McClelland & Stewart, 1998), 328.

22 "Airbus's Secret Past," *The Economist*, June 12, 2003.

23 Lawrence Martin, *Globe and Mail*, March 18, 2004.

24 See the discussion in Kaplan, *Presumed Guilty*, 205ff.

25 Allan Mathews interview, March 26, 2004.

26 Ghyslaine Clément, Assistant Commissioner, to William Kaplan, April 5, 2004.

27 *Ottawa Citizen*, April 9, 2004.

28 *Montreal Gazette*, July 3, 1993; *Vancouver Sun*, July 10, 1993; *Montreal Gazette*, August 8, 1993; *Ottawa Citizen*, December 11, 1993.

On needing money, see Yakabuski, "The Prime of Brian Mulroney": "It was clear he was not headed for retirement when, at barely 54, he stepped down in 1993. Besides, he needed the money. As Iron Ore president, Mulroney evidently never earned more than $400,000 a year. For a decade he had lived on a politician's paltry salary, and his pension on leaving office barely topped $33,000. With four U.S.-college-bound children to sup-port, having himself grown accustomed to finer tastes, and with a new $1.67-million Westmount home and $1 million in renovations to pay for, Mulroney's lifestyle required a salary in seven digits.

"Perhaps it was this pressure that led him, shortly after leaving office, to accept a $300,000 consulting contract from Karlheinz Schreiber, the German-Canadian business-man whose name would come back to haunt Mulroney in the Airbus case. At the time, though, Schreiber had not been accused of any illegal activities. In the end, Mulroney didn't need Schreiber's business."

29 Schreiber interview, March 31, 2004.

30 Stevie Cameron and Harvey Cashore, *The Last Amigo: Karlheinz Schreiber and the Anatomy of a Scandal* (Toronto: Macfarlane Walter & Ross, 2001), 130. See also H. Wittholz and E.J. Grant to MBB, February 24, 1987. Source: *www.cbc.ca/news/indepth/choppers/docs/4-01.gif*.

31 Shannon Kari, "Schreiber paid bribes to foreigners, court told," Victoria *Times Colonist*, December 19, 2002.

32 Mulroney interview, January 9, 2002.

33 Ibid., September 12, 2003.

AFTERWORD

1 After all, as Kaplan notes, "its claim of massive misconduct is seared into the Canadian consciousness, even though the book itself completely failed to deliver the goods."

2 Rereading the column, I realize now that it was primarily about Robert Rabinovitch – today president of the CBC – one of the few public servants Mulroney fired in a late-summer shuffle of deputy ministers. For Cameron, the coincidence of my arrival in Ottawa in August 1986 and his departure must have symbolized the shattering of her world and the arrival of the barbarians.

3 To take but two examples, British Columbia's Jim Pattison chaired Expo 86 for my former boss, Socred premier Bill Bennett. Fifteen years later Pattison hired former NDP premier Glen Clark, positioning himself for any change of government. Pattison, a major contributor to the Paul Martin campaign, is a rarity in business circles: his $2 billion empire is a purely private corporation.

In Ontario, Frank Stronach has Desmarais-like aspirations and, with only 3.4 per cent of the equity, the same secret for controlling Magna International – a dual-voting structure. This year, the board paid him more than $50 million. In addition to Conservative leadership candidate Belinda Stronach, the Magna stable includes former Ontario premiers Bill Davis and Mike Harris, the latter touted by some as a future leadership candidate. Brian Mulroney, who supported Belinda for the leadership, is chair of the company's International Advisory Board. Future Liberal leadership hopeful Brian Tobin recently signed on to manage Magna's sporting and entertainment assets. Tobin has been involved in some other lucrative dealings. A month after leaving the federal Cabinet, he was appointed to the board of CHC Helicopters, owned by fellow Newfoundlander Craig Dobbin. The appointment was cleared by ethics counsellor Howard Wilson, who ruled that the company's efforts to lobby Industry Canada were so negligible that he didn't have to wait the required two years – even though Dobbin hosted a $75,000 a plate fundraiser for Tobin's leadership run.

4 Like Joe Clark, who appointed him to the Senate, Murray had voted against the November 1981 constitutional package because Quebec had not agreed to the terms. I supported the agreement as the best possible one in the circumstances – after Trudeau decided not to await the anticipated election of a federalist government in Quebec before proceeding with his initiative. However, I agreed with others around the table that morning that there was unfinished business. As Privy Council clerk Michael Pitfield observed two years later, "We won the referendum, we said we would give Quebec a new deal and we have not delivered a new deal. If we don't move soon, they [Quebecers] are going to reconsolidate into a nationalist vein." Judy Steed, "Descent from the pinnacle of power," *Globe and Mail*, 26 September, 1983.

5 Chuck Guité, who would later gain notoriety for his management of the sponsorship program under Jean Chrétien, was a mid-level official in the group supporting Murray in his role as chairman of the Cabinet committee.

6 Tassé would later turn up in 1987 as a key adviser to Mulroney in his Airbus defamation lawsuit. See William Kaplan, *Presumed Guilty: Brian Mulroney, the Airbus Affair, and the Government of Canada* (Toronto: McClelland & Stewart, 1998), 96–99.

7 For a fuller description of how one becomes an ambassador, at least in my case, see

Chronicle of a War Foretold: How Mideast Peace Became America's Fight (Vancouver: Douglas & McIntyre 2003), 5–6.

8 One day in Israel, Leo Kolber, the brains in the Bronfman family and a senator, asked for my views on Mulroney, who was lobbying for a seat on their board. According to Kolber, Mulroney had always been helpful and was in the family's good books (unlike me, after I refused to deal with the family trust issue, according to a childhood friend who worked for the family), but the Bronfmans were not sure they wanted him on the board. At the time, I did not know that it was the Bronfman family that had moved the $2 billion out of Canada.

9 As Kaplan notes, "Thyssen money, in the millions, began to flow soon after. Where did that money go? Schreiber considered suing over the letter of intent and even got an opinion from a leading counsel that the German industrial giant had a good case. Schreiber wanted to proceed with the action, but Thyssen said no. Some losses are best just written off."

10 Years later I learned from a key player in Paul Martin's camp that previous service under the Conservative government, far from being a career-killer, was attractive to both David Dingwall and Jean Chrétien because it provided political insulation. As Chuck Guité testified in 2004 to the Public Accounts Committee looking into the sponsorship program, Dingwall was very conscious that he had served under the Conservatives when he offered him the job of running the shop. He also testified that, under both Trudeau and Mulroney, political staff had doled out contracts. Under his bureaucratic leadership, the PMO had only provided "input" on which projects to approve. Though Jean Pelletier, Chrétien's top political adviser, testified that he could not say whether his input had been influential, it seems that Guité, unlike me, had a very "cooperative" attitude.

11 *Globe and Mail*, October 16, 1996.

12 The World Bank defines corruption as "the abuse of public office for private gain."

13 During the Conservative reign, Mulroney's friend and personal financial adviser, Jonathan Deitcher, was promoted to vice-president at Dominion Securities Pitfield; the firm, which once employed Finance Minister Michael Wilson, was the lead underwriter in Petro-Canada's first two steps towards privatization. In 1994 a subsequent tranche went to Gordon Capital, where Chrétien spent a few years as an associate after losing the Liberal Party leadership to John Turner.

14 A few months before I resigned from the public service, the *Globe and Mail* made reference to my conflict with David Dingwall in its weekly Ottawa review, "Who's hot, who's not": "Not: Norman Spector, president of the Atlantic Canada Opportunities Agency. The former Mulroney aide is in hot water with Liberal ministers for dragging his feet over regional development projects pushed by Cape Breton pork barrel meister David Dingwall." Canadians wondering why they learned about the full dimension of the sponsorship program only after Chrétien left office might reflect on the widespread cynicism in the parliamentary press gallery during his decade in power.

15 In 2003 the Treasury Board Secretariat issued a booklet, *Values and Ethics for the Public Service*, which closely followed the recommendations of the working group (which had been chaired by the former deputy minister of justice, the late John Tait), including the appointment of a public service integrity commissioner.

16 Conrad Black later related to author Chris Cobb that Chrétien personally called him about six times in a fruitless attempt to get him to intervene in the *National Post*'s coverage of the scandal, including one 3 a.m. call in Vienna in which Chrétien "blasted" him. According to Black, he simply told editor Ken Whyte that the prime minister was not "delighted" with the coverage, but that it was up to him and he should not make any mistakes. See Chris Cobb, *Ego and Ink* (Toronto: McClelland & Stewart, 2004), 254–7.

17 Ironically, McIntosh had cut his teeth as an investigative reporter working as a research assistant to Stevie Cameron at the time she was writing *On the Take*.

18 As Kaplan notes, "Mulroney offered to come to Ottawa to answer any of the Mounties' questions. He offered to bring all his financial records and income tax returns. He offered everything, but was told that the force was just beginning its investigation. If the offer had been accepted, the investigation could have significantly advanced. The RCMP might even have learned about the Mulroney-Schreiber business relationship. But the offer was turned down."

19 The process was designed by then ombudsman Stephen Owen, who later became public works minister in Ottawa. In British Columbia, the assistant deputy attorney general, a career public servant, appoints the outside lawyer; the minister is simply informed of the decision and may issue subsequent directives only in writing.

20 Ironically in light of its current notoriety, Earnscliffe started out as a Tory lobby firm; indeed, it took its name from Sir John A. Macdonald's Ottawa residence, which now houses the high commissioner of the United Kingdom. Before joining the PMO, Hugh Segal was associated with the firm. During the 2004 election campaign, when favourable polls suggested the possibility of a Conservative victory, Segal was asked to prepare transition material.

21 CBC-TV broadcast transcripts, *The National*, Wednesday, May 8, 2002, "At Issue" panel.

22 "The matter currently being discussed involves commissions paid to advertising agencies relating to a former federal-government sponsorship program. The amount in question is $100-million over a four-year period, or approximately $25-million a year. Based on an annual operating budget of $180-billion, the amount represented .015 per cent of the tax dollars entrusted to government." Allan Gregg, "Why the fuss? A-G's report deals with a drop in the tax bucket," *Globe and Mail*, February 13, 2004.

23 Interestingly, though Cobb writes extensively about the *National Post*'s role in uncovering the Shawinigate affair – a proud moment in journalism for which McIntosh won a National Newspaper Award – he makes nary a mention of the paper's decision to kill Mathias's scoop about Schreiber's cash payments to Mulroney.

24 Unlike the BBC, the CBC board has, for many years, been packed with patronage appointees. Still, the British are also grappling with issues of accountability and independence in public broadcasting. In his report on the suicide of British weapons inspector Dr David Kelly, Lord Hutton provided an excellent analysis of how Tony Blair's Labour government and the BBC interacted in the lead-up to the Iraq war. Unusually, Blair fought back against an inaccurate report accusing the government of lying and ended up with three BBC heads on a platter. As Edward Greenspon noted in the *Globe and Mail*, the Beeb's biggest mistake was not to have corrected its erroneous report quickly (as the *Washington Post* famously did at an early stage of its Watergate coverage).

25 Notably, in her article tracing Martin's key advisers, Jane Taber omitted one of the neighbours who owns "cottages on the same lake in Western Quebec" – Peter Mansbridge. You could call the favour "professional courtesy." Jane Taber, "Ottawa consulting firm called 'Martin's PMO,'" *Globe and Mail*, April 19, 2004.

26 Even CBC defenders like Christopher Dornan, the director of the faculty of journalism at Carleton University, don't dispute its leftist tilt. Writing in the *Globe and Mail*, however, he argues that its role is to provide content that the private sector – dominated by the right, in his view – will not or cannot produce. I don't see why not: the *Toronto Star*, Canada's largest-circulation daily, conveys a similar view of Canada and the world.

27 Diversity and competition are the only protection for journalists too. In my short career as a columnist, I've experienced constraints on expression at virtually every paper in the country. The degree varies, though it's consistent with the findings of an academic survey presented at a McGill conference on the media organized by Michael Goldbloom, now the publisher of the *Toronto Star*. The survey indicated that owner influence in the newsroom was greatest at his newspaper and least at *Le Devoir*. The *Globe and Mail* comes out very well; the Victoria *Times Colonist*, which is unique in having a perfect score in my book, was not included in the survey. See Stuart Soroka and Patrick Fournier, "With media ownership, size does matter: Who's afraid of big bad media concentration? Journalists. And the rest of us should be …" *Globe and Mail*, February 12, 2003.

28 According to a report by Rhéal Séguin in the *Globe and Mail*, one of the advertising companies that profited from the sponsorship program, Groupe Everest, "has had close ties with Mr. Charest throughout his political career … Groupe Everest was founded in Mr. Charest's hometown of Sherbrooke and worked extensively with the former Progressive Conservative Party. The company helped manage Mr. Charest's 1997 federal election campaign when he was Tory leader in Ottawa … Then in 1998, after Mr. Charest was persuaded to quit federal politics to become Quebec Liberal Party Leader, Groupe Everest played a major role in the Liberal election campaign that same year."

In January 2004 Mr Charest hired "the former vice-president of public relations at Groupe Everest, Michel Guitar, as a communications specialist in his office. Mr. Guitar worked at Groupe Everest for 15 years before leaving after major portions of the company were sold for about $120-million to U.S.-based Draft Inc. in March 2003 … According to one source, Mr. Guitar was heavily involved in Groupe Everest's dealings regarding the sponsorship program and communicated regularly with people working in former public works minister Alphonso Gagliano's department." *Globe and Mail*, 19 February 2004.

29 When the matter was raised by the official opposition in February 2004, an official in the PMO indicated that Judge Gomery would be resigning from his position at the Copyright Board before beginning his work with the sponsorship inquiry.

Chronology

September 4, 1984. Brian Mulroney and the Progressive Conservatives sweep to power.

1985. Air Canada decides to buy a fleet of new planes. Three evaluation teams begin to work. Boeing and Airbus Industrie compete for the contract.

1985. Airbus Industrie hires Karlheinz Schreiber through International Aircraft Leasing (IAL) as its agent in Canada. Helicopter manufacturer Messerschmitt Bolkow Blohm (MBB) also reaches an agreement with Schreiber's IAL. Commissions are to be paid to IAL and Schreiber on any helicopter sales to Canada. The German conglomerate Thyssen Industrie later retains Schreiber to promote the Bearhead project.

June 1986. Agreement reached between the Government of Canada and MBB. Commissions, percentage, brokerage, or contingent fee prohibited.

December 1986. Helge Wittholz, president of MBB's Canadian subsidiary MCL, Messerschmitt Canada Limited, learns about the secret commission arrangement.

1987. Government decides to partially privatize Air Canada. Share proceeds to pay for new aircraft.

February 24, 1987. Wittholz writes MBB headquarters in Germany: "The areas that are the most dangerous at this particular time are … Any indication of foreign money that goes into party funds directly or indirectly."

March 30, 1988. Air Canada board of directors approves acquisition of thirty-four Airbus A320 planes at the cost of $1.8 billion.

March 1988. Boeing raises concern about the sale. Government asserts that the decision was made by Air Canada and Air Canada alone.

Summer 1988. Rumours of wrongdoing in Airbus sale. Frank Moores and his firm, Government Consultants International (GCI), said to be involved. Government investigates and determines no impropriety. Rumours persist. RCMP opens file and, in the absence of any evidence, quickly closes it.

1989. Wittholz resigns from MBB.

1991. Schreiber delivers one million German marks in cash to treasurer of the Christian Democratic Union. Payment made in a parking lot.

Summer 1993. Brian Mulroney steps down as prime minister. Enters into commercial relationship with Schreiber. Paid total of $300,000 in cash in 1993–94.

July 26, 1993. Schreiber opens a Swiss bank account code-named "Britan." Deposits $500,000 CDN. Withdraws $100,000 in cash the next day.

October 25, 1993. Jean Chrétien and the Liberal Party of Canada elected to office. Progressive Conservatives reduced from a majority to two seats.

December 2, 1993. Minister of Justice Allan Rock writes the solicitor general, Herb Gray, passing on information received about alleged wrongdoing in the 1988 Air Canada purchase of Airbus planes.

February 22, 1994. Rock advised by RCMP that no grounds found to pursue an investigation.

October 1994. Stevie Cameron publishes On The Take.

Fall 1994. CBC's Fifth Estate begins work on Airbus story with the assistance of documents and other information provided by former Karlheinz Schreiber associate Giorgio Pelossi.

1995. German authorities raid Schreiber's Bavarian estate. Schreiber moves to Switzerland, where he has a weekend home.

January 1995. RCMP investigation resumes after the force comes into possession of "vast information." Sgt Fraser Fiegenwald in charge of the investigation. Solicitor General Herb Gray receives first briefing note about Airbus investigation.

March 1985. Der Spiegel publishes "Tycoon from Alberta," implicating Schreiber in Airbus wrongdoing.

March 19, 1995. La Presse reports that there may have been kickbacks in Air Canada's 1988 Airbus purchase.

March 20, 1995. First Question Period note to Prime Minister Jean Chrétien on Airbus and rumours of kickbacks to unnamed Canadian politician.

March 28, 1995. Fifth Estate goes on air alleging wrongdoing in Air Canada's 1988 Airbus purchase. Schreiber and Moores said to be involved.

June/July 1995. Sgt Fiegenwald contacts Department of Justice lawyer Kimberly Prost and advises her of Airbus probe and informs her that Mulroney is under investigation.

Spring–summer 1995. More briefing notes sent to solicitor general indicating that Mulroney under investigation, that Stevie Cameron has information about Mulroney wrongdoing, and that letter requesting assistance from the Swiss has been prepared.

September 29, 1995. Department of Justice lawyer Kimberly Prost signs and sends Letter of Request to Switzerland.

October 3, 1995. Letter arrives in Berne. Pascal Gossin of the Swiss Federal Office for Police Matters directs letter to Swiss prosecutor Carla del Ponte.

October 26, 1995. Swiss prosecutor del Ponte directs the Swiss Bank Corp. to seize the bank accounts and safety-deposit boxes as requested in the letter. Frank Moores and Karlheinz Schreiber receive notice, and then copies, of the Canadian letter.

November 2, 1995. Schreiber, who has various Swiss bank accounts and who is, therefore, notified about the Canadian Letter of Request, contacts Mulroney. Mulroney retains Roger Tassé to act on his behalf.

November 3–17, 1995. Tassé attempts to persuade Department of Justice and RCMP to withdraw the letter and replace it with one that is less strident and accusatory in content and tone. Gets runaround. Mulroney decides to file suit if letter leaks.

November 10, 1995. Swiss television broadcasts story on the letter and its assertions that Canadian politicians had been paid off.

November 11, 1995. French news service Agence France-Press publishes story on Canadian Letter of Request.

November 12, 1995. Montreal's *La Presse* publishes story that Canadian politicians are under investigation for having accepted secret commissions in the Airbus sale.

November 14, 1995. Swiss authorities confirm that Canada had asked for, and Switzerland had granted, legal assistance, including the freezing of bank accounts linked to secret Airbus payments.

November 18, 1995. *Financial Post* publishes story on letter.

November 18, 1995. Press conference in Montreal. Mulroney lawyers announce intention to file $50-million lawsuit in Montreal on November 20, 1995.

November 19, 1995. Prime Minister Chrétien tells reporters that he had no foreknowledge of the investigation or the letter.

November 20, 1995. Lawsuit filed.

November 28, 1995. *Fifth Estate* rebroadcasts its Airbus show. Pelossi no longer in shadows.

December 2, 1995. Schreiber tells reporters that Mulroney is totally innocent of any involvement in Airbus and that no bank account was established by him in Mulroney's name.

December 4, 1995. Frank Moores declares himself innocent of any wrongdoing.

December 11, 1995. Mulroney lawsuit assigned to Mr Justice André Rochon.

December 16, 1995. Documents show that "Devon" account never held more than $500.

December 19, 1995. Prime Minister Chrétien tells reporters that he "presumes Mulroney is innocent."

1996. German authorities accelerate their investigation.

January 3, 1996. Schreiber initiates legal proceedings against the CBC.

January/February/March 1996. Various pre-trial motions. Government and RCMP invariably lose.

February 13, 1996. Moores sues CBC for libel.

March 1996. Schreiber initiates proceedings in the Federal Court of Canada to quash Letter of Request as an "illegal search and seizure" contrary to the *Charter of Rights and Freedoms.*

March 25, 1996. Pelossi formally interviewed for the first time by the RCMP. He is already on record that the RCMP would be "foolish" to investigate Mulroney solely on the basis of his evidence and allegations.

April 17, 1996. Mulroney testifies in examination on discovery.

April 19, 1996. Second day of examination on discovery.

May 1, 1996. Swiss authorities reject Schreiber's appeal of Swiss prosecutor del Ponte's order directing disclosure of his Swiss bank account.

July–August 1996. Both sides file expert reports.

July 5, 1996. Schreiber receives judgment from Federal Court, concluding that the letter of request violated his constitutional rights. Action on Canadian letter suspended. Government announces intention

to appeal. In the meantime, RCMP receives all banking records relating to Moores, who did not appeal order requiring their release.

August 28, 1996. Trial set to begin on January 6, 1997.

September/October/November 1996. Various pre-trial motions, including unsuccessful bid by CBC to televise the trial and request by RCMP to limit evidence that could be called to trial.

December 1996–January 1997. Subpoenas issued. Government loses bid to exempt evidence and restrict scope of inquiry at trial. Fiegenwald admits disclosing information about Letter of Request to journalist Stevie Cameron. Case settled with the assistance of mediator Alan Gold.

January 6, 1997. Settlement announced. Government apologizes. RCMP acknowledges that any "conclusions of wrongdoing by the former prime minister were – and are – unjustified." Government agrees to pay Mulroney's legal costs. Apologies later issued to Schreiber and Moores. RCMP announces the investigation will continue.

May 1997. German authorities issue arrest warrants for Schreiber. He is wanted to face charges of bribery and tax evasion.

1999. German authorities obtain access to all of Schreiber's Swiss banking records.

May 1999. Schreiber leaves Switzerland for Canada.

August 31, 1999. Schreiber arrested in Toronto. Bail guaranteed by former federal Cabinet ministers Marc Lalonde and Elmer MacKay. Schreiber hires prominent criminal lawyer Eddie Greenspan.

October 20, 1999. The CBC's *Fifth Estate* broadcasts a documentary on Schreiber and secret bank accounts.

November 1999. Secret funding scandal erupts. Liesler Kiep, treasurer of the German Christian Democratic Union, confesses to taking money from Schreiber. Former German chancellor Helmut Kohl (1983–98) admits he accepted secret donations and is forced to resign as honourary chair of the CDU. One senior German official implicated in the payments commits suicide. Another becomes a fugitive from justice. Several ranking Thyssen Industrie officers later convicted of corruption.

December 1999. Search warrants issued for MCL successor company, Eurocopter Canada Limited, in Fort Erie and other Canadian locations. On application of the Crown, Justice James A. Fontana seals all documents related to the case.

Late 1999, early 2000. *National Post* reporter Philip Mathias confirms facts that Schreiber hired Mulroney and paid him in cash over extended period after Mulroney left office. *National Post* decides not to publish story.

2000. Secret, complicated Eurocopter proceedings occur in Ottawa and Toronto. Hearings *in camera* and subject to publication ban and other legal restrictions.

February 2001. Fraser Fiegenwald testifies under oath in Edmonton as part of discovery process in Schreiber's multi-million-dollar lawsuit against RCMP and Government of Canada.

April 9, 2001. Mulroney, Schreiber, and Moores notified of secret Eurocopter proceedings. All three invited to attend. CBC also informed.

2001–3. Proceedings resume and adjourn and resume and adjourn again. Justice Edward Then considers various motions, including application by CBC to open up proceedings. Crown begins to release some of sealed material and asserts existence of confidential informant entitled to privilege from disclosure. Eddie Greenspan identifies informant as journalist Stevie Cameron. Crown advises court that informer will consent to waive privilege "for the prosecution of Brian Mulroney."

October 2002. Eurocopter Canada Limited and two German nationals charged with fraud. Preliminary inquiry under way in Ottawa. Expected to conclude in late 2004 or early 2005.

December 2002. Schreiber's German attorney, Olaf Liesner, testifies in Canada that under German law it was perfectly lawful for Schreiber to pay bribes in Canada in pursuit of export business. Tells reporters outside court that Canadians were among the influential foreigners who had received legal bribes between 1988 and 1993.

April 2003. RCMP announces end of Airbus, MBB, Bearhead investigations.

September 2003. *Globe and Mail* lawyer Patrick Flaherty writes Justice Then and seeks standing in the Eurocopter case.

October 31, 2003. Justice Then orders all documents and records in secret trial unsealed. Parties given one week to appeal order. No appeals filed.

November 7–9, 2003. *Globe and Mail* publishes series. Part one reports on secret trial. Part two, on in-court allegations that Stevie Cameron was police informant. Part three, that Schreiber hired and paid Mulroney in cash.

November 22, 2003. *Globe and Mail* publishes Steve Cameron rebuttal: "Paid police informant? Never. A confidential informant? Are you kidding me?" Cameron refuses *Globe* request to outright reject assertion that she was the confidential informant.

February 25, 2004. Cameron admits to *Globe and Mail* that she was the person identified by the RCMP as confidential informant. Claims it was a "big mistake." RCMP asserts otherwise in sworn affidavits and other materials tendered in court. Cameron referred to in RCMP documents as "A2948."

March 3, 2004. Eurocopter proceedings reconvene in open court. RCMP produces material, including letter from Cameron lawyer Peter Jacobsen in which the confidential informant privilege is invoked: "when our client was designated a confidential informant …"

March 10, 2004. Canadian Association of Journalists "denounce" Cameron for passing on information to police and for conflict of interest.

March–June 2004. Cameron now denies she was a confidential informant.

April 2004 to today. Eurocopter attempts to stay preliminary inquiry. Justice Then attempts to get to the bottom of what went on in his court.

Various legal proceedings continue.

Acknowledgments

Maria Banda, now a Rhodes Scholar at Oxford, did the research on journalistic ethics, while Charmaine Stanley, a doctoral student at the University of Toronto, helped with the research on everything else.

I am blessed by a number of very good friends who are also good readers. Norman Hillmer of the Department of History at Carleton University took a rather poor first draft and patiently explained how to make it better. Former University of Ottawa Law School colleagues Jamie Benidickson and David Paciocco each read two drafts and made huge improvements to the text, as did another former University of Ottawa colleague, Pierre Legrand, now a law professor at the Sorbonne, who read the final draft and, with his legendary precision, pointed out myriad stylistic mistakes (always with an elegant suggestion for change). Other readers who made important contributions include Harvey Cashore, Earl Cherniak, Graham Rawlinson, and Kenneth P. Swan.

Rosemary Shipton, my editor, has been improving my prose for twenty years and did her usual fantastic job this time around. Gillian Watts proved to be a dedicated and careful proofreader. Brian MacLeod Rogers, the *Globe and Mail*'s lawyer when the series was first published and my lawyer for this book, has, I hope, kept me out of trouble. At McGill-Queen's University Press, the three anonymous readers made helpful suggestions. It was a pleasure, once again, to work with Philip Cercone and Joan McGilvray.

The book is dedicated to Robert S. Bothwell, my favourite professor at the University of Toronto, an inspiring teacher, renowned scholar, and, to my fortune, another very good friend.

William Kaplan
Toronto, July 2004

Picture Credits

Index